MY EXTRAORDINARY, COURAGEOUS
Adventure

BELLA PEARCE

BALBOA.
PRESS
A DIVISION OF HAY HOUSE

Balboa Press books may be ordered through booksellers or by contacting:

Balboa Press
A Division of Hay House
1663 Liberty Drive
Bloomington, IN 47403
www.balboapress.com.au
1 (877) 407-4847

ISBN: 978-1-5043-0998-1 (sc)
ISBN: 978-1-5043-0999-8 (e)

Print information available on the last page.

Balboa Press rev. date: 09/25/2017

CONTENTS

Chapter 1

MID LIFE CRISIS 101 – JANUARY - MARCH

THE PLAN

There was that moment; when you knew, life cannot continue on this same path. In my heart and soul, I knew something had to change. My date was the 31st December 2011. Anyone who has had a year, they would rather forget, would know what I am talking about.

The 2011 year started out with deaths of close family members, which coincided with the tsunami and flooding that hit the east coast of Australia in January. The destruction and loss of hope, and an overwhelming feeling, of helplessness was felt world-wide. Between March and August three members of my immediate family nearly died from health issues and a boating accident. In May the suicide of my son's best friend. The failure of my business, due to the impact from the current economic downfall, was the last straw; along with the finalisation of my marriage breakdown.

Out of desperation, on the last day of the year, the decision to walk away from my life, as I knew it, was my only solution, for survival. The hope of finding my sanity, a purpose to live, and a reason to re-invent myself, was my mission. The solution to my mid life crisis, was to travel for eight months, performing volunteer work on farms and properties, in Canada and USA. I Joined WWOOF Canada and USA and started planning the trip; where I'd work for a set numbers of hours in exchange for food and board. My main objectives were to spend spring in Alaska, summer in Canada and fall in Eastern America. I was also toying with the idea, of house-sitting somewhere over winter, but that wasn't part of my original plans.

I spent the first three months of 2012 packing up my life, which included the café I owned; making sure everything was in order and arranging a house-sitter for my home.

Plans for my trip, started with searching for the first host, and then in order of where I wanted to be. I acclimated to the northern hemisphere, spending the first ten days recovering from my exhaustion and working for seven days with my first host, prior to my arrival, in Alaska.

The Universe had an incredible way, of planning my journey; of course I wasn't aware of it at the time. I truly believed the places, events and people I met, was where I was supposed to be, for my greater purpose, and overall well-being. Otherwise, how do you explain, why you're, in a certain place, at a certain time?

You see, I'm a woman in her fifties, not very tall, not very fit and a little overweight. Now these were some of my negatives, but my list of achievements were about two pages long. My life experiences and vocations, led me to hosts involved mainly with farming, as this was my passion. I love gardening and being outside in Mother Nature.

My plan was to wait, for confirmation, from each host, before planning the next location. Waiting for a reply, was the most frustrating part, of my plans. I spent many hours researching each host; looking at the amazing opportunities available to me. Finally, my plan was set, with the departure date of 12th April, the day after my Mum's seventy-fifth birthday. My arrival date back in Australia was set for the 9th December, allowing eight months, to re-invent Bella, the person who loved life to the max, on every level of her being.

THE JOURNEY BEGINS – APRIL

I had had my farewell dinner with the family, as my Mum hugged me goodbye, saying "live your dream".

How did I get to this point in my life at fifty-two years of age? An absolute emotional, mental and physical wreck, walking away from the only life, I'd ever known. The biggest decision was leaving my Thirty-two-year marriage, and grown-up children. Walking away with whatever sanity I still had, before the realisation, was ascertained that I couldn't be saved. This journey started out as trip for self survival; one tiny glimmer of hope, that if I left *NOW,* maybe I could be saved from obliteration.

I had packed into my bags, all of the essential items, including my support system of inspirational books, music, tarot cards and crystals; the link, from my old life to my new one. My large suitcase contained all of my clothes, shoes, toiletries etc which weighed exactly twenty-three kilograms in weight. My small carry-on bag contained my support system.

At the airport I checked my luggage through, receiving my boarding pass at the service counter. Ricky, my soon to be ex-husband, who had driven me to the airport, asked for a hug goodbye. I had absolutely, not one ounce of feeling, for this man, who had been part of my life for the last thirty-four-years.

Walking towards the security check-in I was distraught, with tears welling up in my eyes; overwhelmed with a nervous, excited feeling, in the pit of my stomach, about the extraordinary opportunities lying ahead of me. With very little time to relax, after being processed by immigration and security, I grabbed my last chance to enjoy a coffee, savouring every mouthful of liquid, walking towards the boarding gate and the trip of a lifetime.

I flew directly to the western coast of the Americas, as *I am so over the layovers and delays when travelling internationally*. Next time I travel, I won't mention gluten free, as the meals were disgusting.

My seat, for the flight, was in the middle, of the outside aisle, seeing a little of the sky, before we reached the International Date Line; travelling back into yesterday. During the fifteen-hour flight, I slept a little, plus watched a couple of movies. The passenger beside me was an older Australian woman, travelling to join her husband. They both shuffled the immigration fiasco visiting each other, also spending time in Europe. What a wonderful life they had.

I arrived on the West Coast at 9:00am on the 12th April 2012 two hours before I left Australia. Isn't the world an amazing place, where you can travel back in time, to start again? *Wouldn't it be great if it worked all of the time? A little time machine would work wonders.*

I was processed through customs and immigration easily, only to find out I had to buy a new suitcase, as the wheels had been ripped off, during the transit. I had a couple of hours to wait for the transit bus, to travel over to the island. This was the first time I had arrived absolutely exhausted to start a holiday, but this wasn't any normal holiday. Over the next eight months I would question '*WHAT WAS I THINKING*' when I thought, I would volunteer my way around Canada and America.

I visited the ATM, obtaining enough cash for any unexpected expenses or treats. While waiting at the airport, I found it so hard to stay awake, wandering around, trying to stay active, and stop falling asleep. Even with coffee and more coffee, I was struggling to maintain my energy. Then, with all of the coffee, I had to find washrooms; fortunate the handicapped bathrooms, were big enough, the entire luggage cart fitted in the cubicle with you.

Once I boarded the bus, I slept all the way to the ferry terminal, until it was time to leave the bus, to go upstairs. Passengers weren't permitted in the vehicle bays, while the ferry was sailing; due to a disaster a few years back. Passengers were found in their vehicle, when rescuers retrieved a ferry that had sunk.

I ordered French fries and a coffee, for my lunch time meal; then I really felt like a zombie. I needed sleep, and I needed to be horizontal to do that. I sat at a table, but found it hard to stay awake. I panicked at one time, thinking it was time to re-board the bus, only to realize, we were only half way across the bay. I should have gone outside, onto the deck, to brighten myself up, by looking at the houses and the view; instead of walking around through the shops. I couldn't think straight, as my eyes could see nothing; obscured by my total exhaustion.

I was disappointed my enthusiasm, for this trip, was nowhere to be found. I had always enjoyed the ferry ride, looking out over the inlets, as the ferry manoeuvred between the islands; catching sight of the magnificent houses, on the water's edge, dreaming of a house, to enjoy the beautiful sunsets and sunrises. I'd be searching the waters for whales, while enjoying the fresh air; being excited by the fact, I was here again.

Oh boy, do I need this holiday? I was now questioning what sort of holiday was this anyway, where I'd be working all of the time. I needed to change, the title of this trip, to an adventure, with unlimited experiences to explore.

Are we there yet? As soon as we boarded the bus again, I slept until we arrived at the bus depot. That's a pity, because the whole island was breaking free, from the cool winter weather with everything coming alive. *This time was supposed to be the spring, of my new life's journey; I just wasn't feeling that way.*

I couldn't think about anything. All I knew was I needed sleep – really badly and NOW.

MOTEL ACCOMMODATION SUMNER

I checked into the motel, went upstairs; lay down on the bed and slept for four hours. By the time I got up I wasn't hungry, ending up having French fries and a hot chocolate. French fries twice in one day, was definitely a record, for someone who doesn't normally eat fast food.

The room was clean with a comfy bed and a view of the main street. The internet didn't work in my room; I had the choice of sitting on a step in the stair well or in the bar downstairs. The back area of the reception had a warren of alley ways, leading to bars and restaurants.

That night, I wouldn't have heard a bomb go off, falling into a deep restorative sleep. On Friday morning, I woke up refreshed and starving; searching for breakfast and a new suitcase. I found a shop to purchase my suitcase as well as a new camera, new bamboo socks (*which lasted one month*), slippers and hair products.

I had a fantastic meal at a diner, decorated with white and black checkered floor tiles, you see in the movies. I kept forgetting, to tell the server, no cream on top of the hot chocolate. Why do they do that? I found a shop to buy enough yummy snacks for the next couple of days. Finding the flights and time zones really play havoc, with my eating habits; discovering if I wasn't hungry, had something to do with the fact, I should have been asleep and vise versa.

As this was my third visit to this city, I spent a couple of hours re-exploring the streets, finding the Christmas shop I had visited previously. It was an amazing fact, these shops were open year-round. I just wished I bought a couple of things to send home, but I stopped myself, as I'd be collecting eight months worth of stuff.

Friday night after my afternoon expedition, I enjoyed a nice dinner downstairs at one of the restaurants. The whole ground floor, of the motel, was filled with bars and restaurants and unfortunately my location wasn't the place to be, if you wanted a good night's sleep. I slept well until about 1:00 am, when disturbed by the patrons, who started leaving the bars. I hate my sleep being disrupted, struggling to get back to sleep, especially when I'd been living in a different time zone, staying awake until about 3:00am.

I was shocked, to discover, it was lunch time on Saturday when I finally woke up. I had planned to visit the botanical gardens for the entire day; however by the time the shuttle bus arrived, I had less than two hours to race around to see *EVERYTHING*.

On the return trip back to town, the bus I was travelling on was a 'hop-on-hop-off' bus, with the driver telling us, about the local attractions we could visit. I decided to 'hop-off' in China town, not realising it was a forty minutes' walk back to the motel. It was beautiful spring evening, as I enjoyed walking off my meal of honey king prawns – with left over fried rice for breakfast. *With all of my travels and the different restaurants I've visited, I haven't found a restaurant that serves fried rice better than the one in my home town.*

When I arrived back to the motel, I repacked by bags, ready for departure at the bus depot at 7.30 am. It's a real pity, the guests partying until 3:00am, did not appreciate I needed sleep; once again awake half the night. When I rang the reception at 1:00am, the clerk on the phone said "the motel wasn't advertised, as a quite motel, and if I wanted a good night's sleep, I should've stayed somewhere else".

You can imagine I wasn't impressed, with his answer or attitude, as ear plugs were delivered to my room. The hotel should have offered them, to all guests, as they checked in. Checking out the next morning, I was advised, how lucky I was, as if it was summer time, the roof-top nightclubs were open, and nobody gets any sleep.

The lesson learnt from this experience; before I book anywhere to stay, read the comments of other guests, mentioning the bars and lack of sleep. There were many other motel complexes in and around the city; I could've stayed at, where I'd have had a good rest.

I believe there're three main reasons, for staying at any motel, yes overnight. The first was a clean room; the second a comfy bed and the third, was you actually get sleep, thrown in for good measure. Fancy having a motel where you don't actually sleep; maybe the sleep comes during the day, since you're supposed to be partying all night long. *I added my comments of my impressions and funnily enough it wasn't a favourable review.*

THE GARDENS

Nature was my church; searching to find a special place in the gardens, to pray this year would open doors, to life's wonderful treasures. I desperately needed to find the Bella, buried amongst all the grief, suffering, stress and loneliness. What I needed the most, from this adventure, was the 'freedom' of time, allowing me the space to re-evaluate my life, and find my true self.

Once I overcome the disappointment, of the time factor, I enjoyed the afternoon. There must have been millions of bulbs, planted throughout the gardens. Everywhere I looked hyacinths, tulips, daffodils and many other bulbs were displayed, in their most magnificent glory. Not many people were visiting the gardens, this late in the afternoon. I must admit, the summer visits to the gardens, were more alive with flowers and children, running around, with a heightened sense of energy, laughter, joy and happiness.

Today, there seemed to be a quietness that I needed. The other visitors were quiet, in their own little worlds, exploring the gardens, finding vistas to enjoy the ambience, of the gardens, from different viewpoints, while eating my snacks. The structure of the gardens was different this time, because the trees had bare branches, displaying a unique look. Spring flowering ornamental trees, glistened in the afternoon sun; their dropped petals, creating a beautiful, colourful carpet underneath the trees.

I discovered a merry-go-round located in its own building. Oh to be a child again or just a child at heart, to enjoy the ride, but today the doors were locked; the lights turned off. It would've been lovely, for the ride to be lit up, listening to the fairy tale music playing, as the carousel revolved around, for everyone to see.

Wait a moment, I can imagine it all now in my mind, visualising the lights shining brightly, spotlighting all of the different animals. The children would have climbed onto the carousel, searching for their favourite character, with mum or dad lifting them up. The carousel starts moving; the music in rhythm, with the children, bobbing up and down, on their favourite creatures. The children's laughter, echoes throughout the building, as the parents, stand by, waiting for their child, to come back around, to take another photo. The happiness and joy, this merry-go-round has created, was evident on the smiling faces, of the children and parents alike. The parents would be taken back, to a time, when they were the ones, on the carousel, with their parent's waiting for them, to come back around.

I just loved exploring all of the places around the garden, checking with myself, I remembered it correctly. The walk through the Japanese part of the garden, was interesting, with the structure of the bare tree trunks; noticing the buds re-emerging. My favourite surprise, from the last visit; a 'window' in the hedge, at the bottom of the Japanese garden, allowing a view, of the cove, where boats moored for safety, and a dock available, for visitor to the gardens.

My visit was a wonderful peaceful time, as I was also embarking, on a new cycle of life. My new season, was about to begin, in a display of wonderful blossoms, highlighting my true magnificence. I will be honoured, in a type of 'coming of age' presentation, unveiled to the world, 'this is me'.

The afternoon went by in a dream, as each corner I turned, revealed another amazing vista. After I finished my quick tour of the gardens, I relaxed, near the gift shop, enjoying an ice-cream.

When I downloaded all the photos; I was amazed and truly blessed, to see the garden in spring. The azaleas and rhododendrons, throughout the gardens, were magnificent with their bright colours. How wonderful it'd be, to create and maintain a garden like this. Maybe, this was inspiration enough, to show me, what I could achieve, with the right help in my own garden.

This garden in winter was definitely on my bucket list.

Chapter 2

HOST NO. 1 - THE ISLAND - APRIL

THE MORGAN FAMILY AND THEIR HOME

My first host family; a young mum (Judy), dad (Steve), children; nine year old James and eight year old Anthony. My visit here, was for one week only, due to the impact the 'volunteers' had on their everyday life. A complete stranger would be living in their house, with their children. I know from my own experience; placing a lot of trust in the people, invited into your home. Of course they didn't need to worry about me, as I'm a perfectly responsible mother and grandmother, offering them a wonderful service, for the seven days I was there.

On my farm in Australia, I offer this same experience, where people come to help me in my garden, in exchange for food and board. I have met people, from all over the world, who has helped me create my own way of life, living in rural Australia, living the dream.

I arrived at the bus station, meeting Judy; driving back to the house, where Steve and the boys were waiting for breakfast of pancakes. We enjoyed the brunch, before I settled into my room.

The original owners had lived, in the house, since the fifties when it was built; with Judy and Steve being the second owners. Judy and Steve left the mainland in search of a sustainable, self-sufficient, organic lifestyle, four-years-ago.

The main level of the house had two bedrooms, bathroom and Steve's office, with a spacious lounge room; filled with an assortment of musical instruments, including a piano. The dining room was located off a small kitchen with a little balcony, big enough for one person to stand on. On the lower level, under the back of the house; was the laundry area with clothesline, a guest bedroom, the heating system, storage areas, plus Judy's office.

A two bedroom cottage, next to the main house, was rented out, generating an income to support Steve and Judy's sustainable lifestyle.

The farms' size was five acres, divided into smaller paddocks; the biggest yard was used for the sheep and a bison; fattened up and placed in the freezer. A large chicken pen, located near the cottage, housed the chickens, fed scraps from the kitchen. The two boys collected the eggs each day, as part of their chores.

Within the five acres, an area to one side of the house has remained a natural wooded area, to act as a buffer, between the neighbours. The trees in this forest area were old; spending an hour, one afternoon, talking to the trees, inspecting all of the movement in the forest, becoming aware of the warmer weather. The sunlight in spring was so magical, with the sunbeams shimmering and shining in between all of the branches of the trees. Moving around the forest floor, the light beams, from the sun's ray, are broken by a tree trunk; then reappearing to create a surreal atmosphere. Your footsteps are placed ever so lightly on the path; your presence; unchanging. The crisp green leaves unfurling from the limbs, like a hand, clutched shut, as one finger, at a time, opens, revealing a magical surprise.

Judy and Steve's way of life was different, from the modern twenty-first-century family. Restricted topics of conversation, allowed to be discussed at the dinner table, with the children unaware of happenings, in the greater world. The children attend a private school, not allowing students access to mobile phones, television, radios, computers or any influence from the modern world. No clothing or products, with slogans or promotional gear, were permitted. The parents agreed to these terms and conditions, before the children were allowed to attend, this particular school. Steve was responsible for the children's discipline, taking them to school and their homework. Judy was responsible for meals and their laundry, with both parents sharing the upbringing of their children.

The lifestyle Steve and Judy live, was an inspiration for anyone, wanting a 'basic organic way of life'. What an amazing start to my trip, realising you don't need, material possessions, of the twenty-first-century, for a satisfying life. The changes needed to secure the planet are achievable, with a change of attitude; a bit of little effort, returning to a 'simplistic way of life'.

BATHROOM, WASHROOMS AND THE ENVIRONMENT

Steve showed me around the house, with only one toilet, located upstairs next to Steve and Judy's bedroom. If I needed the bathroom, during the night, I had two options; option one: coming upstairs or option two: 'just pee' on the lawn, without any close neighbours, the outside option was OK. However most nights, it was raining and rather cold, sneaking upstairs, hoping not to disturb anyone on the creaky wooden stairs.

Another part about their toilet system; was using reusable wipes, instead of toilet paper. This alternative method used scraps of material, sterilized, washed and reused again. The things you do for the environment!!

Another rule for the washroom was not flushing the toilet each time it was used. Their water came from a well, using electricity to pump; less water used, equates to less electricity, equates to a lower power bill. If it's yellow let it mellow, nothing new to me, as I practice this at home.

THE WORK WEEK

Each morning I had breakfast, after the children went to school, allowing the family time together. Steve and Judy both worked from home. Judy needed a volunteer, to complete the jobs, without annoying her every five minutes for instructions.

My work week started after lunch on my first day, with Judy and the boys showing me around the property; my list of jobs discussed.

It was a beautiful Sunday afternoon, with all the family, out in the garden working. Both the boys had their own vegetable beds to look after themselves. Steve spent the afternoon trying to start a rotary hoe, to plough up the vegetable beds, but the machine refused to start. By the end of my week Steve had tried several times, but the machine refused to start.

I kept myself busy, changing jobs, when I got bored, or when my arms, legs or back got sore from weeding, I'd go from the green house to reorganising, watering or planting up some new seedlings. I'd collect more newspapers for the rows; or change the jobs from being on my hands weeding, to using a shovel or fork.

My jobs included weeding the peony rose gardens, the garlic beds and other areas already planted. I planted the new seed of beans, peas, beets, quinoa, spinach and chard into prepared beds, using sawdust, for mulch to aid weed control.

A large bed of strawberries; I thinned out, wrapping the extra plants, in newspaper; placing them at the road side stall, selling for fifty-cents each.

One day when it was too wet, I worked inside grinding the thin flat strips of dried garlic, into powder form, transferring the powder into jars; placing them down at the roadside stall. What an easy day's work, especially with my music playing next to me, while preparing dinner for that night. The kitchen was definitely my favourite room in the house; the only thing missing was a glass or two of my favourite liqueur!!!

HUMMINGBIRDS

My favourite highlight, of this home, was sitting at the dining room table, watching the hummingbirds visiting the feeder, placed outside the window. I cannot believe how they flap their wings so quickly; moving between the feeder and their hiding place in the trees. The hummingbirds are smaller than my little finger, with their nests invisible to detect, amongst the branches, of the trees. The syrup to feed them was only water and sugar, made on the stove top, adding it to the feeders, when the mixture was cool.

ALMOST SELF SUFFICIENT

Judy and Steve have a root cellar, located under a large evergreen tree, near the cottage. The small room was accessed by a door, on the north facing part, of the earth mound. The room was lined with shelves, filled with onions, potatoes, apples, and oranges. This week, we were eating the last of the apples, from the previous year.

The orchard and vegetable garden weren't very big, but I reckon, at least seventy-percent of their food, for the whole year, comes from the fruit trees and vegetable patch during the summer months. The previous volunteer, Matt, helped Steve extend the hot house, to grow tomatoes, egg plant, peppers and other crops needing a higher growing temperature.

In the basement under the house, a large storage unit was divided into twelve slots, where Steve and Judy place all of their produce. The preserves are divided into twelve, so each month they have a good selection of food. The freezer was divided in the same way, so they have their own food, year round and only supplement, when necessary.

This was a wonderful idea otherwise their favourite 'something' could all be eaten in the beginning. (*That was what I usually do with my favourites*). The farm grows apples, plums, cherries and peaches processed in various ways. A maple tree, in spring was tapped, to make their own maple syrup. The neighbours within this community, use a barter system, to share and exchange produce, for everyone's benefit.

Judy preserves as much of their produce as possible, using a few different methods. Raw fruit and vegetables, were placed in the freezer directly, or blanched on the stove top. The dehydrator was used to dry garlic, vegetables and fruits. A Christmas gift of a canner would make life, this year a little easier, rather than using the stove top to boil the bottles.

With the chickens for eggs, the bison and sheep for meat, adds up considerably, the amount of food, sourced directly from their property. What an amazing achievement to be almost self-sufficient

DUMPSTER DIVING

One of my most exciting adventures was dumpster diving, for cardboard, as I had 'ran out' of all of the paper and cardboard, stockpiled at the home. One morning Steve and I drove down to the local industrial recycling bins; three metres tall by six metres long, with Steve jumping into the bin, and began throwing the cardboard to me, as I loaded everything into the car. We even tried to steal other peoples' boxes, but said they were too 'valuable'. The shops on the island were reimbursed for recycling their cardboard boxes.

MEALS AND CONVERSATIONS

Food – glorious food it was so good, and so simple.

The dairy the family consumed during the week was obtained from a local, organic farm. Steve purchased cheese; and milk, which he used to make yoghurt. The rest of their diet was made up of lentils and beans. Most of the hosts I visited; living a basic vegetarian lifestyle, used lentils as the main stable part, of their diet. Each morning Steve juices the apples for breakfast, and then adds the pulp into the breakfast mix with the oats.

I used my culinary talents to prepare a couple of meals. Guess which ones I made for them?? My Alfredo crepes: creamy onion, mushroom and bacon sauce; my second meal was Bella's famous lasagne. These meals were enjoyed by the family, especially Judy, having a break from her nightly cooking duties, in the kitchen.

Any dinner conservation was limited because the boys weren't allowed to have interaction with the outside world. Even though the children were oblivious, both parents worked at home, on their computers, accessing online news, as well as local newspapers.

Being protected from everything – like politics, normality with their fellow age group, music, movies, the 'talk' and interests of their peers. It'd be like other cultures, having their own beliefs; limiting interaction with the general population. This education system would be compared to spiritual/religious cults or even remote communities, without a connection, to the outside world.

The world needs communities like this one, to make the necessary changes, for a better planet. Consumerism is out of control, in the first world countries; as we need to step back, to observe what we're creating, for our future generations.

EXPLORING THE ISLAND

Judy mentioned if I wanted to explore the Island; head up to the highway and hitch-hike. I've watched tooooooo many movies, so that wasn't even an option. Maybe if I was young, trim and sexy, I might have given it a go. *Please get a reality check on your life, there's no way I'd ever attempt to hitch hike.*

That was how it was done on the Island, apparently, safe and everyone does it. The day light hours were still short, as I worked from 9:00am and finished about 4:00pm; with little spare time, to go anywhere.

I read a newspaper article about a local man, who late one night, overbalanced on a dock at his home, falling into a river. I believe you've about twenty minutes, before the temperature of the water, takes effect on your body. The water, at this time of the year, was snow melt, with fast flowing streams. While on one of my walks, I came across a bridge, stopping to reflect for a few minutes on the family, grieving their missing loved one, with the authorities still searching.

I managed to explore a bit of the area, on my own, walking to a small park, thirty-minute's walk away from the house. On this particular cold, wet, rainy afternoon, I was geared up with warm clothing and water-proof jacket, spending a few hours reading a book, sitting under a picnic shelter. Even though the weather was cold, I could sense the movement in the trees.

TRESTLE BRIDGE

One afternoon the family and I headed to the nearby trestle bridge, for a picnic dinner. The historic bridge had been damaged, by local youths, who tried to burn it down. The local authorities realized it was cheaper to restore it, rather than knock it down. I cannot believe the Council considered destroying this part of their national heritage. *What the hell were they thinking?*

The trail was used by hikers, horse riders, bike riders, if fact by anyone interested in exploring the country side. While the restoration work was under construction, a detour of a few miles was the alternative path, for crossing the gorge. The bridge recently reopened to the public; the family taking this opportunity to visit. On the approaches to each side of the bridge, were wide access paths and information booths about the area.

The family and I walked to the other side of the bridge, to a platform, leading down to the river, about one-hundred-meters below us. We stayed on the platform, throwing out a rug, enjoying a selection of cheeses, dips, breads and crackers, with the fudge I purchased, as a special treat. It was a beautiful afternoon to be out in nature, witnessing something unique about the Canadian way of life; even the mosquitoes kept us company.

THE HILL

One morning, Judy had an appointment near a park, dropping me off, where I spent a couple of hours, sitting amongst the old growth forest. The forest trees were covered in moss and lichens; with the morning light playing a magical part, in my photos, capturing the sun rays; shinning through the tree branches, lighting up the ferns, on the forest floor. My favourite saying when I'm hiking "it's not the destination that was important; it's the journey".

Other people were using the track this morning, even a woman with a baby-carrier on her back. Yes I would love this track as my daily exercise path to fitness and wellbeing. Any trip you take should never be, about the destination; you have to enjoy the journey along the way, to stop and smell the roses.

It was a great place for me to reconnect, as I stopped about half way, to sit and listen to the messages the trees had for me. *YOU* have to *STOP*, to listen, to nature, to truly appreciate a place like this. My natural therapist Louisa, told me to sit in an old growth forest, if I had the opportunity, which was what I did!

MARINE PARK CENTRE

Saturday morning Steve, the boys and I headed to the official opening, of the marine park centre, with Steve picking up two children, from a friend's place. When we finished reversing the car down their driveway, Steve kept driving backwards in circles, around the cul-de-sac, at least four times. When the car finally came to a stop, all you could hear were screams of laughter, coming from the children in the back seat. Steve finally placed the car into 'drive', as we continued our adventure, with a car full of happy smiling people.

The two children, we picked up, were originally from Chile; where they spoke Spanish. The parents moved to Quebec; where they learnt French and now they're learning English. What an amazing life these children were living in these different countries and communities. Steve spoke Spanish to the children, which helped with the conversation.

We spent a few hours down at the centre with free activities for everyone. The children from Chile were on restricted diets, and when their father arrived, they were only allowed one cookie. Their upbringing was very strict with the parent's values, morals and beliefs instilled in their children. This, I believe, was based on the choices; we can all make for a better planet, a better lifestyle and a better way of life.

A local community club constructed a lookout, built out of timber logs, I'm sure would survive a tsunami. Built like a fort, visitors enjoyed climbing the stairs, to view the wildlife out in the bay. Today volunteers were at the lookout, helping visitors look through binoculars.

The centre had an interactive area, including touch tanks, filled with marine animals from the local bay. Our children explored the beach and rocks, placing any creatures they found, into the touch tanks. The community was well represented, with a large crowd, gathering to take part in the celebrations.

When the official proceedings started, I listened to a lady, aged in her seventies, who'd visited the bay as a child, spending many-a-day out on the water, fishing for salmon, with her grandfather.

This lady, who now resides at the bay, helped campaign local and federal governments, for funding to build this interactive educational facility. Over many years, government and environmental issues had changed the bay. This lady was looking forward to restoring the bay to 'the way it used to be, when she was a child'; going salmon fishing with her grandchildren.

The official part of the day included an aboriginal group of local elders, dancing and singing traditional songs. The elders told stories, of their people, who had lived in this area for hundreds of years.

I enjoyed the time at the centre, with perfect weather; honoured to be part of this community. This experience was what, I wanted from my trip; being connected to the places I visited, so I wasn't just another tourist, but helping the community with their long term plans of being organically sustainable; looking after the planet, for the betterment of everyone's future.

VOLUNTEER WEEK

Judy and Steve only occasionally drank wine and didn't drink tea or coffee. I tried a few different teas, from a variety pack in the kitchen drawer, but I have to admit, I'm definitely a coffee lover.

That week was volunteers' week, with a few local establishments, offering complimentary coffee/tea vouchers. I had an hour's walk each way to redeem the free coffee, enjoying a look around the local stores. I just couldn't help myself, finding a fudge shop, buying a small piece, saving it for the family outing, to the bridge.

THE DUNGEON

Judy and Steve didn't have Wi-Fi, in their house, because of apparent health concerns. My internet was via a cable in my bedroom. This situation was perfect, for me, with my own personal space I reconnected each day, via the internet.

I was lucky to have my own room, as previously, the workers stayed upstairs in the lounge room, on a fold out bed, with no privacy. Steve had just finished the guest bedroom, located in the basement; with its own heater and privacy from the family. My room was like a dungeon, with no windows, and I felt like a bear, in hibernation, when the lights went out each night, I snuggled up under the covers, and went to sleep.

My room was lined with timber; just loving the way the 'knots' add to the character of the wood. I found a few interesting images, on my walls, exploring the odd shapes. The eyes and faces, in the wood, are a point of focus, to ask them, to share their thoughts with you.

As the tree grows, knots are formed, with the memories and life events, stored within its DNA. Trees are part of the creation of our planet; when they change their form, from a tree to a chair, bed, picture frame or panelling on your wall; becoming part of your life. They're still 'alive', having the ability to connect with you, if you dare to ask them 'what they know'. Be brave, make a connection to the wood, ask a question, and then wait patiently for the answer. This idea was the same for rocks and crystals. Crystals once located in the depths of mother earth; now sit on a table, in your house. The belief, they hold memories of their journey, and offer these gifts to those seeking the truth.

There's only one problem, with my room being located, in the basement. Every time someone walked upstairs, I'd hear them, in the kitchen and dining room, especially the boys in the morning, having breakfast and getting ready for school. I was grateful, during the night it's peaceful and quiet.

Steve mentioned *(casually)* the last worker, had a regular visit, from the resident rat. I've nightmares about being visited by rats, as they're the bain of my life, on the farm. I think the rat got the vibes from me, he'd be a 'dead rat' if he entered my room while I was there.

I spent most of the week recovering from jetlag; and the total exhaustion of the last five-years. I believe I gave my first job my all, by completing the list of jobs, Judy had given me. It's a pity we didn't get more cardboard to finish that particular job.

The experience was different for me, as the interaction between Steve, Judy and I was limited because of the work volume. As a result I spent a lot of time alone with no one to talk to. *Poor ME.*

THE GOODBYES

Sunday morning, it was time for goodbyes, as Steve and the boys had hugs of appreciation. Judy was working in Sumner that morning, so it worked out well for me. The weather was glorious, as I breathed in deeply; the beautiful spring morning air. I cannot help being thankful to witness the glory of spring in the northern hemisphere.

I enjoyed my trip, down the centre of the island, to Sumner with Judy. A truck accident, last year spilled fuel into the stream, I had visited before. The truck driver was drunk and the environmental committee, were still processing, what affect the accident, will have on the local salmon spawning for the coming years.

As Judy and I pulled up at a taxi rank, it was time for our goodbyes. Judy thanked me, for my help, and left me with these parting words "I hope you find, the things you're looking for, and some things you weren't".

THE REASON AND LESSONS LEARNT

I often think about Judy's quote; definitely finding more than I'd ever anticipated. The messages I received all throughout my trip; was 'life was too short' so make the most of it. Enjoy each day, as if it was, your last day, on earth. Appreciate everything.

I truly believe the places; I have chosen to stay, were the places I was meant to visit, lessons to be learned and shared. The whole work experience idea was based on the sharing of talents, expertise and cultures.

So what was the lesson learnt here? Definitely the 'back to basics lifestyle'; as what this family was doing; was needed on a global scale. Living a minimalistic lifestyle was the key, with little or no impact, on the environment and human society as possible.

Flying from Density to Windstrome, seeing the sun rise up over the islands in the bay

Chapter 3

IN TRANSIT TO ALASKA APRIL

TIME OUT

The taxi transferred me to a motel near the Density Airport, as it was only 8:00am, on a Sunday morning, I couldn't book into my room until after lunch. I was able to store my luggage with the clerk, until I returned. The same cabbie dropped me down town in Density, where I was surprised; this town was certainly quieter and a lot less touristy than Sumner.

I spotted a little café with a queue out of the door, thinking it must be popular for breakfast. A man in front of me appeared to be dining alone; my little voice said, I should ask, if he wanted company. *No I wasn't brave enough yet!* I finally made it inside the café door, the man reached over for the Sunday paper, offering me a section. I replied "no the paper is toxic".

I didn't ramble on too much about how depressing it was reading stories from around the world; published to bring people into despair each day, upset while watching the news on television. All of the injustices around the world with murders, wars, rapes, bombings, etc etc etc. *DO NOT GET ME STARTED. See more of this in Chapter 21 – In Box.*

After waiting for about thirty minutes, I was offered a bench spot, along a window, with a view of the street, with a sign in the café' 'children left unattended will be fed espresso and given a puppy'. I enjoyed my breakfast omelette, as much as I enjoyed people watching; wondering about their conversation, as I studied the expressions on their faces.

I really miss having someone to share my life with – all of those years without someone to enjoy such occasions like this one. Living in an isolated rural area, for all of those years, as Ricky worked away, supporting our family. Many lunches, movies, and many other occasions and events I attended alone. This year I need to find someone, to share my life with; new friends to enjoy socialising with. Desperately, I need a new beginning, a new peace and a new attitude, to be brave; and more open, allowing people into my life.

Bella Pearce

I watched a movie with a comment "we all need someone to witness our lives, so we know we exist" – how true is that statement.

After breakfast I roamed the streets, window shopping, discovering a lavender shop, producing all of their products; from the ingredients grown, at their farm. I purchased a jar of hand cream as a reminder of my visit.

I found a rock museum/jewellery shop, with a cave; you walked into with rocks on display. The jewellery store was filled with crystals displayed, on glass shelves, lining the windows around the outside of the shop. The inside counters had jewellery and crystals in glass display cases, for you to wonder around and admire. I love when shops display their items in colour sequences, and this shop did exactly that. I spent some time chatting to the staff, while looking at stones and picked out a large rhodochrosite crystal and a green jade ring, to take home, as mementos of my time on the island.

A visit to the aquarium filled in some extra time, as I enjoyed watching children and their reactions; when they saw all the sea creatures in the tanks. The aquarium had a touch tank, noticing how well the creatures handled the crowds. The time spent, watching the marine animals, swimming around had such a calming effect, on anyone who stops to see, with the creatures having no worries or concerns. What a life, knowing their meals are delivered, with their days filled, with menial duties, like swimming around in circles. The aquarium had a gift shop, purchasing a book about a seagull, and a fancy pair of coloured glasses for the grandchildren.

After the aquarium I spent a couple of hours walking along the water front; a beautiful spring day to spend outdoors, with a light cloud cover and calm water. A yacht race was taking place out in the bay; a few boats were ready at the starting line, as a group of people on the wharf watched the activities. People were fishing, off the wharf, looking over the side of the railing, the water was so clear, and you could see the fish swimming around, also noticing it was a bloody long way down, to the water.

After I left the jetty I walked along the foreshore, inspecting a row of waterfront houses. I could imagine, witnessing the sunrises and sunsets, from the verandahs, of these houses. I continued to walking, until I came to a ferry terminal. IF I had my passport and luggage with me, I could've taken the ferry over to Windstrome, that afternoon, to spend the night. Had I known what I was doing, it could have been a better plan, than spending all day roaming the streets, with the early morning flight the next day. *You don't know it at the time, but there's always a reason for the current course.*

I found a nice café to indulge a delicious cake and coffee, as a substitute for lunch, before returning to the motel. The taxi fares for the day totalled ninety-dollars; made up of fifty-dollars from Sumner to the motel, and then twenty-dollars, each way, from the motel to Density. Boy of boy, it's expensive, but there wasn't an alternative.

I walked to the restaurant next door, for dinner, before re-organising my luggage, for the flight. What was I thinking? I wasn't impressed with such an early flight; having two days rest, before my next job started, easily travelling on a later flight.

The taxi arrived at the airport in record time, clearing check-in and security, with almost two hours of time to kill. What do you do, when you have nothing to do? Eat of course! Coffee with some fruit for breakfast, but who wants to eat breakfast at 5.00am; but of course you do it anyway, just to fill in time.

My most favourite pastime was 'people watching' with a group of soldiers, sitting nearby. They obviously knew each other, as I watched their camaraderie, sharing jokes and stories, ready to begin some mission or adventure. Oh, how the mind, races off to conclusions, wondering what their plans were today.

Even though I had been complaining about the early flight, my attitude was soon replaced by amazement, witnessing the best sunrise of my entire trip, from an elevated view, of about 30,000 feet. I was seated next to a window, watching the sun, peak through the clouds, on the eastern horizon.

In the eastern sky, the magnificent clouds were multi coloured, their glow reflecting on the still waters. With the rising sun's rays, penetrating the spaces between the perfectly formed clouds, I was speechless. The darkness of the islands, scattered in the bay, were silhouetted against the rainbow of colours, spotlighting the entire view, before me. As the flight continued, I witnessed the changing light, as the new day began.

Sometimes I had to pinch myself, to remind me, how blessed, to be on this amazing journey. How could I have asked for anything more in life than to witness nature's true magic?

I almost missed my connecting flight, with no idea how big the Windstrome Airport was. The underground system of trains were amazing, and if I wasn't totally panicked, about getting to my next flight, I might have enjoyed the experience.

I was almost running to get to the next flight, pissed off, because I didn't get a coffee and something to eat, before boarding the plane. Getting up at 3.30am certainly turns your stomach into knots, when it comes to food. Of course you have to understand, it was only 7:00am. *I felt like I had been travelling for days.*

NORTH TO ALASKA

The flight north was one of the best flights I have ever taken. With a window seat, at the back of the plane, I headed 'north to Alaska', registering the snow-capped mountains monopolising the entire landscape below.

The air was so crisp and clean; the earth celebrating a brand new day, with the outside temperature at -50C, on a beautiful spring morning in the northern hemisphere. Looking out the window I was humbled and truly amazed at the beauty of our planet, as I started the second leg of my adventure.

As I left my seat, the air hostesses assumed I was Alaskan and said "welcome home". I told the hosties I was an Australian, working as a volunteer, for an eight month period in The States and Canada. People's reactions were shocked, bewildered, astonished, and envious I've chosen to do this midlife crisis, gap year adventure.

I found my way around the Saarland airport, collected my luggage, phoning for the motel shuttle. Each accommodation establishment was allocated a number, picking up the courtesy phone; dial the number, which goes directly to their reception. The airport was located in the town prescient, I didn't have long to wait, for my ride.

Leaving the main airport building, I quickly found a jacket, noticing a difference in the air temperature, of probably twenty-degree Celsius. The trip from the airport to the motel was only a few minutes, noticing snow banks on the side of the roads.

My accommodation was in an apartment building, with a spacious room, including a desk and large bed. The desk sat beneath the windows, with a view, of a large snow-capped mountain. Once I was settled into the motel, I hailed a taxi to the nearest movie theatre, for an afternoon escaping reality; one of my favourite pass-times.

For dinner I found a café across the road, ordering a green side salad with fish and chips. The meal was big enough for breakfast and lunch the next day; spending the whole day lazing about, reading and catching up on sleep.

For dinner, I walked down the road about fifteen minutes, hoping for some wild caught Alaskan salmon. My anticipation was satisfied, walking back to the motel for an early night. I was meeting Bree, the next morning to continue my adventures.

THE DECISION

Bree and Marcus had been completing, all of the pre-staff and pre-season jobs, themselves, for the previous three years. I pushed, for them to accept my help, this early in the season. The work staff arrived in mid May, two weeks before the first guests arrived. This amount of time was sufficient, for the entire centre, to be functional and open for business.

Because of my travel restrictions I wanted to be in Alaska for spring; after a multitude of emails, and a phone interview, I was accepted as their first volunteer. I told Bree Aussies are bred pretty tough, especially coming from a farming back ground, having to deal with rough conditions; such as camping.

Bree explained; this process was based on a job interview. I wasn't just a worker, but a staff member. I had to be the right person, with the right attitude, capabilities and attributes, to work there.

Because this was the first volunteer place I had applied for, I just wanted to go there and didn't know what all the fuss was about. I did learn the process, of what volunteering, was all about after that. The hosts had to pick the best person for the job, and that's why I got knocked back by a few of the hosts, because I wasn't what they needed.

Sleeping on the Docks in Alaska

Chapter 4

HOST NO. 2 THE LODGE SEAL BAY APRIL/MAY

FIRST DAY

I woke up early, anticipating meeting Bree, as she checked in the motel last night. When I hadn't heard from her by 7.30am, I went out for breakfast. Bree and I met up at reception, loading my gear into the truck, before spending an hour driving around town, delivering posters, to businesses, to advertise activities at the centre for this year.

Our next stop was a trade show, for the distribution of food and equipment to the northern region. The trade centre was filled to the brim with companies promoting their products. I could've saved myself, the cost of breakfast; with hundreds of free samples and taste tests available.

Bree and I did our own thing, both looking at different products, for different reasons. Bree was looking for new products, for the centre; and I wanted products, organic, and free of gluten and soy. Yeah right! There were heaps of products for me to taste. I'm not sure what Bree thought about all of the products here, as I guarantee, ninety-five-percent of the products were extremely processed.

I managed to fill the sample bag with bits and pieces, mostly for Marcus and Annabelle. It must have been my intuition to collect more, as these were my dinner that night.

I enjoyed the wine tasting, at lunch time, since I wasn't driving. When Bree was ready, we headed to the wholesaler, spending $3,500 on the grocery bill. Bree had notes on her phone, with prices and quantities, of the items, she needed to purchase. Bree compared the prices with the shops in Scanar.

Last year, Bree spent her only day off, from work, over at Scanar, shopping for supplies for the centre. This year the pantry would be stocked, with enough supplies, for the entire season. Of course, Bree still had to shop for supplies, not available from their garden.

I was the trolley girl, (I forgot they call them carts); filling ten carts, during the afternoon, with a production line going through the checkout; Bree and a worker loading the items onto five large flat-bed carts, transferring the shopping into the car, was a precision exercise, with the whole back of the truck; filled to the brim, also using the back seat, with half a meter of space available, just in case.

Finally, we started heading towards Scanar, a four-hours-drive away. When we pulled in for fuel, I purchased yoghurt and a baby Ruth chocolate *"Just because it was from my favourite 80's movie"*. Because I had a big breakfast, I wasn't hungry at the trade show. However, Bree had used the trade show taste testing, as her food intake for the day. I can't live without three meals a day; probably why I'm a happy, healthy, over-weight person☺.

The trip driving through the mountain ranges was amazing, as I studied the scenery; I knew exactly what I'd seen out of the window of the plane. The plane's route flew south to north; looking at this area, from the plane, I couldn't make out the landscape. The scenery was set in black and white, with swirling designs, like milk and dark chocolate melted in a bowl with white chocolate, creating an incredible scene. It's hard to describe, what looked like mud plains, at low tide, with a snow melt river, running off a nearby glacier, and a bridge crossing over the flood plains. Bree was actually driving, on the exact roads, I had seen from the plane. With the snow covered mountains, snow melt, and the tidal plains, the scenery was quite extraordinary.

Bree realized after we left the fuel station, we weren't going to arrive home that night; arranging for us to stay in Scanar, in the studio suit, belonging to Ian and Barbara. I realized my luggage was behind, all of the groceries, with no way of accessing my clothes. No makeup, toiletries, or change of clothes for the night. Bree took the sofa bed downstairs, in the lounge room; giving me the upstairs bedroom.

I wondered about dinner; when Bree didn't mention anything, I found cheese and crackers out of my sample bag. I was lucky the unit had soap, shampoo and moisturiser, enjoying a really long hot shower, with a good night's sleep, after an exhausting day with the groceries expedition.

SECOND DAY

The next morning I was awake early, going for a walk around the resort and marina. The first thing I noticed, across the bay, was the amazing snow covered mountain ranges. The view was breathtaking and truly awe inspiring, pinching myself, I was in Alaska. How unbelievable was this. I was so grateful.

I walked around the area, stopping briefly at the marina, looking at the fishing boats moored there. I love reading the name plates on the boats, to see where they're from. As I stood there looking at the boats, little did I know, an eagle was resting on the railing, three-metres away. Had I known he was there, I would have taken some great shots; but it was only, when I turned to look, in that direction, I noticed him. Unfortunately, the eagle had flown away, before I grabbed my camera. *Each time I came back to Scanar, I'd see the eagles at the docks.*

The resort wraps around, the edge of the bay, with a motel, function and restaurant areas located at one end of the complex. On the southern end, a row of multi-coloured, multi-storey town houses were located. These were privately owned, with the owners returning, to enjoy the northern summer.

Located near the marina, a cargo shipping terminal, delivered supplies, along the coastline, to towns without road access. I would've loved to go exploring, on one of these ferries, if I'd a chance.

A coast-guard base, also located at the marina, reminded me of a movie, with my favourite actor, Ryan Jones.

The crisp morning air filled my lungs, with my eyes taking in the breathtaking view. Anyone staying here would be truly appreciative, of the true beauty of Alaska, in spring. When I returned to the room, Bree was ready for breakfast; and as I finished eating, Bree spotted 'The Aurora' coming across the bay, jumping into the car and heading to the marina. Now this was where the fun was about to began? You reckon? NOT!!!

The process: load the groceries, into the totes (large plastic containers with slides underneath, with a rope handle attached). Gravity, along with the weight of the load, worked together, holding onto the rope, walking behind the tote, down the ramp. The ramps are the link between accessing the land to the docks; the ramps floating up and down, with the tides. When the tides were full; the ramps were easy to navigate, but when the tides were low, the ramps were steep. Can you guess how steep the ramps were? Of course, the best solution was to wait for the high tide, but that wasn't an option.

Lucky for me, Bree's husband Marcus, and Ian the owner, helped load the groceries into the boat. Bree lost the grip, of a tote's handle; the tub flying down the ramp, as we yelled out to a lady, walking on the ramp; running to get out of the way. The tub scooted down the ramp, continued along the dock, finally stopping. Luckily Jenny was near, the bottom of the ramp, and wasn't injured.

The newspaper headlines would've said 'ran over by a tote of groceries'. It's definitely no joking matter, but it was funny. Was it my weird, Aussie, sense of humour, seeing the funny side of the situation?

Once all of the supplies were unloaded, Bree drove the car, along the street, to a car park. "All aboard" says Ian; setting off on the next phase of the adventure. The bay's waters were calm, with an even low swell, with smooth sailing in 'the Aurora', a luxurious cabin cruiser. I sat up next to Ian, sharing stories, about his time in the area, as a pilot.

I enjoyed my two hour's rest, crossing the bay; as the next phase of 'operation food drop', continued for another three hours. A good system was created, with the boat unloaded and the supplies, finally stored away.

Ian was in charge of the bobcat, transferring the supplies from the cart, into the front of the bobcat bucket. A railing, on the second floor balcony, was removed for this exact purpose. As Ian lifted the bucket full of groceries; Bree and I walked up the stairs. By the time we finished unpacking one golf cart, Marcus had returned with a new load. We still used the stairs, each time to load and unload the bucket, I don't know!! About a million times.

After three hours the supplies were placed, into their final home, on the shelves or in the fridge. Some items were handled up to eleven times, before reaching their final destination.

What a busy morning at work, but it wasn't over just yet, as it was only lunch time. After placing all of the supplies into the kitchen, lunch was provided at Ian and Barbara's home. Barbara had been looking after Annabelle, Bree and Marcus's four-year-old daughter, while both were working. I enjoyed a lovely lunch, with my whole body, in shock of where I was, as I couldn't believe the view from the house.

After lunch my luggage went down on the hydraulic platform lift, to the staff quarters; as I discovered my room, on a dock. I was sleeping on a dock, in Alaska. Please do not wake me up. I definitely, wasn't in Kansas, anymore.

My first day wasn't over just yet, touring the entire complex; Bree making lists of jobs to be completed. I was pre-staff assistant to Bree and Marcus, to help in any way. This year, the centre was using volunteers, as workers, for the first time. Bree cooked dinner that night; I was unconscious, before my head hit the pillow.

As I lay awake in bed, one night, I thought about my first day with Bree. We couldn't have completed the grocery drop, in one day. 9:00pm we arrived at Scanar, then one hour loading the boat, then two hours travelling across the bay, and then WHAT? Were we supposed to unload the groceries at midnight? Crazy, Crazy, Crazy. I'm glad it worked out the way it did.

THE MOTHER HOUSE AND ART STUDIO

The one-eighty-degree view, to the south east, from Ian and Barbara's house was across Seal Bay, with majestic snow-capped mountains, right in front of your eyes. Ian and Barbara's house was built on two levels, on the side of the hill, with an earth bank, constructed for protection, from the western weather. A wrap-around verandah, on the top floor of the house, created an amazing vista over the entire landscape. Ian's room, on the main floor, had clear glass windows, like a conservatory, allowing uninterrupted views, of the stars, during the night.

In summer, blinds covered the windows, for Ian to sleep. *NOW* if I lived here, the curtains would be open every night, no matter what. What I would've given, for a chance to sleep there, just one night? A dream comes true; my perfect bedroom, and star gazing all night long. Making the dream even more perfect, would be the northern lights. Then I'd know, I had definitely, died and gone to heaven.

The art studio perched on the hill, above Ian and Barbara's house; had three-sixty-degree views around the township, over the whole complex and the mountains. If you were a 'sticky beak', you'd have uninterrupted views of the 'goings on'. I'd absolutely die, for a space like this, to call my own. Ian had been encouraging Barbara, to visit her studio, to start creating again; as ill health had kept her away, over the last couple of years.

I was called to the mother house, as Barbara needed assistance. *It was funny they called the main house, 'the mother house' as my daughter calls me 'the mother ship''.* The pantry and kitchen cupboards needed sorting out, organising and throwing out anything not needed. Barbara and Ian had only recently turned vegan, with products in the pantry, to be removed and taken to the staff kitchen, or the food bank in Scanar.

Bree asked me to help Barbara's for a couple of hours, cleaning out the fridge, with a black liquid coming out from under it. I smelt something 'bad' a couple of weeks ago, but didn't want to offend her. However, Barbara lost her sense of smell, when she had cancer treatment. After I cleaned out the fridge, we chatted, about who I was, and what I wanted from life. Talked about my struggles over my marriage breakup, my daughter Kristy's death, with too many emotions held onto, for too long.

Barbara always dreamed of having a centre, where people find themselves; conducting meditation sessions, in the chapel during the retreats. Barbara shared details of a technique, she uses in her sessions.

Barbara asks a person to go for a walk, around the grounds, to search for 'something' that catches their eye. It could be a piece of bark, a flower, a pebble or a feather. The item itself wasn't important; as you return to a spot, where you have a note book. Study your item, writing down the thoughts and feelings, the objects reveals. Keep looking at your item, hold it to your heart, turn it over, smell it. The exercise can bring up sadness, hurt, grief and anger. Keep exploring the feelings revealed to you, as you release the emotions.

I have used a similar exercise, using my crystals. I walk past the glass tray where my crystals are on display, search for the one, speaking to me today. I read my crystal book, for information and place the crystal into a little pouch, placing it in my bra and wear it for the day.

THE LODGE

When Ian and Barbara first purchased land here, it was to build their house and art studio. An opportunity presented itself, to purchase the neighbouring property, where the centre was now located. The staff quarter's dock and buildings; one self contained cabin and the hydraulic lift system were included in the purchase. The dock, with the hydraulic lift, received the delivery of supplies for the buildings. The construction workers used the staff quarters for accommodation, while they built the cabins; then used the cabins as accommodation, while they built the lodge. The short building season here, due to the extreme weather, made the construction of the centre, a two-year project.

The lodge had a peaceful atmosphere, and each time entering the lounge, I chose a stone out of the inspirational message bag. Eclectic items I studied, before choosing one, to hold or read or play. This was a time of quiet contemplation and reflection to calm my soul.

A beautiful, decorative wall hanging; situated on the wall of the lounge, caught my attention. The creation was made from a hand-dyed piece of fabric, with items sewn and decorated, to resemble a women's figure. Whoever created this wall hanging used wool, buttons and ribbons; capturing my imagination. I'm going to attempt, something similar, with a piece of fabric I purchased in Canada. *See more of the details of this in Quilting in Chapter 21.*

THE STAFF QUARTERS

OK stop dreaming and get back to reality. After lunch, on that first day, my luggage went down on the hydraulic lift, to the staff quarters, attempting the first of many trips, down the sixty stairs to my room (*stairway to heaven*:-). I was living on a dock, how about that!! I just loved waking up naturally, with my alarm clock, being the morning sun, rising up over the mountains. Each morning, I would pinch myself; watching each brand new day, start with the magnificent sunrises. When I sat up in bed, I witnessed the tides and the activity of the cove.

I enjoyed escaping to my room; just sitting quietly, on my bed, watching the world goes by. Life here never stood still, with the flow of the water, never stopping, the tide was either going in or out. The sun either shone or not, the stars and moon were out, and the snow on the mountains was melting, then a sprinkling of snow again. The hill, behind the staff quarters, blocked out the afternoon sun; but I still captured photos of the sun-setting clouds, reflected on the water. The whole area was coming alive with creatures, welcoming us each morning; as our bird feeder, at the staff kitchen, fed the squirrels as well as the blue jays.

The staff quarters consisted of four separate buildings; two buildings for the bedrooms; one building housed two separate bathrooms, with a shower and bio toilets. The main building was the common area for the staff, with a kitchen/dining/lounge room; and washroom with shower and toilet.

The staff dock was located below the staff quarters, with a float house attached. Marcus, Bree and Annabelle lived in the float house, along with the nanny. Looking at the float house on a high tide, almost level with the dock, and then surprisingly, on the next tide, was sitting in the mud.

What amazed me the most, about living here, was looking out to the view; the next time you looked up, the view was totally different. We had a small island, just out in front of our dock; one minute seeing most of it, and the next minute it's almost submerged.

Wi-Fi for the internet, kept me connected, with the rest of the world. I looked forward to receiving my daily astrology forecasts; hearing from family and friends, with news from home. The internet didn't work in our rooms, so we mostly sat around the dining table. The staff room didn't have TV reception, but we could watch videos or DVD's. I bought a couple of movies, Heather and I watched, after Annabelle went to bed.

In my room, in the afternoon, if Marcus was working nearby, Annabelle would lie on my bed to play with my crystals, while I read my book. My nine chakra crystals were lined up along the window sill, with my bed located beneath the window. Annabelle just loved playing with the crystals; her favourite was a carnelian. Annabelle would just lay there for ages, without saying or doing anything, as Marcus checked on her occasionally. One day, she did go to sleep; so angelic and peaceful to watch, as I placed a blanket around her.

Bree, Marcus and I decided we'd take turns at cooking dinner; preparing my favourite food: salmon. Last summer, Bree went salmon fishing, with their freezer full of fish. Or should I say, *WAS* full. I was in heaven, with wild halibut included on our dinner menu. Marcus and Bree owned their own smoker; used to smoke the salmon.

The centre was basically an organic vegan/vegetarian establishment, with lots of lentils in our meals. I reckon I ate more lentils and beans, over that six week period; than in the rest of my entire life combined. The food was good, with fantastic flavours. Marcus cooked breakfast, and for the first time in my life, I ate porridge with dried fruits, nuts and topped off with maple syrup - yummy.

The nights were still pitch black, during the first couple of weeks of my stay. If I needed to go to the bathroom, during the night; I stuck my head out the door, check for bears, ran as fast as I could, to the bathroom; and repeat the same, on the way back to my room. The temperature was still in the minuses, not very warm, to be running around in your jarmies. I was glad I didn't come, face to face, with a bear on the dock. I don't know what I'd have done? Or who would've been more frightened.

Maybe I could've jumped overboard, to escape the bear; in the hope the tide was high, and probably dies in the water from exposure, as the water was still freezing!! Or land in the mud and die instantly#@%!!! *I'm so glad, I have such an active imagination, and so relieved I didn't have to resort to any of the above measures.*

THE WORK SCHEDULE

Bree had set up the hot house with vegetable seeds, for a head start, for the seedlings to be a good size to transplant into the garden, during the working bee. With the overnight temperature still below zero, electric heaters were hooked up, keeping the temperature at eighty degrees. During the day we'd check, and turn off the heaters, if the day was warm enough.

Marcus and Ian transferred the float house, into its summer position, near the staff quarters. My job involved cleaning the float house, ready for Bree, Marcus and Annabelle, to move into. Currently, the family were staying in two rooms, in the lodge, usually used for Bree's office and the massage room.

With the float house ready, the next exciting job was transferring all of their belongings. We loaded everything into the golf cart, placing the cart on the hydraulic loader, to travel down to the staff quarters, and then manually carrying everything, down into the float house. OMG by the end of the day I could hardly move; walking from the lodge, down the sixty steps; down the ramps numerous times, unloading the entire cart; with the ramps getting steeper and steeper, as the tide went out. I'd walk back up to the lodge; starting the sequence, over again; all afternoon.

Bree and Marcus had cut a small hole in the wall, between the two rooms, so Annabelle could come into their bedroom. The other alternative was Annabelle leaving her room, going onto the dock; entering their bedroom, via the main door. It would be a rather scary scenario for any parent, especially as Annabelle was only four-years-old.

Ian had ordered some new foam flotation boards, to go under the main dock. When they arrived in Scanar, Marcus picked up the order, transferring it to the mail boat. One afternoon Marcus and I went over, to the mail boat, to pick up the supplies; balancing them nicely on the skiff. Marcus and I stored them in Ian's boat house, ready to complete the job of stabilizing the dock.

When I first started gardening, I found the ground was still frozen, so I left that particular job for another week or so, in hope I had better luck then. As the weeks progressed, the weather warmed a little, the snow melted as the ground was thawing.

A small pond, located near the lodge, was covered with snow and frozen, when I first arrived. Ian scared me one morning, turning on the pump, to recycle the water through a hidden waterfall. I couldn't believe how bad the water stunk, with the smell disappearing after a week. I sat on the bank of the pond, on my bum, with my feet almost touching the water, pruning the roses. At the other end of the pond, Barbara placed a bench seat; for visitors to enjoy the colourful view of the roses, flowering next to the waterfall.

I was given the perfect job, or so I thought! To apply a sand/lacquer mixture, to the main stairs from the dining room, the front foyer and the washrooms. These stairs were polished wood and during the previous year, a few people slipped; as socks were worn inside. Marcus had all of the supplies to complete the job, I volunteered for.

At the same time I was lacquering the stairs, Marcus was repairing the inside pond. He wore protective clothing and a mask while working, as the fumes were toxic. I had opened all of the windows, for ventilation, thinking I wouldn't be affected. As it turned out, I wasn't far enough away and felt nauseous from the fumes.

Marcus instructed; how to set up the tape to apply the lacquer. The job proceeded well over two days, and on the second afternoon, I asked Marcus about applying another layer of the grit, and he said yes, go ahead.

Well the next morning, he wasn't happy, advising me the stairs looked terrible; blaming himself for not checking on my progress. Marcus was angry, ranting about how Barbara wouldn't be happy with the job. Marcus said the lodge cost over $1million to build and I'd ruined the stairs. Bree, Ian and Barbara were inspecting the property that morning, which included the stairs. Marcus wasn't sure what was going to happen.

I spent the morning in the garden, on my knees, weeding, crying my little eyes out, because I'd stuffed up. How were we going to fix the problem? Or more importantly, how was Marcus going to fix the problem? When Ian came by later, he said the problem can be fixed, and not to worry about it. I was still upset and he said "don't worry, as we all make mistakes". Marcus used a wood chisel and hammer, and the new lacquer was removed quite easily. I just had to clean up all of the mess, re-tape it all and start again.

So the job took five days, and Barbara didn't really like the finished job, because it was rough. That's the purpose of the strip, in the first place, so no one slips down the stairs. The best alternative was a suitable adhesive tape, applied in strips, in one day, instead of all of the drama and mess. Annabelle was my little assistant, working with me on the stairs, helping with the tape placement.

Marcus mentioned he learnt a good lesson, from this situation, as he'd always been the worker; realising, workers needed to be supervised. This was a new level of responsibility for him. Marcus should have inspected my work, before I applied another coat. This was a lesson for me as well; as hosts have the right to demand, what they wanted me to do.

Each morning I greeted Ian with the phrase "another beautiful day in paradise" and he replied "yes and this location suits you". The snow-capped mountain loomed directly behind me, as Ian viewed me working in the garden. I would have my red-tinged-hair glowing in the sun; my eyes were bright with laughter and happiness. Who wouldn't want to be here, on this earth, in Alaska, this time of the year?

The time I spent in the garden, was like a breath of fresh air, as this was where I loved to be; with my hands in direct contact, with mother earth. I cherished the days I spent in the garden, with just the birds and nature keeping me company, and of course Annabelle, if she was behaving herself.

With Bree and Marcus busy with their jobs, Annabelle was with me a lot of the time, not to look after, but she was just there. She was a beautiful bright girl, full of energy, not stopping all day, following Marcus around, while he worked. Bree's job was in the office and/or with Barbara, so most of the time Annabelle was with Marcus. Unless she couldn't go with him, then she spent time with me. I really didn't mind, as long as she was not annoying me or misbehaving.

Annabelle and I had one great day together; pulling all of the summer growth from the steep bank below the vegetable garden. All of the last year's growth, of the fireweed plant had been crushed under the snow. As I continued to remove all of the rubbish, I got a delightful surprise finding a tiny pansy, with a flower on it. The pansy was sitting there, full of life, after surviving the minus temperatures, with two or more meters of snow, placed on top of it. The snow wasn't compacted, but light and fluffy, so I believe the flower just sat there, near the rock, waiting for the sunshine to appear again.

Barbara had mentioned to Bree, if I didn't slow down, there'd be no work for the volunteers at the working bee weekend.

Finally, the ground was defrosting; as I started working in the vegetable patch below the lodge. One particular day, ripping out the old vegetable plants from last year, Annabelle cracked a spas attack. I had rested, on one of the large rocks, in the garden, and Annabelle started screaming, I wasn't allowed to sit there. Barbara says "no one's allowed to sit on the rocks, because they were special". After a few minutes of this inappropriate screaming, I walked away, telling Annabelle, 'if she continued acting like this, then she wouldn't be spending time with me in the garden'. I worked away from the vegetable garden, until Bree came by to take Annabelle away. As they were leaving, Annabelle asked Bree, why she wasn't allowed to stay with me and Bree told her "because she wasn't your Nanny".

After lunch on the same day, Marcus was working in workshop, as I continued to work in the vegetable patch. I had moved onto the strawberry patch, when Annabelle came over and started screaming again; saying I was doing it all 'wrong'. Marcus walked over to me, wanting to know what Annabelle was screaming about, as I explained; Marcus lead her away. Annabelle apologized for upsetting me, and I told Marcus, privately, about the morning's episode, as I was concerned by her outburst. I think Marcus was concerned as well.

Sometimes I wondered what 'they' thought of me. What was my relationship with Bree, Marcus, Ian and Barbara? Did they just think of me, as 'hired help' or a friend who was helping them achieve their dreams of running a retreat centre? A couple of times I felt like I was 'substandard'; not on the same level as them. Ian and Barbara were very wealthy and me just an Aussie surfer chickie babe from the Gold Coast.

There were only a couple of times I felt this way, and this instance with Bree, was one of them. I would have preferred Bree say that "Bella's not your Nanny" rather than "she". But I just let it slide – because I know all humans are created equal. However, what I wouldn't give, to have the opportunity, to live the life Ian and Barbara had created for themselves.

One thing for certain; the forty-hour-week limit, was definitely, not in place during my first few weeks, working over eight hours, each day, for the first nine days. Except for the Saturday when we went over to Scanar, but I still had to help, collect the freight, from the mail boat. My first weekend off was while Bree and Marcus spent the weekend in Scanar, meeting the nanny, Heather, who started work on the Sunday.

With Heather here, everyone would be able to work, without the responsibility of looking after Annabelle. Annabelle wandered from the staff quarters to the lodge, the work shop; all around without supervision. Surrounded by water, a child of four-years-of-age; was unsupervised and left unattended, especially now the bears were awake.

Marcus had wanted me to do some jobs over the weekend, but decided I wasn't going to do very much at all; having worked more than enough hours, since I'd arrived; deserving my two days off. During the first couple of weeks, I just kept working, feeling like I was being taken advantage of. One of the jobs Marcus wanted me to do, that weekend, was removing all of the electric fence wire from around the main dock. I removed all of the fibre cording, but didn't know about the hard wire, until a couple of weeks later, when we were using the kayaks. Oh well!!

One morning, I geared up to work up near Barbara's art studio, where four large, constructed wooden frames, were used as a strawberry patch. Today's job was reorganising the beds and planting the strawberry runners. From the strawberry fields, the view was overlooking the township and the main dock area. Today the weather was cold, bleak and wet, with not much activity going on anywhere, except for a few dogs barking, somewhere down in the village.

When I first visited Ian and Barbara's house, I questioned whether anyone helped clean the mother ship house; which looked neglected. I was asked, by Bree, if I'd like to help clean out the kitchen cupboards and pantry. I enjoyed the change of pace, from what I had been doing; cleaning the staff quarter's bedrooms, for the arrival of three new staff members. I didn't think the rooms had had a good clean for a few years; so I made it all special for their arrival.

YOGA

Within a few days of my arrival, Marcus and Bree decided, they would start the day, with yoga. I have often thought about joining a yoga class, so this was a perfect opportunity to learn. Marcus had spent twelve-weeks, during this last winter, learning to be a yoga instructor. Our morning sessions were the perfect opportunity for Marcus to learn a routine, with a small group of two (Bree and me); and during the retreats, this was one of Marcus's jobs each morning. With all of the problems with my stomach, the morning yoga class was just what I needed. I just wish I'd recorded one of Marcus's sessions, as a guide to help me start the day, with his encouraging words.

TIME OFF AND EXPLORING

The first Saturday morning Marcus, Bree, Annabelle and I went over to Scanar, in their skiff, shopping for supplies. Annabelle was dropped off at Mona's, (Marcus's sisters) for a play date with her cousins. Annabelle had very few chances for socialising, with other children; as Marcus and Bree enjoyed the opportunity for a break.

In Scanar, we gathered supplies; then dropped them off at the mail boat, for delivery to Seal Bay. We spoilt ourselves, stopping for lunch at a Thai place, ordering my favourite dish of pad Thai. We stopped at a garden centre, where I purchased some begonia bulbs, which Bree planted into three different hanging baskets; my 'living' gift so they'd always remember me, their first Aussie worker.

During my first weekend alone, I visited all of the cottages, pretending to be a guest. My favourite cottage sleeps just one person, with a large deck; perfect for entertaining, and included stairs, leading down to the beach. A larger cottage, located directly behind the single cottage, was included in the land package, when Ian and Barbara purchased the property. The cottage had its own kitchenette and shower, which was a luxury. When the new cottages were built they connected electricity only, using bio toilets, as they're a lot easier to manage than a sewerage system. All guests used the luxurious bathrooms, at the lodge for showers and a bonus of flush toilets.

I spent my first two days off washing clothes, exploring, reading my books, resting and meditating. I spent time sitting in the deck chairs, at the lodge, looking out at the view to the west, which included the main area of the bay; with the restaurants, cafés, the mail house, and the docking system. There was no activity today, with the weather, cold, wet and miserable; the summer visitors still at their homes, somewhere else. Most of the businesses didn't open until the Labour Day weekend, which was when I leave.

My love of reading was rekindled on this trip, as I discovered second hand book stores and swap shelf in café's, where you donate the same amount of books you take. I was able to read books from authors I wouldn't normally purchase. I fell in love with one particular writer, whose books, were transformed into several well known movies. I started to read his repertoire over my travels, unfortunately not keeping the books, as I didn't have the space to carry them around with me. It was cheaper to leave them behind than pay for the excess luggage costs, and the reality was, my bags were already full to the brim.

CAMARADERIE

Marcus graduated from university in California, where he met Bree. Marcus was full of wisdom and knowledge; usually over lunch, he shared stories about his life's interests. Annabelle would happily be drawing or playing, as we chatted.

I remember one of my conservations with Marcus; I used the quote 'I don't know' once, with Marcus explaining, one of his professors told him the meaning of the phrase. When you end a conversation with 'I don't know' you are, if fact, not sure or believe what you've just said. This analogy has stuck with me ever since. Mean what you say, and say what you mean!

Marcus's sister Mona moved to Alaska, quite a few years ago, with her husband and their two children arriving later. Marcus secured summer work building the docks; relaying stories, about his adventures, were hilarious, as he had me in stitches of laughter. I told Marcus he should write a book, about all the things that happened, while working as a labourer. Being so well educated, it amazes me; Marcus now works as a handy man and yoga teacher. Go figure.

I suppose, you start your life with education, and see where it leads you. Life changes along the way, and who knows where you'll go, or what jobs will be available in the future. Marcus has many talents that can help secure any job, anywhere. In the beginning, Marcus travelled from California to Alaska alone each summer, before Bree joined him. When Bree secured the job at the centre, they spend the off season back down in California. During the winter months, Bree works from her computer 'anywhere' planning the summer schedules, working on the website and staff interviews.

Marcus and Bree had to commit, to living permanently, 'somewhere' as Annabelle was starting school at the end of this summer. That summer they purchased their own home in Scaner; to go to work, they jumped in the boat or stayed in the manager's house near the lodge. Ian and Barbara had been looking for a house, to buy near their property, for a carer to be close by to help them. Just after I left Seal Bay, an opportunity presented itself and the manager's house was purchased.

Marcus had an interest in crystals, so we had a crystal sharing evening, showing off our collection of crystals. Marcus and Bree had rock hounded most of them, unlike me, I walked into a shop. Oh what fun, to go out in nature, digging up your own. The stones in the shops; they talk to me and say 'take me home'. What can a girl do?☺

During this trip, I picked up random rocks from each of the places I visited, the glaciers, beaches, river and streams. I added them to my collection of crystals, to I carry a little piece of each place with me, forever. I never realised I was already a rock collector, until I was sorting out at my collection, from this trip. I purchased a large spaghetti type vase, to display my collection in; amazed at the rocks I had collected from New Zealand, Africa, Egypt and all around Australia.

THE NANNY

When Bree, Marcus, Annabelle and Heather arrived back on that Sunday, I knew the dynamics of our little group had changed. Heather was in charge of Annabelle, from 9:00am until Marcus or Bree finished work in the afternoons. Heather had the mornings as her free time, not participating in our yoga group. Heather was a native Alaskan, spending most of her adult life living in native communities. Heather had strong religious and political views, had a great sense of humour, with a wonderful outlook in life.

There were four people, to prepare meals, with Heather added onto our dinner roster, with the five of us together each night in the staff kitchen. The pressure was on Bree to get the centre fully operational and organized, as we set times for dinner.

When Marcus, Bree and Annabelle were together as a family, Heather had a chance to relax each night, heading up to the lodge; the atmosphere was quiet and serene, sharing stories of our lives, over a cup of tea. The sunsets, from our view point, were magnificent, saying goodbye to another day in paradise. Heather was a physic of sorts, sensing the presence of a little boy, at the lodge. Barbara and Bree liked the thought of having a spirit there, but I didn't see or feel him.

SEAL BAY

Seal Bay has one of the biggest tide changes on the planet, with the land mass facing the east/west direction; with up to twenty-feet in difference; usually during the new and full moon cycles. I witnessed these tides, noticing one of the float houses, in the main area of the bay, sitting in mud and the entire cove, empty of water. It was an unbelievable sight, then without noticing any changes, the house was floating again.

Marcus and Bree use their mobile phones, with tide applications, to plan trips which involved water and/or a boat. Sometimes our plans were cancelled because of the wrong tide. The staff quarter's dock wasn't permanently accessible by boat, as a large sandbank was located just off shore, created a narrow channel at low tide, which didn't include our staff dock. At Ian's boat house, the dock was accessible at all times. Life in Alaska was ruled equally, by the weather, wind and ocean swells. At certain times of the year a large fog mass arrives, staying for days.

At the end of the summer season; the staff dock and float house, are towed over and stored at one of 'all tide' docks. The structures were secured to the dock, for when their extreme weather, of up to minus forty hit the region. The float house was winterized; disconnecting power, with all windows and doors locked up tight.

Ian and Barbara, along with about twenty other people, live here year round. Most homes in the bay are not heated; used during the warm summer months, and it really wasn't that warm. During winter, Ian and Barbara go to Scanar, on the mail boat, for supplies, twice a week, connecting with the other residents, during the journey.

I call them 'crazy people'. Haven't they heard of the tropics? Ian explained; someone had to stay, to make sure the centre was safe. One winter, the roof, at one of the cabins was damaged, with emergency repairs needed, before the proper repairs were completed in spring. Ian also had to supervise the float house and dock, checking it was secure during the winter months.

Each resident pays a yearly fee, for access to the mail boat, for freight deliveries and passengers, including staff and guests. How lucky to have free passage, each time, we travelled to Scanar, (*It was only twice a week:-*) only during the cooler months. During summer the Blue Bobby Bay, an open deck schooner, travels three or four times each day, transferring passengers to the cafes, restaurants and accommodation places in Seal Bay.

One morning, in early May, I woke to find the whole area, covered in a fresh sprinkling of snow. Just like a winter wonderland photo; transferred to a Christmas card scene. I just needed a pack of huskies, with a sled, to take me for a ride. *The husky ride, to the interior of Alaska or Canada, was on my bucket list, for another trip.*

The postal office was located, down on the floating dock system, in the main part of town, where the mail boat moors. I visited the post office one day, to purchase stamps, to send letters home to the family.

Sitting up in lodge, I enjoyed an unusual experience, hearing an engine noise approaching from the east. Suddenly a seaplane flew past the window, landing near the postal office. Ian was a pilot; with Barbara, they flew here in their sea plane, to visit. When their home was built they continued flying here, until Ian retired his aviator's hat. *I would have loved to enjoy a scenic flight over the area - another thing to add to my bucket list.*

The waters were full of marine animals, as I regularly spotted sea lions, frolicking about. During winter, Ian sets up electric fences around the docks, to stop the sea lions using his dock, as a resting and birthing place. Apparently, creating an absolute mess, which was very hard to clean up. Ian and Barbara use the docks, all throughout winter, not wanting any dramas, when boarding their boat.

The ocean water, in this part of the world, was pristine; perfect for oyster beds. One of the owners lived up past the staff quarters; each day travelling in and out, checking on his plot. Early one morning, I stood on the dock, surveying the area, after a wild storm the previous night. I noticed the oyster rig, had broken free of its mooring, and was now a mangled mess, up on the bank, after the high tide. Marcus had spoken to the man; saying it would be repaired and operational again soon.

The Oyster Shack Restaurant had the annual get-together meal for staff from both businesses. I had wanted to explore some of the township, but there hadn't been an opportunity, because of work commitments. Bree arranged for a group of us, to leave early for dinner, to explore. We spotted horses Jenny used as part of her pony club business, for youngsters during the summer.

Bree guided Ian, Barbara, Billy, Rob and I for a walk, to visit the grave yards. The graveyard site was situated on the highest point of the area, with a three-sixty-degrees view of the area. This place was perfect to rest, for eternity, for those who'd found this amazing place, during their living years.

I remembered times, when I stood at a similar place, burying loved ones. At death; lay in the earth, or soaring in the wind, like the eagles; free and wild. We spent twenty minutes, reading the plaques; identifying the people who rested here. I had tears in my eyes, knowing they were loved and missed by their families.

The same emotions come to mind, every time I think of my daughter, Kristy and how she was loved and not part of my life anymore. I believe my heart will never completely heal, from her death; at three months of age. She will always be the missing part of my life, every single day, including every family occasion; all of the Christmases, mother's day, birthday's, weddings, anniversaries and parties. Kristy, will always be, the missing piece, to the 'jigsaw' of our family.

We continued our tour, with a visit to the new light house, built as a B&B. The lighthouse, with its incredible view across the bay, will be a 'welcoming' beacon, for anyone travelling.

We walked back to the main area of town, wandering into the art studio of a lady, who had painted all of her life. Lucy's studio had incredible views of the township, in the foreground, being insignificant, against the backdrop of the huge mountains, directly behind it. The three storey complex consisted of the art gallery, on the first floor, set up as a memorial to Lucy, who had recently passed away; buried up in the graveyard. The second level, Lucy conducted art classes, and the third floor, was Lucy's personal space.

After the art gallery, we shared the amazing food, prepared for our supper. Marcus, Annabelle and Heather joined us for dinner, and it was a really fun night with good food and companionship.

Seal Bay consisted of a large island, creating a safe harbour; protecting the township, from the direct force of the Pacific Ocean. The island was divided into two separate pieces of land, joined by a narrow sea wall, consisted mainly of sand. The town centre was linked by a road, to access the dock system, mail house, restaurants and shops. The residents used four wheel motorbikes and golf carts for travelling around.

A few years back, bad weather, with rough seas and strong winds, threatened the sea wall, by the extreme force of the ocean, as a bull dozer repaired the wall, as it was being damaged. The effort by the bulldozer paid off, as the sea wall was still intact, and continues to protect the township from the ocean swells.

The whole dock system starts at the northern end, beyond the first restaurant; with staff quarters and continues on past all of the shops and cafes. The boardwalk allows access to 'everything' on the same level; several ramps going down, off the boardwalk, access the individual docks, which rise and fall with the tidal activity. At low tide, the boardwalk must be at least thirty-feet, from the water level.

Jenny and her husband are potters; operating the Oyster Shack restaurant. Unique ceramic plates, created with bright colours, sea creatures and shells, are used in the restaurant. The plates are raised in texture, with the year written on the bottom; the broken plates are recreated as mosaic- tables in the restaurant. The small alfresco tables, plates, mugs and cups in an assortment of sizes, were for sale in their shop.

The waters are used by an assortment of motorized crafts, as well as canoes and kayaks. I could imagine the summer months, full of life, excitement, laughter and activities. The story of a couple, visiting the bay, had tied their kayak up at the dock, to go exploring; and on their return, the kayak was up in the air, a few meters, due the tide changing.☺

WEEKLY ESCAPES

Heather and I had Saturday's off, to go over to Scanar, on the mail boat. We had three-hours to spend, either shopping or just cruising around. The mail boat arrived at 10.30am and departed at 2:30pm. The boat didn't wait for anyone, so if you're late, you're stuck there until Monday afternoon's mail boat. Or another way home, was hiring a water taxi costing about eighty-dollars. In summer, the open deck schooner The Blue Bobby Bay delivered passengers across the bay three or four times each day.

My weekly escapes with Heather were a highlight for me, visiting op shops and yard sales. One of Heather's friends, Nelly joined us in our adventures, with one of our most memorable days; involved a church group. The preacher conducted a special ceremony, blessing all the motorcycle riders, travelling the northern roads, during the summer months. Heather and Nelly knew the preacher, so we invited ourselves along for lunch of sausages and salad.

Another time Heather and I picked up a young hitch hiker from the harbour, as the fishing boats dock was five miles from the shops; so rather than taking a taxi, the workers hitched into town and back. Oh to be 30 years younger!!!! Boy we could have had some fun. The guy was having reservations, by the time we reached town, but we dropped him off safe and sound.

One of Heather's habits, while driving around town, was beeping the horn and waving to all of the people walking. I sat there dumbfounded and embarrassed; well not really. It was a hoot, as we laughed at people reactions, as they waved back, trying to work out if they knew us or not. 99.99 percent of the time Heather didn't know them, but it was her way of being friendly. Just go with the flow and enjoy the riiiiiiiiiiiiiiide baaaaaabbbbbyyyy cruising around town, in her van.

Nelly, Heather and I travelled over to the neighbouring town of Edmund, to visit a market stall, where I purchased three quartz crystal pendants. At the time I had no idea why I'd bought them, however they were gifts to people, for their healing and not mine. I gave two away as gifts and the other one; I lost in the airport at Garland.

One of our Saturday adventures on the mail boat didn't work out well; as the boat was about to dock, everyone was anxious and eager to get off the boat. This was the first time I'd been outside on the deck, when we were docking, as I didn't know you weren't allowed on that side of the boat. A lady with a dog and I were shuffled along, towards the back of the boat. Had I known the consequences, I would have kept well clear, of that side of the boat, as I was hit in the face with the end of the rope; the deck hand had thrown my way. I was literally stunned, as the rope landed, just between my eyes. I stepped back in shock, as the other passengers, asked if I was ok. I was, but what really pissed me off, when the woman, didn't even apologize for hitting me.

The impact of the rope had broken the skin with a little bit of blood, nothing to worry about, but I was upset, the incident was ignored. Since it was a Saturday, I decided not to mention anything to Bree until the Monday. However, Heather had told Bree, who then spoke to the owner of the boat, with the lady deck-hand being sacked. I felt sad for the lady, but she needed to be more aware of new people, travelling on the boat. I mentioned the incident to Bree about my ordeal, mainly so other staff were prepared, especially if they weren't accustomed to this way of life and avoiding this incident happening again.

When I was travelling on the Blue Bobby Bay, the deck-hand went around to all of the passengers, advising them to remain wherever they were, until the boat came to a complete stop. Just like the instructions given, as an airplane was preparing for take-off.

One Saturday, Katie (a staff member) came back with us, in the skiff, from the mail boat. Heather was learning to get the forty-five-degree angle, for directing the boat towards the dock. But today, Heather had trouble parking; attempting to dock three times. One attempt, the point of the boat, wedged itself tightly in the wooden pylon; as I went up to the front of the boat, to rock it out of position, of course, without tipping the boat over. At the same time, Katie almost had a heart attack, screaming at us, as I tried to free the boat. When we finally docked, Katie stormed off in a huff, as Heather and I were hysterical with laughter, about the whole event. I'm not sure, what the reaction would have been; if the boat had sunk, and we all suffered hyperthermia☺.

OUR NEIGHBOURS

Bree, Marcus, Annabelle, Heather and I visited neighbours for a social evening. We crossed the cove, in the skiff and docked directly opposite the staff quarters. We climbed up this slippery and muddy hill, with our gum boots on. Bree mixed up the times, arriving late for dinner, with the pot luck already over; eating left over's. After dinner, the adults played cards, while the children watched a movie. Annabelle was memorised, by the television screen, as she rarely watches any movies.

There were three generations, living at the house, operated an oyster farm, all year round, and during summer ran a bed and breakfast. The house was perched on the top of a cliff's edge, surrounded by a large fir tree forest. The outlook, from the house had unbelievable views across the Pacific Ocean; scattered islands in the bay; and their oyster beds. The family had built the house themselves, finishing sections of it, as they could afford to. They didn't borrow any money to build the house, using whatever profit they made each year, to complete more. During the summer months, the lady of the house cooks all of the meals, for the guests. The daughter takes care of the servicing the rooms and cleaning, as well as looking after her two small children. During summer separate areas of the house, were for the guests, with the main loft guest bedroom, having a full-length, black bear skin, lying on the floor. The owners told me; guests staying with them, woke up to find, their four young children had a wonderful night's sleep, on the bear mat, instead of sleeping in the bed. They'd used a blanket from the bed to cover them and snuggled up all together.

The husband and son operated the oyster beds, hiring workers when needed. The parents lived in the B&B year round, working very hard, for their lifestyle. During the off season the son, daughter and their two children move down to a rental place near the dock.

I enjoyed the night out, with Heather meeting some new children and Bree, Marcus and Annabelle catching up with old friends. I had bought a new pair of mud boots, specifically for this job and they didn't fit very well, and by the time I got back to the boat, I had blisters.

Mona, her husband, Jock and their two children, visited one afternoon, as a play date for Annabelle. We all sat around the staff kitchen, chatting about life in Alaska. This year, Jock had taken over the fishing licence, from his father, with access to one of the rivers. Jock was getting ready to fish for the next few months, while the season was open. I would've loved to live here, eating salmon, as part of my diet.

RECYCLING AND GLASS BEACH

Everyone who buys groceries should be wary about rubbish and recycling. Whatever supplies are taken home, with you, have to be dealt with environmentally and thoughtfully. What do these residents do with their rubbish, you ask?

Arriving in the port, at Scanar; large industrial rubbish bins, are available to dispose of your general rubbish, plastics and glass jars. At the lodge, the incinerator, near the top of the hydraulic lift, was used for all cardboard and bathroom paper materials. All food scraps, egg shells and peelings are broken into small pieces, and placed in the compost area. Eventually, after many years, the scraps are used as compost, on the vegetable garden.

The green garden waste was disposed of by having a bon fire on the beach. The climate, doesn't allow waste to decompose quickly, and with the threat of fires, during the summer months, excess green waste was burned.

The berry patch, near the staff kitchen, had been planted by the previous owner, and over the years, become out of control, with dead foliage. I spent a few days, removing all of the old canes; as this year's new canes, would shoot, with the warmer weather. Over many years, trees surrounding the staff quarters had trunks and branches, trimmed and removed. These were all stacked up high around the side of the building.

With the huge differences in high and low tides, around the new moon; I picked the day, and started throwing all the green waste, over the railing of the dock, as the tide started to recede. When dinner was finished, we restacked the rubbish, before starting the fire. As the tide came in, the fire site disappeared, and all the remaining debris that didn't burn, went out on the next tide.

I also had piles of green waste, stacked close to the hydraulic lift, that were too difficult to remove. During the working bee weekend, workers came along on the hydraulic lift and collected the rubbish, placing it in the compost bin.

Marcus and I cleaned out beneath one of the verandahs at the lodge, filling two large drums, full of empty wine bottles. Each business, in the bay, was committed to recycling their bottles in a particular manner. What was this method, you may ask? The surprises just kept coming; my next exciting adventure was to glass beach, with Bree, Marcus and Annabelle.

We loaded the two large drums, into the front of the skiff; and it didn't take long, before we were out in the bay. The foreshore was constructed of rocky outcrops, as Marcus steered the boat towards the spot, where we landed on the beach. We found a tiny patch of sand, to park the boat, as Annabelle grabbed a bottle; throwing it at the rocks. If you throw, the bottle, hard enough, it smashes into small pieces. If it doesn't break, you fetch it and throw it again. This was fun and a good way, to get rid of your frustrations, you had bottled up. *Did you get the pun – bottled up!*☺

We spent, about thirty minutes emptying the bins; and looking down, in the sand, you'd find glass, tumbled by the waves, were now all smooth. Over a period of time, the movement, of the waves, removes all evidence of the broken bottles.

Marcus, Bree, Annabelle and I hopped back, into the skiff and headed back home. I turned to look back at glass beach, from a distance, finding it hard, to determine, exactly where the beach was located, along the foreshore.

As the sun was going down, on another wonderful day, in paradise, we did our bit for the environment, and stopping the landfill. I thought it was a novel way to recycle; thoroughly enjoying the afternoon expedition.

NEW STAFF

On the morning of the new staff's arrival, I travelled over to Scanar by the Aurora. Ian and Barbara, Bree and Marcus all had appointments, so I was left to my own devices. I savoured a real cappuccino as I visited the shops that were open. I headed towards the sailor's memorial; honouring all of the men and women, who had lost their lives at sea. The intricate gazebo housed a statue, to reflect and pray to. The pillars of the gazebo, listed the names, in family groups, of those who perished; noticing the dates of their demise, going back hundreds-of-years.

I waited at the restaurant, for the luncheon, while I enjoyed a coffee and studied my crystal book. Rob, the gardener, had flown overnight from Miami; Billy, the chef, had flown in from Hawaii; with Katie, the house maid, had her own RV and was already in Scanar.

I always love meeting new people, and it was a nice relaxing lunch, unfortunately, most of the food ordered, for the first course, I couldn't eat, and the main meal wasn't much better. The deep-fried-frozen-food was disappointing, especially when the fishing boats were docked three-hundred-meters away.

After lunch, the staff got settled into their new home. I purchased a bunch of tulips, creating a small arrangement of flowers, for each staff member's rooms – including mine. I handed my room over to

Rob, as he was staying for the whole summer season. The experience, of waking up, to see the sunrises and witnessing all of nature's magic, was truly extraordinary. For my remaining two weeks, I slept in the back room, of the other accommodation building.

We all met, again, for a welcome gathering, in the lodge, exchanging our own stories, and after the introductions, walked up 'the boot camp trail'. This trail included a very steep hill, located on the southern part of the township. Snow was still on the ground, in places, and after the climb, we enjoyed walking along the range, for about an hour, before arriving at the lookout. The view encompassed the main dock area; around the bay and out into the Pacific Ocean. The sun was still high in the sky, as we headed back to the staff quarters, for dinner.

The next day was filled with paperwork; a different induction, from when I arrived, more official. I was only, a temporary worker, so it probably seemed pointless. The forty-hour-week being enforced would have been nice, because I've worked more than forty hours, every week.

As I'm not an American citizen, I wasn't allowed to work for money or get tips, as it forms part of your wages. Dan and Billy were planning on staying for the entire season; receiving a $1000 bonus. Billy, the chef, was the only paid employee, with everyone else, signing a work trade contract.

Katie and I were paired to work together, preparing the cabins and lodge, ready for the guests. The first day working with Katie went well, but the second day, I was on my own, as Katie went to Scanar, to move her car. The local council had enforced the summer parking restrictions; with vehicles not permitted to be parked, longer than seventy two hours. When Katie got back after lunch, we still had to finish all of the rooms before the end of the day.

The third morning I was on my own again, as Katie spent the morning, talking to Barbara about the list of rules, regulations and the unsuitable accommodation, she's had to endure. Katie had been constantly complaining, about the noise on the stairs, used all throughout the night. Staying in the room, next to Katie's, the noise wasn't worrying me at all. We were living on a dock, constantly moving and squeaking.

The other staff members were night owls, staying up past midnight. Each night Billy would go for a walk along the water's edge, and when he couldn't sleep, he baked. I know this, because some nights, when I went to the bathroom, I'd see a lonely figure silhouetted, against the midnight haze of dusk, out along the beach, walking. The smell, of freshly baked bread, wafting out of the kitchen, while we were doing yoga, was so wrong. The yoga sessions were moved up to the lodge, as we viewed the snow covered mountains each morning.

One morning, Katie was in the staff kitchen, as I arrived for breakfast and I said "good morning" and started to ask, how she'd slept. She rather bluntly told me "she wasn't a morning person and to stop the chit chat", then marched out of the room. Katie would sit on the dock, in solitude; which was a beautiful way to start your day. Bree made the mistake, one morning, of saying "good morning" to Katie, while she was sitting there alone. Bree had to tell us privately, that when Katie was sitting out there alone, she doesn't want anyone talking to her.

Katie and I continued to work together in quiet solitude, having decided she wasn't worth the worry. Katie was supposed to stay for six weeks, but had handed in her resignation, and leaving the following week. Bree was upset by Katie's departure, as she was now one worker down, with only three people to complete all of the work.

We were all glad Katie spent her days off, in her campervan, at Scanar, because we were on eggs shells, while she was here. One night, at nearly midnight, Heather and I were sitting in the kitchen chatting; when we saw Marcus walking down the stairs, with his shoes in his hand. The next minute, Billy comes down the stairs, tip toeing; and then Rob, walks out of his room, using the side steps to enter the kitchen. Heather and I were beside ourselves with laughter; with everyone making such an effort to please her. Billy offered her his room, because he's a night owl, however, she refused the offer.

The staff had to be trained in the fine art of waitressing and dinner services; with instructions in the correct manner, of setting up the tables, with glass wear and cutlery, and how to serve food and wine. We had practice sessions, to perfect our performances, with official guests of Barbara, Ian, Heather, Marcus and Annabelle.

Bree had sourced little swan shaped vases, in different colours, for each guest to 'own' during their stay. Each staff member decorated the vases, with flowers and greenery, from the garden. When the guests first arrived, they chose a vase at the first meal; then for each of the following meals, the vases were placed in different positions; giving the guest, the opportunity to sit next to someone new each time, to socialise and get to know, their fellow guests.

FITNESS AND EXPLORING

I wanted stronger legs; to attempt the walk, up to the glacier, without being too fatigued and too slow. *I wanted to be like Annabelle; no whingeing or whining, and get smores at the lake and watch a DVD when I arrived home☺.*

The stairs, from the staff quarters to the lodge, were sixty steps; each time you went down to the staff quarters, you obviously had to go back up again - sixty steps each way. By the end of my stay I'd make it to the top without stopping, I just had to pace myself. The stairs were just like a stair master machine, except real life ones. Come here to work, to create strong legs and a trim butt! Ha!

There were a few adventures with the staff; calculated as 'team building', as Rob and I, with Katie and Billy, got lessons on how to use the kayaks. It was a fun afternoon, paddling around the cove and coming back past the mail dock. What was even more exciting, we didn't end up wet, which was a bonus. During summer, if you wanted to leave the centre at any time, the kayaks were the only escape.

Located at the boat house, a notice board, recorded your expedition; writing down your name; where you were going, and what time, you were due back. There were no restrictions, to where you could go, and if you didn't arrive back, they knew where to look for you. I didn't have to worry about this, as I was leaving; not sure I'd have handled the kayaks, on my own anyway.

Ian and Barbara were always doing deals, with people, who offered 'a service' in exchange for accommodation. One man, who had stayed the previous year, was a graphic designer, designing the new logo, for the centre; in the shape of a conical shell. The man enjoyed his stay and the design, was now part of all the centre's promotions.

A couple of young women, in their twenties, arrived to spend the weekend as guests, in one of the cabins. The exchange; for the accommodation, was the task of helping, carry two inflatable kayaks, up to the glacier storage shed. The girls spent the morning exploring the area, using the kayaks, before joining the group, at the bottom of the stairs, leading into the park. We started the hike up the track, while Marcus tied the boat up to a buoy; using the kayak, to row back to shore.

The climb up the switch back track was very steep; hiking for about forty-five minutes. I always have a saying, when I'm doing this type of hiking 'it's the journey, not the destination that's important'. It's my excuse to stop and catch my breath, with the view along the journey, sometimes, more spectacular than the destination.

Everyone had stopped at the parks notice board, to regroup, before continuing on, at our own pace. There were many different trails to explore the park; as I'd have taken the trail, to the area directly above the glacier; a much longer hike, whereas the lake was about five-kilometers or was it miles, from the glacier face.

We continued on the easy walking track, for an extra hour-and-a-half before arriving at the beach. Annabelle was in the lead with Billy, carrying one of the packs. Annabelle was so funny, if she didn't complain, or need to be carried, while on the hike, she got 'smores' at the glacier, and at home she could watch a movie. Oh the bribery of some parents!!

The story of the kayaks goes like this: a friend of Ian's, with a helicopter, lifted two large drums into position on the banks of the lake; for the storage of all the kayak gear. During summer, the guests at the lodge have the opportunity, to use the kayaks, on the glacier lake.

Arriving at the lake, Marcus inflated one of the kayaks; loading the rest of the gear onto the kayak, rowing over to drum's location. The two girls and Billy walked around the shoreline, to meet up with Marcus. The rest of the group stayed behind, collecting wood to start a fire for smore's (melted marshmallows, a piece of chocolate, sandwiched between two biscuits/cookies). You eat the biscuits, when the chocolate was all mushy. The group spent a wonderful afternoon, exploring the shoreline, or sitting on the beach, keeping the fire going. We spotted a black bear up on the hillside, not close enough, for us to worry about. Since this was a national park, everyone had to be aware, this was their home.

Marcus, Billy and the girls spent a couple of hours touring around the lake, having a closer look at the face of the glacier and circling the icebergs.

When we were sitting around the fire, Bree told us a story; fifty-years ago a large section of the mountain, collapsed into the lake, causing a tidal wave that wiped out, all the vegetation, on the valley floor. Nature was a force to be reckoned with, as the reforestation of the valley floor, was evident, with young trees growing here now.

After an enjoyable few hours visiting the glacier lake, we trekked back, towards the boat, to return back home. It was a lot easier hiking downhill, than the climb up. Ian came over in the Aurora, to collect some of the staff, as there were too many people for one boat. The extra girls with their kayak got a lift back with my boat.

MESSAGE IN A BOTTLE

I had an idea to throw a bottle, with a message in it, into the ocean. At this time in my life, I was starting afresh; purchasing my favourite bottle of wine, and thoroughly enjoyed drinking it. I wrote the letters; addressed to Kristy my daughter, who had died; Ricky the ex-husband; as well as other members of my family. The letters were written, sharing deep and meaning thoughts, and feelings, and 'closure' for me.

In the boat, on the way back from the glacier, the tide was perfectly staged, for the bottle to reach the Pacific Ocean. What was its destination? Maybe Australia; you never know, where the currents move the flow of water. I believe 'messages in a bottle' aren't meant to be opened. You send the bottle out, on its journey, to drift for eternity, on the currents, without being opened. The girls made me open the bottle, to write my phone number, on the notes, so whoever finds it, can ring me. Deep down, I hoped, the bottle was never found or opened.

This gesture signifies the start of a new chapter in my life, a new beginning, forgiveness and understanding. The letters were about letting go of the pain, anger, grief, sacrifice and all of the hurt. It was a very emotional time for me, as I sat in the boat, looking back at the spot in the ocean where the bottle landed. It's now time, I released my life's struggles, and everything I had endured; to move forward, to a bigger and better future, full of infinite possibilities. I turned to face the front of the boat, as the wind wiped away the tears.

EATING, POOPING AND BIO TOILETS

Marcus was the chief faecal officer (*ha ha*) dealing with all of the bio toilet systems located in the cabins and staff quarters. The lodge had flushable toilets, as we were 'encouraged' to use these facilities, whenever possible. I know this was too much information, but I just have to share with you the fascinating details about human waste. The bio toilets should be used, under specific conditions, otherwise Marcus has to deal with the problems, and it wasn't his favourite job.

The two most important things to remember are; firstly the least amount of liquid the better; and secondly absolutely no paper added into the system. The staff ladies' had a pee bucket, with all paper products, were placed in the burnable rubbish bin.

We disposed the contents of the pee bucket, over the edge of the dock. I had an emergency, early one morning, when one of my crystals, fell into the bucket of pee. Oh yeah! The crystal got caught up in my shirt, going 'splash' into the bucket. Oh boy, what was I going to do? So I poured the contents of one pee bucket into the other (this was at about 4:00am) and rescued my crystal from the bottom.

At this hour of the day, I wasn't emptying the pee, over the rail, and possibly wake up Bree and Marcus. That morning, Heather had beaten me to the task, and I then had to explain, why a full bucket of pee, was in the washroom. There's no way, I was going to throw my crystal, out over the edge. Even now, every time I look at that particular crystal, I have a little chuckle to myself, about how I saved it from the bottom on the pee bucket.

Heather and I had numerous discussions about our diet of lentils. We laughed about the length of our 'deposits'; looking into the bottom, of the bio toilet and reckon, it was usually over two-feet long. You ask "how do I know this?" With the bio toilet system, you rotate the blades, after each deposit, to make sure the blades, were working correctly.

One morning, while I was up at the lodge, making a deposit☺, I blocked up the toilet because there was so much waste. I had the plunger out, and it was not a pretty sight. Oh Heather and I were in stitches of laughter; as I shared this wonderful piece of information. When people asked me, where my favourite place was? I would always say 'sleeping on the dock in Alaska and my adventures with Heather'.

TOP VALUES

One afternoon, everyone was invited to attend a session on 'top values' which Katie was presenting. I was excited, as I'd never participated, in any of these activities before. Actually I didn't know the programme existed; finding it interesting, to discover what it's all about. Katie was a wonderful presenter, as I wondered why, her teacher's personality, didn't transfer into her normal interaction with people. Bree had commented; most of the people, who came to work here, were introverts – *WAS I ONE OF THEM é#%+?.*

My top values as at 19th May are:

1. Passion – to have deep feelings about ideas, activities and people
2. Genuineness – to act in a manner that is true to who I am
3. Family – to have a happy loving family
4. Faithfulness – to be loyal and true in relationships
5. Loved – to be loved by those close to me
6. Intimacy – to share my inner most experiences with others
7. Spirituality – to grow and mature spiritually
8. Inner Peace – to experience personal peace
9. Hope – to maintain a positive and optimistic outlook
10. Health – to be physically well and healthy

After we had finished with our own list, we shared the information with the others, emphasizing each one of us, was a truly unique soul, on different journeys in life.

THE SUMMER SEASON

Thursday the 24th May, the weather was perfect, to showcase the area, with a luncheon, for the whole community, to celebrate the new summer season. The Blue Bobby Bay arrived, with people the mainland, representing tourist associated businesses. Ian and Barbara, along with other local residents and business operators; representing B&B's, the Art Gallery, oyster growers, a water taxi service; coming together for this special event.

Each business person presented an introductory speech, sharing information about their business, and their offerings, for this summer season. Several oyster growers were represented, with one family venturing into producing mussels this year. The mussels and oysters would definitely be a treat, for the diners, sampling the delicacies on offer.

It was really interesting, seeing the young children, running around on the docks, wearing life jackets. It's part of their clothing, when they're near water. The surface of the water, at low tide, was quite a distance, from the boardwalk; and if anyone fell over the edge, they'd be injured. The consequences, if a child fell, without a life jacket; err on the side of caution. I had seen Annabelle wearing a life jacket, on the dock, at her float house.

Businesses, along the boardwalk, were open today, with dessert being served at the art gallery. We had a sneak peak at the new exhibitions, with the official opening, the following night. The exhibition displays artists, exclusively from the Seal Bay residents. Bree was given the opportunity to showcase a painting, this year, after she was accepted as a local resident. Mixtures of talents were displayed, showcasing jewellery, glass wear and pottery; different mediums of paintings were also displayed. I purchased a beautiful plate, featuring hollyhocks, as my memento of Alaska.

MY SPECIAL VISITORS

A few months prior to my trip; I attended a life-changing weekend retreat, with the two days filled with sessions based on information about chakra balancing, meditation and crystals. This information was the acknowledgement; I needed that meant I wasn't crazy for all of those years. I lacked the knowledge and understanding, of what I'd been experiencing.

I've always been intuitive, and during the last few years, members of my family have passed away; and while I was staying at Seal Bay, they visited me.

Number One

Bobbie, my cousin, had helped me set up my restaurant, intending to be business partners, before she got sick and passed away. After her passing Bobbie, on a regular basis, would visit; watching me preparing the food. I'd say 'good morning' as I felt Robyn presence, as I continued to work; as her presence was a comforting and reassuring feeling.

One morning, lying in bed, watching the sun rise up over the mountain, I felt Bobbie's presence. It was a beautiful spring morning; knowing she was checking on me. "Yes Bobbie, I am doing OK" as she noticed my surroundings, jealous (in a good way) I was here, and then she left. I knew this was the last time she'd visit me, as I'm already so much stronger.

Number Two

My ex-mother-in-law Anne regularly visited me, over the first few months, of my trip. Every time I felt her presence; I'd tell her to leave me alone, and go spend time with her son. Over the thirty-four-years I'd known Anne, I felt, she never completely accepted me into the family, and hardly ever treated me in a nice way; NOW she was concerned, about, how I am going. All of the work Ricky and I had done for the family, over the years, was thrown back in our faces. The whole family was displaced; with the soul destroying decisions, made after her death. I'll find it hard to forgive, the injustices, I felt I received.

As Anne continued to visit me, during my trip, I asked a few people for advice. They told me 'maybe she was concerned because she knew how badly she treated me when she was alive'. Anne also could see the emotional, mental and physical pain I was in. Anne wanted me to know she was there looking over me. Maybe, it's her way of saying sorry, but I wasn't buying any of that bullshit. Maybe Anne discovered how badly her son and husband had treated me over the last thirty years. All of the secrets were now out, in the open, for everyone to discover.

Number Four

One night in May; as I lay down to sleep, I felt someone breathe their last breath. I was so scared my Mum had passed away, as she'd been very ill. I sent an email to my family, asking them 'if they were all ok'. Most of the family sent back positive responses, but it took a long time before Christian, my youngest son, wrote back to say, it was the first anniversary of Dominic's death.

Dominic and Christian's were best friends since they were four-years-old. Dominic committed suicide in May the previous year. Of all of the situations, I'd dealt with that year; Dominic's death was the hardest, as he chose to end his own life.

I had a really hard time acknowledging, the fact, Dominic had died. My heart was going out to his family, as well as my son Christian. When I arrived at the church for the funeral, I felt overwhelmed with grief, as I watched the video of his twenty-five-years play across the screen. I didn't know why I felt so overwhelmed, until I finally went to a clinic the next day, because I wasn't coping. They told me, Dominic had attached himself to me, as I knew how he felt, as I'd committed suicide in a former life. It took a whole afternoon of sessions at my local healing centre to calm me down. Dominic's death was still the hardest thing I've EVER had to deal with, besides my own daughter's death.

Number Five

During my stay in Alaska, I experienced an event that changed my life as I knew it. Waiting on the dock, with the rest of the staff, to greet our guests; the excitement was building, as the first glimpse of Ian and Barbara's friends, arriving on the Blue Bobby Bay. The open-deck-schooner, crowded with people, manoeuvred to line up with the dock; as a familiar face came into view. He was higher than everyone else; my heart started to beat faster, our eyes locked and my breath got shallower. Searching, for a million answers, in the space of seconds; overwhelmed with strange emotions, looking around, to see if this was actually real.

My eyes reconnected with him, in a familiar scenario; of the same proportions, as the dramatic events of a historical romance movie. This was definitely a déjà vu moment; I believe I've met him twice before, waiting for him, both times, to arrive in a boat.

My first memory was from the 1800's, where he wore a fancy hat, with a plume of feathers, like a pirate. This man arrived on an open-deck-vessel, standing up high near the bow, holding onto the ropes of the sails. His mouth was formed in a huge smile, with his mischievous eyes connecting exclusively to mine. I felt this meeting, was a long-awaited return, of my lover.

The second time, I was standing on a wharf, searching for his familiar face amongst the thousands of soldiers, lining the decks of a ship, returning from war; the soldiers were all waving and yelling. This was an occasion for celebrations, with streamers connecting the dock, to the decks of the ships. When the ship finally docked, and the ramps lowered in place, the rush of the crowds, from both directions was crushing. The men and women returning home were welcomed by loved ones, as I felt my brother's arms wrap around me, as we reconnected.

And now here he was again. I was overwhelmed with confusion. *Who was this man?* Never before in my life, have I had this sort of experience. I wonder whether he felt the same. *Did he remember me from another time as well?* What was he feeling when he noticed me standing on the dock? Did his heart and mind go back to the times we'd met before? How can this be and what am I going to do?

A million questions were running, through my mind, but all of this has to stop, because I had a job to do. Guests were disembarking the Blue Bobby Bay, and I had to leave NOW.

My mystery man was to stay a mystery, as unfortunately circumstances over the weekend didn't allow me to find out how he felt because he was travelling with his wife. We did chat occasionally over the weekend in a friendly manner, as his wife's mother was Australian.

I wasn't able to have a private conversation, like I'd had hoped; however, he was drawn to me, as quite regularly I'd find him close by, with his camera, taking photos or just looking at me. We also found ourselves, at the same table, for lunch each day. Now if he'd been there alone, then the circumstances would've been different, as I'd definitely made time to sit and chat with him.

This event was the beginning of a new life direction and purpose. Learning to be aware of 'what' my intuition was telling me, to take a chance on what I'm discovering about myself. It's scary to take that first step, towards the unknown; and this was definitely a huge step for me. I've always been very intuitive or even physic. At certain times, during my life, there's been this big voice inside my head that's said stop, or look here, do this, or watch out.

Mostly my intuition felt like a warning system, to keep me safe; but this incident was on a totally different level. I'd been meditating and soul searching, for the last eight weeks since I left Australia. I'm finally finding peace and my eyes were being opened for the first time, to see the beauty inside me.

OUR FIRST GUESTS

Finally our first guests had arrived, just after lunch on the Friday. They weren't just any ordinary guests; they were all friends, of Ian and Barbara's. Each year the friends arrive on the Blue Bobby Bay, helping to prepare the centre, ready for the summer season. They're basically volunteers (like me) who arrive at their own expense; and in exchange for a weekend's adventure, meals and accommodation, they work around the centre. Without this help, Ian and Barbara wouldn't be able to, maintain the property. This was especially true, for all the gardens and heavy yard work, the men accomplished with chainsaws and bobcats.

Twenty-five guests disembarked the Blue Bobby Bay; as I left the dock, leading a small group up to the lodge. A formal gathering welcomed everyone, as the guests were allocated rooms, and given the run down on the weekend's activities. Each staff member was responsible for a small group; to complete a list of tasks, over the weekend. Ian's list was quite comprehensive, which involved chopping down trees and clearing road, needing machines and men's muscles.

The women completed a variety of jobs in the different gardens around the property. Many native perennial flowers, mostly the beautiful fire-weed, returned each year, for a magnificent display, along the road ways. The old flower heads were removed, as the new flowers welcomed the arriving guests.

Billy was in charge of the kitchen, preparing all of the meals for the weekend. A group of ladies helped with the meal preparation; and cookie dough's were created, shaped, then frozen ready for future retreats; to be defrosted and baked. This idea was certainly a time saver, when the centre was busy.

Katie's job was cleaning the windows and mirrors in the cabins; and she was on *fire*. Katie had a couple of ladies in her team, with their slogan 'No streaking", completing the job on the first day.

Rob was in charge of the food garden, using his expertise with micro vegetable growing. Barbara was an artist; and the vegetable garden needed 'an artistic effect' using colours and textures, creating different patterns. When standing on the verandah, looking over the vegetable garden, you're supposed to be amazed, by the creativity. A wonderful group of ladies were helping Rob with the new design.

My little group was responsible for cleaning the outside of the building. As high up, as we could reach, we used brooms, to brush down all the sides of the building, under the stairs, and the railings, to remove cobwebs. We cleaned all of the decks of dust; making it all look a million dollars.

The weekend wasn't just work, work and more work. The long daylight hours, allowed plenty of time for fun; with the kayaks available to use; exploring 'the boot camp trail'; the state park and the glacier. Yoga and meditation, in the chapel, was held each morning. Plus the fantastic meals prepared by Billy and his helpers. Remember the meals were all vegan, with the salad vegetables grown in the gardens on site. The food was good, but you could tell there weren't any eggs or dairy in them. Soy was used in the meals, making it difficult, for me to eat everything on offer. Billy made a special effort, on the last night, making me a special dessert.

My second visit to the glacier was with the volunteers, on my last weekend; when Marcus, and a couple of young men, carried survival suits. Marcus thought it'd be a great adventure swimming in the freezing waters, of the glacier lake. Marcus was the first person to go swimming; with photos of him sliding down an iceberg, like a slippery slide.

How many times in your life do you get offered this type of opportunity? A continuous stream of swimmers donned the suits. Two of the young guys, aged in their twenties, swam out to one of the icebergs, undressed down to their boxer shorts, planning to jump in the freezing water. I looked at Marcus to see what his reaction was, because I didn't think it was a great idea. I could see Marcus thinking of the emergency situation, activated, when they had about five minutes, to restore his body temperature, back to normal. The possibility of these men, going into cardiac arrest, was extreme, with the consequences, deadly.

Some of the people, on the shore were, encouraging them to jump; taking Marcus about thirty-seconds, to jump up and say NO, NO, NO; as Marcus didn't have a suit, to rescue them, because there were only two suits. It was a very tense few minutes, before the guys redressed, and came back to shore; a relief to everyone, in the group.

After the survival suit incident; the group were standing by the fire, when we heard a loud thunder noise, coming from the direction, of the glacier. We turned around, just in time to see an iceberg roll over. The indescribable majestic-blue colour; of the glacier that was previously submerged, was now sitting on top of the water. After fifteen minutes, a six-inch tidal wave, reached the shore near us. Just think, how massive the mountain slide would've been, to create the tidal wave, destroying all the vegetation, on the valley floor.

I'd been down at the water's edge, looking at the lake water, which was littered with particles of debris. Usually in Australia, you'd refill your bottle with water, out of the lake. But this lake's water was toxic; and drinking the water, could make you extremely sick or dead.

We walked back along the path, spotting some bear droppings, before we reached the boat. The park's notice board, mentioned a black bear, was spotted in the vicinity, as everyone was 'on' alert, because we're in the bear's home. This situation wasn't something I wanted to be faced with, so I was glad we only found his poopey doopey, instead of him.

On the second day with the volunteers my job was to clean the brass railings around the dining room, lounge room and the stair cases. Bree had seen a tip, for cleaning the brass, using a mixture of lemon juice and salt. It was a big job, and from my point of view a total waste of time. The air changed the railings back to a darker colour, even over night.

My time here was coming to an end with Sunday being my last work day. As I entered the centre, via Bree's office, I noticed a letter from Katie to Bree. The letter stated; Katie's hours for this week were almost up, and she wasn't coming to work today. Katie mentioned she would save the hours for tomorrow, for housekeeping duties.

Bree had mentioned to keep our roster within a forty-hour work week. During my stay, I worked more than forty hours *every* week. Were they bucking the system, of what volunteering, was all about? You know what? I am just one of those 'types of people', doing what needs to be done, to get the job finished. Katie was definitely not a team player.

Over the two work days with the volunteers; an incredible amount of work, was achieved, in all areas of the property. The entire vegetable garden was fertilized and planted out with new seedlings. The edges of the roads were trimmed, with the removal of excess growth and weeds.

The labyrinth was restored to 'perfect'; ready for the visitors, to enter the spiral walk, around the roped area. The 'marked' trees were removed, chopped up into logs, for the fire place. One of the balcony railings was removed; the bobcat bucket full of logs, was lifted up to the second storey, with the logs placed, near the door, to the lounge room.

Ian and Barbara kept the main lodge building operational over the winter months, as it wasn't feasible to shut it down. The cabins have their electricity and bio toilets switched off, and all bedding removed. With the new staff crew in action; only three days was all it needed, to restore the cabins ready for the new guest's arrival.

During the last week of my stay, I started reorganising; emptying the cupboards; and planning how everything was going to fit, back in my suitcases, after being here for nearly six-weeks. Sunday afternoon I finished packing my suitcases; and laid down to rest for awhile. Heather came over to see where I was, as I ran up to help with dinner. I thought maybe Bree had a talk to Katie about working, but she was nowhere to be found. I was very tired, but couldn't escape the farewell talk, as Ian and Barbara thanked everyone, for our hard work.

I could see the tension and stress, in Bree, as the weekend came to an end. Cindy, one of the volunteers, from the weekend, would move into my room. With Katie leaving, Bree had to find a new worker, pretty quickly, with back to back retreats, for the entire summer. The retreats usually lasted anywhere from two to six days. The staff had their days off, when there were no guests.

At the end of each retreat, all of the bedding was changed and the rooms made up. I really think the forty-hour shifts would've been nonexistent, over the summer, as it would be impossible to clean the cabins, and maintain the whole centre. Add to the mix the meal preparation, serving and cleaning up. AND only work a forty hour week. I think Bree would've taken advantage of the system, because they had no other choice.

This was the first year Ian and Barbara were using volunteers to run the centre. I have no idea how successful it was or whether it worked at all. The volunteering programme was not designed to replace, normally paid work. The programme was designed, to help farmers and businesses, engage workers because of their lack of resources. Just maybe The Lodge fits the bill.

FINAL DAY

On my last morning I attended yoga and meditation; arriving back to my room, to find a bottle of salmon was sitting on my suitcase. I had to squeeze the jar in, for Marcus to transfer my luggage, over to the Blue Bobby Bay. Arriving at our dock, I'd missed my ride over to the main dock, but luckily another boat was just leaving, so I hitched a ride.

At the dock, there was a last chance for a staff photo, and goodbyes. I hate goodbyes, as I'm too emotional. Heather and I had our goodbyes, at the staff quarters, crying out to her "I'm leaving on a jet plane and don't know when I'll be back again", one of my favourite songs. We had a huge hug, with a sad farewell, to an amazing woman, who shared all of my thoughts and dreams, in this incredible short space of time.

Some of the volunteers had arrived, in their own boat; who would spend the day cruising back home, while enjoying the holiday break. Taking my seat on the little cruiser, I turned back, to see Bree and Marcus standing on the dock, arm in arm, waving to me. I waved back, with a sense of overwhelming peace and love, for the opportunity, to be part of this incredible place. As Bree and Marcus figures faded into the distance, the huge mountain range, behind the lodge, loomed above, creating a breathtaking view.

NEWS UPDATES AFTER I LEFT

Bree, Marcus and Annabelle moved into a house, near the retreat centre, freeing up three bedrooms in the float house. This would ensure extra staff be hired and everyone would get their two days a week off and only work a forty-hour-week.

Heather updated me, after I left; mentioning everyone was exhausted, including her. Heather looked after Annabelle; and forever looking after other people's children, who came to play with Annabelle. Heather also missed out on all the meals, waiting at the house until Marcus or Bree came home, which were very long days.

The staff also had to clean and look after the staff quarters, along with their normal duties. Heather was asked by Cindy, to clean the staff quarters, for twenty-dollars, because she had no energy left. Cindy agreed to stay the entire summer, instead of the original few weeks.

LESSONS LEARNT

Anything was possible, if you've the money and the support, of a partner and friends, to help you achieve your dreams. I've spent most of my life, being the only person; I was able to rely on, since Ricky was hardly ever around to help me. What'd been missing from my life; was a special someone, there for me, to rely on, and look after me, for a change. I always had to be the 'strong' one, to make all the decisions.

With a partner, supporting me, I'd be a totally different person today. Was that a good or a bad thing? I truly believe past events, have made me, the person I am: a strong, determined and independent person. Go girl☺.

Chapter 5

IN TRANSIT TO CANADA - MAY

TIME OUT

I had a wonderful time, sitting out on the deck, of the Blue Bobby Bay, heading back to Scanner. I kept a jacket with me, in case the wind was cold, but the trip across the bay, was just perfect. The Blue Bobby Bay was a unique way to travel; with smooth even swells, spread across the massive expanse of water. The soft breeze tousled my hair, the warm sun shone on my face; breathing the ocean air into my lungs, the fresh cool air, rejuvenated my heart and soul. I talked with a lady on the boat, who mentioned, most of the volunteers were from the local area.

Oh course, you wouldn't believe the tide, when the Blue Bobby Bay, docked in Scanner. The ramps were steep, but luckily for me, there's only one trip up the ramp this time. I waited for the luggage to reappear out of the storage hole; with two bags, plus a backpack, plus a carry bag to manage up the ramp. I was very grateful, when a lady offered, to help me with my smaller suitcase. I struggled up the ramp, basically dragging the suitcases, as the wheels weren't big enough, to roll over the steel design.

A huge line of people were following me up the ramp; when suddenly, a strapping young lad walked down, from the top of the dock, grabbing both of my bags. He lifted them up, as if they were the weight of feathers, marching back up the ramp ahead of me. I thanked him for his generous act, as he met me at the top.

The same lady, I was talking to on the boat, offered to drive me to the motel, where I was staying the night. I checked in at 11:00am, with my room on the first floor, directly above reception. I had booked a room with a view; opening the door, I had a view overlooking the car park. I walked back downstairs, to reception, paying another fifty-dollars; for a room with a better view. $180US for one night's accommodation was total extortion.

The view of the bay and the mountains; was worth every cent. I had a great day of relaxation with a sleep, then lunch, and a massage. The massage was my reward, for all the hard work, over the last two months, and it felt SO GOOD, all wrapped up in hot towels, like a burrito baby. All the senses were switched on with the smell, touch and feel of the lotions and healing hands massaging my body.

After my massage, with the sun, still high up in the sky; I walked around the marina, looking for salmon, on the dinner menu. The little restaurant had breathtaking views, of the elements of the bay. Watching the seagulls, enjoying the last of the sun's rays, as the sunset clouds reflected on the water.

I rang home to Australia to catch up with news from mum and dad, as they weren't on my newsletter list. It's always good to hear Mum's voice. When I got lonely, I'd look at photos, taking me straight back home; I just had to close my eyes, and I was with them all again.

A few people were wondering around on the docks, as the summer season had officially arrived; bringing the whole area, into a busy metropolis, for the next three months. Looking around; it would've been great to spend the summer here, to experience the real Alaska. Barbara asked me to stay, to help them out, with Katie's job. But then I'd be letting down my next hosts, by cancelling on them, so close to my arrival date. I would've had to change all of my flights, and that wasn't something, I was prepared to do.

I walked off my salmon dinner, returning to the motel, to enjoy the vista from my balcony. OMG what an amazing 'once in a lifetime' experience I've had. I slept like a baby, in the huge queen-size-bed; as the motel was quiet, with no interruptions. I was emotionally and mentally prepared, for the next leg of my adventure, with an early morning flight south to Canada.

The taxi ride to the airport was only ten-minutes, with a very relaxed airport security (what security). I checked my bags through, and would see them again at Stapleton. Whooooooa!! Lucky for me I didn't have to pay for the extra weight charges. I need a bigger bag to distribute my growing collection of 'stuff', as my smallest bag was chock-a-block full and my big bag was overweight.

There was no café in the terminal, moving around the airport, waiting patiently (*or not so patiently*) before a very small plane taxied up. The plane was so small the pilot greeted us on his knees. It was ok for me, as I'm short, grabbing the first seat available, with a blocked window. Hand luggage was stored, at the front of the plane, with the pilot giving us the safety instructions while kneeling down.

I think there were about twelve seats, no toilet, no moving, just sit there and hold on. The weather this morning was perfect, with crystal clear skies, beautiful sunshine, visible from the window opposite me. With the flight only forty five minutes, it didn't take long, before landing safely and disembarking the plane.

I had a quick breakfast, before boarding the plane, travelling back to Windstrome. I didn't have a window seat and rested for the entire flight, really needing to catch up on some sleep, to rejuvenate a little, before I arrived at the next host. I can now sleep anywhere, including planes as I felt a little better with some extra shut eye.

Upon arriving at the Windstrome Airport, I was better prepared, for dealing with the train system, than my last visit. I had a couple of hour's layover before my flight to Canada, with no rush finding the right terminal. Now realising how exhausting; travelling and waiting around airports, can be. Time does fly by quickly, stretching my legs and of course, people watching. My favourite pastime when out in public places, wondering what they're thinking or talking about. Are they travelling alone? Or will they be meeting someone special at the other end?

FAMILY

I felt like I'd been travelling for days, with such an early start; finally arriving in Stapleton at 4:00pm, greeted by my nephew Bevan, Susie and Xavier. Bevan drove us back to Linden Grove, where I stayed the night with them. Bevan and Susie moved to Canada a few years ago, with Xavier, their twelve month old son, born here.

The changes they'd made to their house, since I'd visited them last year, were amazing. Bevan had finished the basement and started work building a garage. There was a back alley, behind their house, accessing their backyard and garage.

Bevan spends the autumn months hunting deer, at a friend's property up state, with the meat being a stable part of their diet. We had venison for dinner; catching up on the news, in their lives, over the last twelve months.

I mentioned to the new hosts, my dietary requirements; they suggested I shop in the city. Susie kindly dropped me off at the supermarket, before dropping me off at the bus station. The bus company recommends, arriving one-hour before the bus schedule, which was pathetic. I just sat there doing NOTHING. Oh what joy to just be sitting!

I was very tired, also excited, about my expectations of the new hosts. On the bus I tried to keep my eyes open, to look around, but they refused to stay open. Boy do I need a holiday☺.

First night at the Horse Stud

Chapter 6

HOST NO. 3 THE HORSE STUD – MAY/JUNE

THE ARRIVAL

On the bus, I half slept with one eye open, not wanting to miss my stop. The tiredness might have something to do with the amount of hours; I'd worked, for the last six weeks, and the time difference ahead of Alaskan time.

At the little corner store, I hopped off the bus, waiting for Trudy. While waiting, outside the shop, a lady asked "who are you and what are you doing here". After telling her my story, she said she knew Trudy, and we chatted, until a lady waved at us, as she stopped her car. The lady I was talking too said "oh do you know that person" and I said "No, but I hope it's Trudy". The lady said "that's not Trudy". I replied a little anxiously, "Well I hope it was".

Trudy and the lady spoke for a few minute; the lady admitting, she hadn't seen Trudy in awhile. I know sometimes when you don't see someone; especially women, who change their hair colour and style, put on weight and just get old. You can age beautifully or tragically, depending on what's going on with your life.

After we loaded my luggage in the back of the pickup, my first duty for the afternoon was unloading bags full of recyclable cans and bottles; cashing them in, at the recycling centre. Even cardboard was worth money, as I found out on the island. The recyclers pay money, for a lot of things, in Canada, that for us, in Australia, was landfill. After the recycling centre Trudy and I went grocery shopping. The shop was an eye opener, situated in an old building, with limited varieties, in the type of groceries, they sold. The township reminded me, of rural Australia, before modernisation, started to take over old townships. Residents who lived here travelled further afield, to buy their weekly supplies.

On the way out to the farm, Trudy casually mentioned the stable meat, for their diet was horse and would I mind, having it as part of my diet. I was rather shocked, replying "ok I'd give it a try". Trudy said they didn't kill their horses, for meat; they were culled for other reasons, such as breeding, as a male or female. The farm was currently overstocked; because of a downturn in the economy. Eating horse had only been practiced, for a couple of years; when they didn't want to waste, the meat of a horse, they put down. It's called sustainable living, living off a product they're producing, just like the sheep, pigs and chickens.

Arriving at the farm I was in shock, as the main overall impression was unwelcoming. The main, barn style house, looked at least twenty-years overdue, for a paint job. 'Dead cars' littered the area; the grass was one meter tall, with little cabins doted along the rim of the river, in urgent need of major repairs and a coat of paint.

THE DECISION TO STAY

Well the first few hours at the farm were an eye opener. I'd painted a particular picture in my mind; what the horse farm, would be like. The 'picture perfect farm' was nowhere near the expectations I'd set up for myself; as I laid down that night, in bed, deciding what I wanted to do.

Fifteen other workers were there to help, however I was the only one working in the garden. I was just, number sixteen, on the wall chart of workers, with no special treatment, just one extra person helping Trudy and Doug live 'their dream'. Promising Trudy five weeks, I considered the choice; of taking up the challenge, to see what the time would offer up to me OR leave and find a new place to stay.

THE HOUSE

After I settled into my room, which was about five minutes; I took a deep breath, heading back down, to the main house, for Trudy to show me around. I passed the hot house, near the main dorm room, with seedlings planted in trays, ready to be planted out in the gardens; and shown the paddock that needed to be ploughed, before we could plant the vegetables.

My heart sank when I was shown the Reiki studio; a disused building, never finished. The building was basically an empty shell. The location of the building, sitting at the edge of the embankment, overlooking the river; was the only reason to get excited. What a wonderful spot to have a session; away from the main house. Unfortunately, it'd take at least a few-thousand-dollars, along with a lot of hard work, to get the studio operational.

My vision for the renovations was sewing new curtains, repainting and reorganising the rooms. I was very disappointed, with this picture; starting to question why I was there. Exchanging emails, we discussed the work plan, forming a mental picture of the farm, *AND THIS WAS NOTHING LIKE IT.*

I truly believe the hosts, accepted me, because I was needed for a reason. I had to trust the reason was all part of the journey I was on. I worked out the first host was for 'a back to basic lifestyle'. Alaska was for the meditation, the mother earth connection and to arouse my intuition with my encounter with a former soul mate. I was here at this host for a reason, so I needed to see where the experience leads me.

The house was originally an old style barn, with extensions added on, in every direction. The entrance to the house was via the mud room, a fully enclosed glass-walled verandah. This area had year round use, with storage shelves, cupboards and chairs; removing all of your excess clothing, before entering the house. In winter, it's the perfect area, coming in out of the cold, before you enter the house and in summer this area was quite warm. *I have to mention the summer temperature, in Canada, was nothing like our extreme hot summers in Australia.*

Entering the main house, via a foyer, you access the kitchen area, via a set of stairs. To the right, a wash room, laundry room, freezer and a cold store room. A large staircase leads to the upper levels with a bathroom, bedroom, a lounge room and library, with Trudy's bedroom located in the loft above the library.

As you entered the kitchen area, a table and chairs were used for breakfast dining. The kitchen had lots of storage areas including a pantry; dishwasher and large stove and oven. *I would get accustomed to every part of the kitchen over the next five weeks.* The office area was located on the western side of the kitchen, with a connecting corridor, leading into the lounge and dining room. There was certainly plenty of room, for everyone, to find a place to eat, sit and relax.

In the lounge room, a grand piano and an assortment of instruments were available, if you had the inclination to play. The lounge room, located on the northern end of the house, was much cooler than the kitchen area. This room was all glassed in; as I cannot understand why they didn't have opening windows, in the house. The glass walls were floor to ceiling height, with a beautiful natural light entering the room. The lounge room had higher ceilings, than the dining room, as it was on ground level, accessed by a set of stairs.

Doug's had his room above the kitchen, accessed by a spiral staircase. A couple of nights we left the kitchen area, because Doug was going to bed early. The mares were being closely monitored during the night, because it was breeding season.

Another wing of the house was accessed through the mud room. This wing included a shower, washroom plus four bedrooms. Kathryn (the mother) and Audrey (a full time worker) had one room each; and two spare rooms were used by visitors, guests or workers. Kathryn's corner room had windows on two outside walls. One window had a view of the paved area, which Kathryn accesses for daily walks, using her wheelie walker. The other window viewed the grassed paddocks, where the pregnant horses are currently staying.

THE FAMILY

Over dinner that first night, I met the other volunteers; most of them female, aged around twenty-years-old from Germany. An older group of Alex, Veronica and Lindsey were French Canadians, and Lindsey's boyfriend, Phillip was from Germany. Lindsey previously worked at the farm; now had a job in a café, in Boulder. I met Doug, the brother and Kathryn, the mother over dinner. A second brother, Martin, his wife Paula, and two small children, lived on another part of the property, where the sheep, pigs and chickens were farmed. Currently the two spare rooms, in the east wing, were accommodating Paula's parents, visiting from Germany.

Martin had an older son Sam, from his first marriage; and Sam spent A LOT of time here at the main house, with the young single girls. And why wouldn't a young-red-hot-sexy-male, want to spend time, with the young sexy girls from Europe. He was extremely good looking, and hey if I was thirty-years younger, I'd have been chasing him as well.

Trudy was in charge of running the house, meal preparation, and the business paperwork, including organising the volunteers, who arrived to help out. Trudy was also responsible for the care of Kathryn. What a wonderful caring relationship, they shared with each other. Each morning Trudy would make up their breakfast tray; taking it to Kathryn's room, spending time alone together. I could see how much they both cared for each other, as this is what I want for my mother, a close bond, going beyond the ordinary.

Doug was in charge of breeding the warm blood horses; Martin was in charge of fields, crops, pigs and chickens. Martin was an ex-ballroom dancer, daring to hope, he'd teach me a step or two in their dance studio. However, there wasn't a dance studio on the property; so please add this, to the list of disappointments, about my expectations, from my visit to the farm. Obviously, I watch toooooooo many movies. Paula, Martin's second wife, worked as a ballet teacher, and looked after their two young sons.

What I discovered; the reality of life in Canada was the same, as in Australia. Families struggle financially to remain on their farms, chasing their dreams, of a sustainable rural lifestyle.

On my first night, after dinner, a massive storm cell passed through the area, creating a huge rainbow decorating the turbulent skies. With the northern summers, it was still day light, with everyone outside enjoying the cool night air. The young ones stayed outside, every night, drinking and smoking. For the week I stayed in the main dorm, the girls disturbed my sleep, all night with their comings and goings. I felt like their grandmother, not wanted or acknowledged, so I just kept to myself, reading on my bed and trying to get as much sleep as possible.

ROSTERS

One of the first things you're introduced to, when you arrived was the 'duty list'. The list included kitchen duty, preparing meals, house duties, and the most important information, 'your days off'. The meal times were approximate, each day waiting for the barn staff to arrive for lunch and dinner depending, on what tasks they're doing.

Lunch break was between twelve and two o'clock, which included eating your lunch, cleaning up all of the dishes, and resetting the dining tables for dinner. Everyone contributed in one way or other and Veronica made sure I did as much as everyone else.

The hours of work were from 8:00am until midday. The afternoon session was from 2:00 until 6:00pm; calculated as an eight hours a day, for an eleven day fortnight. What happened to the forty hour week?@#$%&*. Living in such isolation, I had no way of escaping the farm, except on a bush bike. My rostered days off were spent helping Audrey with the market, or just chilling out in my room.

I asked Trudy why she didn't get more help in the house; changing the rosters, with help in the house all day long. The current roster was only for morning help, which involved cleaning the bathrooms, floors and helping with lunch. The afternoon shift included helping with dinner and looking after the veggie garden. I mentioned to Trudy that when I left, someone would've to look after the green house and water all of the vegetables; to weed and pick the fruits of our labour. I can tell you; when the girls found out, about the roster changes, they weren't happy, missing out, on their afternoon with the horses. For god's sake, it's only one afternoon every two or so weeks. Stop complaining. What fuss pots they were. Poor little girls it was all about the horses.

ACCOMMODATION

I settled into my accommodation, sharing with five other girls, all about the age of twenty. The room was big, dark and untidy; sleeping in the bottom bunk bed, near the door. With no bathroom or shower; all the facilities were down at the main house. My stay here was only temporary, so I basically lived out of my suitcase. If I needed to go to the bathroom, during the night I just squatted out near the hothouse, as it's too far, to walk back to the house, plus I'd have to get dressed.

My second week at the farm I moved into the east wing, where Kathryn and Audrey stayed. It was good to have my own space; a window opening to the east, with the sun shining into my room in the mornings. I placed my bed on the south side of the room, in case there were any northern lights. Trudy had an alert, from an online aurora tracking app; sending me a link, but most nights, by the time the alerts were notified, I was in my room, too far away from the server, to receive the signal.

One night I hopped up to see if I could see the northern lights. I went to the area near the dining room; getting confused. *WHERE EXACTLY WAS THE NORTH AGAIN*. I keep telling you this chicky babe, from down-under, gets confused about where her true north was.

I really enjoyed the breeze through the window, with the curtains open, especially the view, of the pregnant horses, grazing just outside my window. I loved having the horses near my room, feeling their energies, during the night, as they munched on the grass. I assumed the area was private until one night, just after a shower, I noticed Doug walking across the grass in front of my room. I wondered how many nights, he had walked past; with a strange feeling, he'd looked in on a previous nights. I made sure I was dressed respectably after that time.

THE KITCHEN WORK

Audrey, who usually helped Trudy in the kitchen, was away for two weeks, looking after a handicapped boy. Trudy asked me if I knew how to cook bread. I said "it had been a few years, but I'd give it a go". I ended baking at least six loaves of bread a day, not big loaves, but they sure smelt good when they're baking. I changed the mix; from white, to multigrain, to wholemeal and maize. Veronica commented on how nice the bread was; thinking she was just being nice, because I was just following the recipe. After a week of baking, Trudy realized how much butter, eggs and milk I used, changing the recipe to just flour, water, sugar and salt. What a difference it made to the taste, compared to adding the butter mixture. Trudy was cutting the costs, the best she could, as I seriously didn't know how they afforded to feed, so many people, without the income of selling horses.

One afternoon I was cooking dinner; lasagne, and boy do I know how to make a mess. One pot was for the meat sauce; one for the béchamel sauce; one for the pastry mixture, plus a skillet to make the pastry. I had alternative meals for gluten free, and the girl's who won't eat horse. I was having a wonderful time, putting the meal together, with my music playing – all that was missing, was the wine.

This particular day I was baking bread at the same time and I had the entire kitchen full of pots and pans. Guess who was on the afternoon shift? Veronica!!! As she walked into the kitchen, she looked at me, then the mess, then turned around and walked back out again. Veronica went to ask Trudy "whether she had to clean up my mess in the kitchen" and Trudy said "yes". Veronica came back into the kitchen, cleaned up everything, without one comment. While Veronica was washing up, I was making more mess, by creating a dessert of rhubarb and apple crumble and home-made custard for a treat.

One of the mornings out in the garden, Andrea came over to tell me, I had to prepare lunch as there was an accident at the barn. Trudy had to go to the hospital with someone, who had crushed their finger. I had no idea what Trudy had planned for lunch, so I went with spaghetti bolognaise (one with horse and one without) with tube pasta. I had the sauce prepared, but didn't know how much pasta to cook up for the workers. I put in a handful of pasta, for each person, and when the girls arrived, there was nowhere near enough food for everyone. I told them to stop whingeing, and be patient, as I boiled up more pasta. They just had two small plates, instead of one large one, with most of the girls only eating, the 'non horse' sauce.

My payment for helping Audrey, with the markets, was a packet of ground bison. I used the meat to cook up a bolognaise sauce; frozen into small amounts, to have with my rice pasta. I made a lasagne, out of the bison, for one dinner, with Doug and I both having gluten free pasta sheets. Doug had trialed a diet of low gluten, to see if he gained better health. The girls were asking why there were so many different meals; sighing with jealousy, when I told them, my meal was made from bison. Tough bickies baby.

THE WORKERS

Life on the farm was one big adventure, after another, saying goodbye to one girl as we welcomed another, in an orderly fashion. There were teary goodbyes for the popular girls, and so mean and bitchy, when someone didn't fit in. Meal times were interesting, with the German girls, sitting at one table; with Trudy continually reminding them to talk in English. I sat with Trudy, Doug, Kathryn, Audrey and whoever didn't want to sit with the young ones.

A French girl, stayed for awhile, but the French-Canadian language was quite different from the European French. Well for me, I just spoke English, and when travelling; the Australian English was quite different, from other countries. Our terminology was quite bizarre whereas Canada was influenced by America. There were times, when a person would look at you 'with a blanked out expression' on their face. I found these conversations fascinating, because they had no idea what I just said. You would have to ask them, what part of the conversation, *DID they NOT* understand.

THE HORSES

The horses were certainly, magnificent creatures; watching the power of their bodies, as they ran, was an amazing sight. *I love a scene out of one of my favourite movies, where a horseman has a group of horses, in the high country, with snow on the ground. He uses his whip, to control the horses, as they move in a fluid movement, all together and change course like water starting to run down a dry river bed. The photography from that scene, was spellbinding, and that was how I felt, looking out over the paddocks, watching the horses. Another scene, from the same movie, filmed from the opposite river bank, as the sun shines behind the horses, capturing a golden blanket reflection; on the water. As the horses enter the river, glistening droplets of water, rise into the air, the sun catching each droplets of water, as the horse continues across the river. Both of these scenes are mesmerising.*

The farm had two hundred horses, as I wondered '*WHY*' so many. My next question was what activities involved all the fifteen girls working all day? Each day, someone was rostered off, with ten to twelve girls, working each day at the barn.

The barn duties in the morning were for cleaning out the stalls and feeding the animals. After lunch each day, was 'play time'; according to Trudy. The girls ride the horses, sometimes out on the trails, other times around the ring. I believe this should still be classified as work. I had questioned Trudy about the hours of work, and why they needed so many workers, apparently the horses needed a lot of attention. I also questioned Trudy about why I was working such long hours as my work was all 'hard work' with no play time.

One of my gardening jobs was removing, an invasive grass, from the flower garden beds. I gathered the grass in my little trolley, and feed the horses near the house. The three female horses were pregnant; with a couple of stud male horses, also resting in this paddock. The horses were huge as I patted them most days, if they let me, especially if I had grass for them. After the first couple of days, when the horses noticed me, coming their way, they'd head over to the fence hoping for gifts. At least I got to spend time with them to feel their energies.

The three female horses all gave birth to three little girls, so they would stay together in the same paddocks as they grew up. Early one morning, when one of the horses gave birth; Audrey had her camera, photographing the birth, and the first few moments of the foal's life. There was one particular photo; the steam off the afterbirth, was rising in the cool morning air, with Alex and Veronica standing, behind the steam, watching the foal. It was a very special moment for all of us.

At the gate, I stood watching the horses, in the river paddock, and all of a sudden they'd take off running around the paddock. I was curious as to why they did this? Trudy said horses had a lot of energy to 'run' off. The horses would be near the gate, altogether in a group; and I think, one horse, says to the others "let's go", heading towards the river, around the paddock, in formation, like paint being brushed onto a canvas. The pack of horses would have their manes and tails flying in the wind; coming back, to where they started from, settling back into quite conversation again, as if they had never left. If you were away, for those ten minutes, you would have thought, they hadn't moved, at all.

Everyone from the barn was extremely late for lunch, and those of us at the house decided to eat. Doug drove up to the house, asking everyone to follow him, back to the barn, to help him with an emergency with the horses. A gate had not been closed properly; with the colts now mixed up in the same paddock, with the young fillies. Apparently, a total disaster, as the colts were not 'cut' and the young fillies were too young to give birth.

The farm was divided into different holding paddocks; linked by a corridor, about one kilometer long; leading into the holding pens and barn. The horses were in the end paddock, with workers placed, along the corridor, encouraging them along. We spent a couple of hours getting the horses back into the yards. I was the gate control keeper, closing the gate, as the horses entered the yarded area, where a small, hexagonal shaped pen, had gates leading off, into different pens. Doug would advise us, which pen each horse, was to go into, with that person, opening their gate. Each pen was allocated to a different horse, depending on whether the horse was young, old, male or female.

Doug was stressed out of his mind; not capable of giving good verbal instructions, to get the help, he needed; from the team, trying to help him. Doug decided to place all of the young colts into the stables, in the barn; locked into separate pens, to calm them down. Audrey was in a power struggle with Ann, who wouldn't listen, for instructions from Audrey, about how to handle the colts.

My time at the gate was stressful enough, when Sarah, asked ME to go into the pen to separate a young colt, before he mated, with the young mare. Since I was the closest person, Sarah must've thought it was a good idea. *THERE WAS NO WAY IN HELL* I'm going anywhere near a horse. Without even one second of experience, dealing with any horses, especially a young colt with one thing on his mind. We all just stood there, leaning on our gates, watching them and when the colt was 'finished' he was easily, led away, without any resistance.

I know what I was thinking – wow I'd love sex, but with only thirty seconds worth of action. The male would say "thank you very much and have a great day"☺. I definitely needed an hour or so, for my afternoon delight, not just thirty seconds.

It was an eventful day, working with everyone at the barn; knee deep in muck trying to open and close gates. I had to contend with nearly getting electrified (I mean electrocuted☺) placing a metal chain, on a metal post, 'alive' with 210 volts of electricity. I didn't know it was 'alive' until I was struck, with a lightning bolt and momentarily motionless, literally in shock. "Oh well" said Doug and Audrey, with not one ounce of sympathy, as I was expected to keep working.

Finally, we breathed a sigh of relief, with the horses safely in the yards, and the worst of the situation was over. The barn girls, still had to separate a few of the horses, but the job was mostly finished. The barn workers were absolutely starving as it was 3:00pm before we arrived back to the main house, and cleaned up for lunch.

FOOD

Our main ingredients for meals were bread, rice, pasta and horse. Breakfast was usually toast, yoghurt or cereal; as the volunteers bought their own food, if they didn't like what was provided by Trudy. A couple of cars, belonging to the workers, were used for expeditions to town for beer, cigarettes and nutella.

I had bought nuts, dried fruits, rice pasta and snack bars; I kept in my room, except for my yoghurt. I purchased a few gluten-free bread packet mixes, cooked and sliced up for the freezer.

Trudy had a canteen with soft drinks, chocolates and chips for sale; which we could buy at a minimal cost. The young ones had a good supply of beer, kept in a fridge somewhere; I didn't see where. A few of the girls mentioned, the chocolates and chips should've been included in their food allowance. I didn't buy anything from the canteen, as I was trying to lose weight.

The meals were basic, without desserts; however there were many birthday cakes. Dining in style with baked ham and pork, were definitely my favourite meals, with rhubarb growing in the garden as well.

At lunch time one day, word spread, dinner was going to be in town, for anyone who wanted to go. Chip in money for fuel and car pool, rounding up the troops and headed into Sandalwood. Pizza was our target food, for our dinner, but settled for a diner. I'm sure Trudy was delighted to be cooking for a few people, instead of twenty.

During my stay, volunteers were holding a B-B-Q, for any workers in town on Thursday and Friday. It's 'Beef week', as we jumped into the car, headed for town. The food was so good; the workers went back for seconds, on the Friday. The free meal included a BEEF hamburger, with a soft drink; a great change for everyone.

THE GARDEN WORK

I woke up, on my first morning, full of excitement, about the challenges of the new job. I found all of the equipment, I needed to start my projects and went to work. I always love it, when you have lots of jobs to do, as you change to suit how you're feeling; working on my hands and knees, weeding, until my knees or back hurt; changing to a job standing up with a shovel. An invasive grass, had taken over quite a few of the garden beds; my main job was for the gardens to be 'weed free'. This was an almost impossible task, with the grass grown, in and around all of the flowers. I replanted a few flowers, from one garden into another, prepared other beds for veggie planting. I removed whole beds of flowers, from the back of house, because a deck was going to be built there.

Trudy had a hand-held, motorised, cultivator SHE was going to plough up, the acre of ground. I said I wouldn't be able to help her, with that job, as my back wasn't strong enough. Trudy and Doug tried to get the cultivator started; in the end, a tractor and plough was used. Alex and Phillip completed the job in less than thirty minutes. A task was made so much easier, with the right equipment.

Trudy's hot house stocked with seedlings, were ready to go out in the garden. Packets of seeds needed to be planted around whole area, with a huge list of tasks to keep me busy.

An electric fence, confronted me, every day, going down to the 'patch'. If I was quick enough, I would reach the paddock, without being too frightened by the horses. Animals know when you are scared of them. I wouldn't say I was exactly 'scared' just cautious, because they were SO big.

With the paddock ready to plant, Suzanna, who was on light duties, with a sore back, was able to help me. We planted the whole patch of vegetables, with a seed planter, in one afternoon. There were rows and rows of different types of beans, peas, kale, spinach, chard, beets and lettuce. Most of the ground had good soil, however one part, was one-hundred-percent horse manure and when it rained this area got flooded.

With the seeds planted, we needed rain and moisture to get everything moving. Planting some of the seeds; the packet mentions, 'that by mid June, make your final plantings', and here we were, just beginning. It's a pity the vegetables were not a priority, with a house full of willing workers. Had the vegetables been planted in May, they'd be more established, when I left. The gods were looking down on us, receiving a shower of rain, just after we finished planting.

Each morning, my first job, was raking the entire area, between the rows, to stop all of the weeds from coming up. You wouldn't believe it, but overnight, a whole new batch of weeds sprung up. I completed this task at almost a walking pace, I found it so therapeutic. The job was similar to a Japanese or Asian sand pit, creating your decorative design into the sand.

If I needed extra muscles, with any jobs around the garden, Trudy arranged with Doug for someone to help out. Trudy and I decided to move, a few of the old bath tubs, laying in the paddock not being used; placing them near the hot house, filled with soil, for vegetables growing near the house.

Doug arranged for Veronica and Sarah to help with the soil, for the tubs, as we headed to the 'manure tower' behind the stables. The manure tower was about fifteen metres across by ten metres high, with the tower being added to daily, over the last twenty years. A narrow spiral track, lead to the top of the stack; where the latest droppings were placed.

The tractor and trailer were parked, at the bottom of the tower, with Veronica in her whining and whingeing voice wanting to know "how much manure was needed, and how long was it going to take"? I stood there, leaning on my shovel, and said in a matter of fact voice "It's only going to take about fifteen minutes of your time". I felt like adding "stop the freaking complaining and get on with it". Instead I just started shovelling; and there's, no way in hell, I was stopping, until after Veronica did. Veronica was about twenty-four; half my age, but there was no stopping me. I was like a crazed maniac, on an important mission; manure mission. I earned a little more respect from Veronica after that, probably not, because she was the first to stop shovelling. Sarah had a sore back, attempting a reasonable, but pathetic effort. The whole job was completed in less than ten minutes, as I timed it. All I can say, about this job was, I can shovel shit, like the best of them.

Veronica drove the tractor up to the house; with borrowed workers and wheelbarrows from the barn. The wheelbarrows were used to unload all of the manure into the tubs. How amazing was it, when everyone works together. By the next afternoon, all the seeds and seedlings were planted out in the tubs. There'd be so many vegetables, to feed, the entire house hold for months.

The pity of it all was, why the garden, wasn't made a priority, before I arrived on the farm. As by now they could have been eating salad and vegetables fresh from the garden and supplementing their food bill with all of this fantastic produce.

During summer the mud room was steaming hot, because of the wall of glass; mentioning to Trudy about using big pots, placed at the posts, creating a wall of green beans, climbing up the ropes in a fan design; making a nice entrance. It was my lucky day, as old wine barrels were planted with beans and lettuces; wouldn't you know it, before I left; the beans were already winding their way up the rope.

While I was weeding all of the gardens, I mentioned to Trudy, about the entrance to the house; where a nice little corner was filled with tubs of flowers. The plants lived outside in summer, but lived in the mud room, during winter. I asked Trudy if I could 'pretty up' the entrance, by placing small river stones, along the edge of the mud room; a dual purpose of stopping the weeds growing, and giving a more welcoming and attractive feel to the entrance.

Veronica was on afternoon duty, as I needed some help with carting stones. I asked Veronica if she would collect the stones, from the paddock, in the little trolley and bring them back to me, while I placed them along the glass panels. The afternoon shift was mainly to help me with any jobs I needed to do. Veronica was not a happy camper; by her attitude, making her collect double the stones I required – just because I could!!!

AUDREY AND THE MARKETS

Audrey and I shared a passion for photography; with her camera a really expensive digital one, with interchangeable zoom lens. My camera, for this trip, was a drop proof, freeze proof, water proof little number. Audrey's photos were incredible; especially the horses and bison, taken in the snow. Every time Audrey checked the fences, she photographed the horses or anything else interesting.

Audrey was British, a little bit younger than me; employed full time at the farm. During summer she helps a neighbour, selling their bison through market stalls, on the weekends. One weekend Audrey asked; if I would like to help; since it was my day off, I said YES.

We travelled over to the neighbour's house; loading up the van; driving one-and-a-half to two hours to the markets; set up the stand, ready to start selling by 9:00am. I helped Audrey set up the marquee;

carrying the tables and eskies full of frozen meat. The organisers were very strict, NO ONE was allowed to start selling, before the horn blew; unless you were a stall holder, then you could. In the afternoons, no one was allowed to pack up, before the horn blew, whether you had sold out or not.

The first market, was the first time, I had seen any shops, over the last couple of months. I went crazy for crystals, hand creams, magnets and some beautiful handmade cards. I bought Trudy an Asiatic lily with a beautiful flower. The gift was conditional; while it was flowering, I would look after it; Trudy could then plant it in her garden, for next year's flowers. I ended up buying Trudy three plants, as they're one of my favourite flowers, and now each year, when they flower, she'll think of their Aussie volunteer.

I enjoyed my time away from the farm helping Audrey with three markets. As soon as I opened my mouth, the customers knew; I was Australian, and would say "just keep talking". *It wasn't until September in Quebec, that I ran into my first Aussies. All I kept thinking was "do I really sound like that"? Then in November, in California, I was really shocked when I met up with Tasmanians and nearly died at their strange accent. The accent was so pronounced, no wonder everyone knew.* So after a while I would just say a quick 'hi' hoping the accent didn't come through. Not that I'm ashamed of being Australia, I just wanted to sell bison and have a good day talking to people.

CONVERSATIONS AND CELEBRATIONS

Kathryn, the mother had been unwell, spending time in the city with Thomas, another son; so Trudy was a little lost without her companion. Thomas and Kathryn arrived back to the farm in time for the celebrations; where the whole family, celebrated Doug's sixtieth birthday. Trudy and I cooked up a storm, with the volunteers contributing 'something' in the form of a dish, from their homeland. The occasion was celebrated with Doug coming down to dinner, in a tuxedo.

Our meal had a five-star rating, with five courses. The event started with nibbles; then a soup with fresh bread rolls I baked, including gluten free bread, which impressed Doug. Our main meal, for twenty-five people; consisted of roast pork and vegetables. I baked a Pavlova, served with strawberries and cream. I believe the Pavlova was Australian, but some New Zealanders say, it's *THEIRS*. The evening had a great mood of excitement, with wine and good cheer; including a group photo, with the dogs and cats included.

I really didn't spend much time with Doug, as I wasn't part of his 'horse groupies', but occasionally we would have conversations, around the dinner table, about life in Australia.

THE WATER CRYSTALS

Trudy and I were having a chat, when she mentioned a book; about a man who prayed for world peace. The man had taken microscopic photos of water, before and after, the water was blessed. The man had photographic proof, the water crystals were a different shape, after the prayers. A prayer from his book; you say before you drink or eat anything, helps with your life. I'd tell people about this story; what a difference, a little prayer, can make to our lives.

A story, out of the book, details a shuttle mission into space, where thing goes wrong with the spacecraft. Grave fears were held, for the ship, and the men on board, who might perish before, landing back on earth. Over a period of three or four days, people all over the world, prayed for the men's safe passage, with the astronauts surviving the re-entry back to earth. The man who wrote the book, believed their survival, was due to the fact, three-billion people, on the planet, were praying for them.

I remember this story from back in 1970. I believe anything's possible, if we all join hands and pray. Let us pray for world peace.

EXPLORING THE FARM

With a day off, after a massive sleep-in, I explored the paddocks, around the farm. Martin and Paula lived about one kilometer away, so I walked over, to see where it was located. I didn't disturb them, but they saw me and asked Trudy why I didn't come up to the house. I really should have rang or arranged to say hi, otherwise I thought it's rude to just turn up. Martin had a marimba guard dog, acting protective, immediately, as I approached the paddock, near the house. He followed me, with his eyes and body, continuing to watch me, long after I passed the sheep paddock.

I patted a couple of friendly horses, until they realised I didn't have treats, in exchange for a pat. With the recent rain, the roads were mucky and very slippery; managing to navigate the bog holes, to dry ground. I picked a spot, at the edge of a clearing, perfect for resting and reading. It was very peaceful, except for some ants and other insects that decided I needed to be investigated. I spent a couple of hours in solitude, with the cool breeze and birds chattering off in the distance.

SPEAKERS

I emailed the Club, enquiring about the location of the nearest one; forty-minute' drive away, with no possibility of attending a meeting, without access to a vehicle. I kept my options open, when Lindsey was working, a meeting night. I arranged for the afternoon off, and spent the afternoon shopping and looking around the township of Boulder.

I bought a journal to start recording my trip, to maybe make sense of it, one day. I visited a shop selling fudge and *REAL* coffee, ordering a cappuccino. My only other coffee experience in the last three months was, at the markets with Audrey, so this was an extra treat.

In a little arcade I found a shop full of crystals, spending a couple of hours, and a couple of hundred dollars, on a multitude of crystals. I'd been reading the crystal books, about the healing powers of crystals, so I was on cloud nine. The crystals connect with you; so what can a girl do, I had to take them home. That's my story; and I'm sticking with it.

I found a tavern, with a wings deal, which I'll never understand, why chicken wings are so popular. Bars everywhere, had happy hour with wings; and this place was packed. I ordered fish for dinner;

excited beyond belief, at my treasure trove of crystals, studying the information about my new stones. When I had finished eating, I hired a cab to go to the meeting.

At the meeting, the man I had emailed was there, setting up new clubs, with the Boulder Club being chartered that night. Their first official meeting, was professionally run, with most of the members associated with the local council management or were in fact, councillors.

At the meeting, I gave a small speech about my volunteering plans for Canada. One of the members knew Doug and Trudy, who knew them as well; sharing the information when I got home. Doug was interested in joining the club, but had other commitments, on the night of the meeting.

The theme of the meeting was 'patriotism'. I was privileged to witness, how passionate Canadians are, about their country. I was presented with a mini Canadian flag, as a memento of the meeting. The man, sitting next to me, was an Australian from Ipswich. Steve has lived here for the last twenty-years, working as an executive chef, at the local casino. What a small world it was, as Steve drove me to reconnect with Lindsey.

Lindsey was a crazy, nervous driver, travelling the gravel roads at forty-kilometers-an-hour, the whole distance, to and from the farm. The reason for the nervousness was she had damaged her car the week before, hitting a deer, and currently driving, a replacement car, from the insurance company. I was so appreciative of the ride, with an amazing sunset to watch, on the way home.

REIKI

Trudy was a Reiki master, my main reasons for visiting there. I wanted to help with some treatments, as I said earlier. I thought I'd be helping out in a Reiki centre, already established. Completing my level one course, needing a mentor, to help practice on patients. I practiced self-healing, with the help of crystals.

During a conversation with Trudy, she mentioned the Reiki centre had taken a backward stance, for several reasons. Her marriage dissolved; and the down turn, in the horse industry, were the main reasons. Over the years, the whole property became run down, with an unwelcoming and unpleasant appearance. Trudy mentioned its tough work, managing all of the volunteers with meals, shopping, paperwork and taking care of Kathryn.

I was so happy when I revisited here in 2014, with the roster, for full time help, in the house was still in place. The whole property was once again profitable, with renovations, including a large deck on the northern side of the house. I was surprised at the overall appeal of the farm, compared to my first visit.

BUCKING THE SYSTEM

After the second week of working nearly sixty hours, which included the garden and kitchen work, I said it wasn't fair. I changed my work day, around what needed to be done. I wouldn't be able to continue, at this pace, for the whole five weeks. I spent more and more time in the kitchen, working more than eight hours each day, which was enough, especially when I was providing most of my own food.

This farm, and the Alaskan hosts were definitely pushing the limits, of what the volunteer programme was all about; not following the rules, of a maximum forty-hour-week. I could've done a 'Mary' and refused to work, but that's not who I was, or what I do. The volunteering programme was NOT designed, to take over, normal paid work.

I discussed with Trudy, changing the details, about their sustainable practices on the volunteering website. The last time I looked at the farm's blog, there still hadn't mentioned horse as part of their diet. I don't think the farm would attract many young, impressionable girls from Europe, who arrived exclusively to work with horses. It's disappointing, Trudy also mentions Reiki.

I updated my volunteer profile making comments on my host's sites, with honest comments about my individual experiences on each of the farms. *(I didn't mention horse as dinner, as that wasn't my place to do so)* I found these comments very valuable, when I was looking for places to stay, and taken the advice of other volunteers, when making a decision.

SPECIAL EMAIL DELIVERY

Along with volunteering I took the opportunity to look at house sitting; really wanting to spend winter somewhere. A nice place with snow, clear beautiful blue skies and cold temperatures. I had been speaking with a couple from Colorado, who were now permanently heading to Puerto Rico, as they had finally sold their house, which had been listed for over two years.

I received an email from Steve and Lauren, asking if I was available, to look after their house from late December to April the following year. I replied YES; agreeing to visit me, while I was staying at Grosvenor, at my next host's location. I now have to extend my trip, from the end of November to the beginning of April. Wow I'm going to spend a winter in Canada; OMG how amazing was this.

THE REASON FOR THE VISIT

During my stay, I realised why I was here. The relationship between Trudy and Kathryn, the love, care and concern they have for each other, was the relationship, I need with my mum. Kathryn, with her failing eyesight, failing health and the decline in her mobility, now relied on Trudy.

It's a true gift, to look after another person; as I need to be there for my mum, in all ways that matter. I've often thought about this statement; caring for my mother, was just as important to me, as it was for her. To repay the service of life, the unconditional gift of love, from me to my family.

One perfect Day

Chapter 7

IN TRANSIT VIA TRAIN, BUS AND CAR -JULY

FAREWELLS

Trudy and Kathryn were waiting to say goodbye to me, as I left with Audrey, heading for the markets. My luggage had to fit in the back of the van, along with all of the meat and market supplies. I waited until the end of the markets, helping Audrey repack, before I said goodbye; meeting up with Bevan and Susie. The weather was so hot; visiting a water park to cool off after the markets. The first time I'd seen a water park, of this magnitude, with families having an incredible amount of fun. What amazed me the most, about the visit; Xavier was covered head to toe, in sun clothes with sunscreen and a hat. The rest of the children, in the park, were just wearing swimmers. Either Susie was over the top cautious, or the Canadians haven't heard about skin cancer.

I've heard reports from medical authorities; claiming children in Australia were deficient in vitamin D; as parents restrict children, without sun protection. Parents have been told to slip; slop, slap with schools enforcing strict rules, about playing in the sun, without sunscreen and hat.

The Canadian children only experience warm weather for what? About two months, when it's hot enough to visit the water parks. I say let them play, having fun, whatever your views.

After the water park we dined at a Thai restaurant, before Bevan, Susie and Xavier dropped me off at the motel.

THE TRAIN TRIP

The first time visiting a place, it's all new; discovering the more I travel, the more comfortable I feel about, visiting new places. Had I looked at the map, I would've discovered the train went through Linden Grove; Bevan and Susie's town. I could've saved myself a couple-of-hundred-bucks in motel accommodation and taxi fares.

The morning was grey and wet boarding the train; relaxing for the five hours, before the arrival into Greensboro. The train trip showcased the landscape, and at one point of time, I had a sleep along the way. At Greensboro, the rental car company had restricted kilometres, on their vehicles; a ridiculous figure of one-hundred-kilometres-per-day. I had no choice, but pay for the additional costs, for my mileage. I wasn't happy Jan!!!

THE RENTAL CAR AND ACCOMMODATION

The first time climbing into the driver's seat, *THE STEERING WHEEL'S ON THE WRONG SIDE OF THE CAR*. I am always nervous, the first time I start driving, on the right-hand-side of the road, hoping I didn't hit anyone or anything. Ha Ha!! My accommodation was seventy kilometres from the national park. I would've found a closer motel, but they're just way too expensive for my budget; as the peak-summer-holiday-tariffs are charged. One bonus was my national parks voucher, from last year trip; saving me a few dollars.

I booked the motel online; ringing to change the booking, from a king size bed to two queens, as Audrey joined me for a couple of days, arriving by bus. I arranged for a key, waiting at reception; not realising the town had two motels, with the same name. Of course the bus dropped her off at the wrong one; driving to the other side of town, to pick her up, from the side of the road, at midnight.

The plan was finding, as many wild animals, to photograph and explore the surrounding area. Audrey purchased her camera a while ago, but never had the time to check out all of the settings, as she usually photographed animals. Now she was taking photos of lakes and mountains; with settings on the camera, she never knew she had. How exciting!!!!

We travelled over 2,000 kilometers during the five days, continuously pulling the car over to the side of the road, investigating what, all the people, from the parked cars were looking at. A large brown bear, over in the fields, about five-hundred-meters, was eating something. People were asking "what's the bear eating"? I said in a matter of fact voice "the bear was eating the last human who got too close to him". One lady was clearly upset at my remark, but it's true. We had no right to be this close to a wild predator.

I love driving, planning to drive nine-hundred-kilometers in one day. We arrived at our first lake, where it'd just stopped raining; luckily scoring a parking spot. I'm always speechless driving into this valley; with the mountain formations, above the lake, spectacular, especially the reflections, on the surface, of the incredible colourful lake. The track onto the moraine had dramatically improved since my last visit there in 2008. Instead of scrambling over rocks, all the way to the top, steps and paths were constructed for easy access. The whole viewing area had landscaped walls, with seats to relax on. Both of us were amazed at the intensity of the glacier lake; me with quiet reflection; Audrey with her camera.

Tourism was big business, with tens of thousands of people, visiting these lakes *EACH DAY* and if you're very lucky enough, to secure a car park space, which we did. The weather had turned bad, with black skies, threatening to rain any minute. We didn't escape the torrential rain, running for our lives, back to the car, as we headed back home.

Audrey only brought with her high-heel-boots to climb up and around the mountains. A particular lake became our favourite place to visit; close to the car park. The colours, in the deepest part of the lake, were a dark navy blue. We visited the lake in the afternoons, after the sun rose above the large mountain range. We explored incredible canyons with waterfalls; created by the force of the water, over a period of millions of years.

We photographed a huge moose; not in the slightest bit interested, in the people, who were photographing him at a rather close distance. Audrey had a few really good shots of him, as I enjoyed a new location. *(Audrey sells her photographs at the markets, with some new exciting specimens captured on this trip).*

The national park was certainly an interesting place, and every time you spotted a car, on the side of the road, you'd also pull over, to investigate what they were looking at. We were blessed to witness elk, deer and bears; almost witnessing a bear attack some idiot who walked too close.

When we pulled up, there was only one other car; but within a few minutes there were ten cars. Everyone was watching the bear, from across the road, behind their cars, at a good distance, with the bear happily munching away on foliage, as he walked along the side of the road. With the bear heading in the same direction, one guy crosses the road, hiding behind a very small tree. When the bear spotted him; the bear growled, his annoyance that the human was in his way. A couple of people honked their horns, to distract the bear, as the guy headed back across the road to his car. What an idiot. I told Audrey to place his picture on social media, so he gets the message.

Do you know what would've happened to the bear, if he had attacked the man? The bear would permanently be relocated to heaven, because of this man's stupidity; which was so wrong. The national park was for the animals, to live their natural lives, with as little human contact as possible.

THE WILDFLOWER FIELDS

My reason for choosing the Greensboro area for a break; was to spend time at the wildflower fields and glacier located there. Decked out in my hiking gear, to go exploring, I arrived at the car park, to find a notice, advising hikers, the walk was closed, because of snow. I was so pissed off, as in September 2008 the walk had already closed, because of early snow.

My second visit here and I still couldn't climb up to the wildflower fields. Audrey was taking photos, along the valley floor of the glacier, as I climbed up higher to capture better photos of the glacier. I started on the walk towards the wildflower fields; to see how far I could travel, turning around too early that day (*as I discovered in August when I returned. See Chapter 9*). The track, to the wildflower fields, travels along the top of the moraine, before ascending the mountain.

The snow melt that year had been higher than normal, with the streams and rivers wild and almost overflowing. After leaving the bitumen, basically four-wheel-driving, in my little car; slipping and sliding, our way to the car park, six-kilometres from the main road. We immediately spotted a sign, stating bears could be in the areas, be safe when walking through on the tracks. The other thing, attracting our immediate attention, were the million mosquitoes, hanging around to suck our blood. We sprayed ourselves, quickly walking down towards the lake.

OMG the lake was breathtaking, nestled between two long ridges, protecting it from the winds. A small boat was tied up to the little jetty; imaging spending the day drifting, while we caught a boat load of fish. The presence, I felt, was of peace and tranquility, as we enjoyed the ambiance. On the track, back to the car park, I was in front of Audrey, power walking. Suddenly, I caught movement, through the bushes, out of the corner of my eye. My heart stopped beating as I drew a deep breath, before I started singing "I come from a land down under" in the hope that *IF IT WAS A BEAR*, it would've been terrified by my singing, and run in the opposite direction.

My next breath was one of relief, when I noticed the movement, was in the shape of a young family, who had just arrived on the track. So glad to see them I didn't ask what they thought of my singing talents; explaining why I was singing. Audrey, being British, definitely struggled with my explanation of the events.

ONE PERFECT DAY

The weather on the Tuesday and Wednesday was terrible, with the photos having a dull grey, cloud reflection. Finally on the Thursday, the gods were listening; out the door at 4:00am hoping to catch the reflections on the lakes before the sun rises. At the first lake the mist hovered above the water, as the eastern sky, started to glow with the rising sun. We spent an hour taking photos, from different angles, including a pair of wild ducks, swimming in the calm water.

We had two sunrises that morning, travelling over to the western side of the range. The photos from this location had an almost picture-perfect-reflection; of the large snow capped mountain, reflected in the lake. The photo turned around and viewed, finding it hard to know, which 'was the right way up'.

Because Audrey was on a budget, our meals were heated up TV dinners or take-away. After breakfast on Thursday, Audrey wanted to hitchhike back to the farm; but I didn't want her to do that, so I drove her back just in time for lunch, with a chance for a second goodbye.

After I arrived back at the motel; I slept and chilled out in front of the television, ordering a movie, and dined at the restaurant downstairs. On Friday I headed into Greensboro, shopping before I returned my rental car; checked my luggage in, boarding the train mid-afternoon.

TRAIN TRAVEL CONTINUES

While I was waiting at the train station, I met a young girl Nikki, travelling with her dad Henry. We started talking; discovering Henry and I were born on the same day and year; except he was born in Canada and I was born in Australia. What were the chances of meeting your twin? Nikki captured a photo of us with our driver's licence, to prove we were twins. On the train I spent the whole time, in the observation car with Nikki and Henry; where Henry entertained the entire car with his stories and charisma. There was alcohol available, so the time passed quickly, with a few drinks.

Eight incredible hours spent in the viewing car, looking above the train, at the scenery, with the train slowing down at one of the biggest waterfalls in the Rockies; only visible from the train.

Train travel was a truly unique way to see any country; with Dad and I enjoying the experience back in 2005, travelling from Edmonton to Halifax. Dad and I enjoyed our two days travelling from Winnipeg up to Churchill; spending two days exploring Hudson Bay, before returning back to Winnipeg. We really enjoyed the hospitality of a local Portuguese café with Jon and Ben; the brothers from Winnipeg, entertaining us with their adventures. On the train today, I met a man, who travelled up to Churchill by train from Winnipeg. Apparently, the rail to Churchill was stopping, so this man took the last chance, to ride the train.

When the train arrived at Ploomaks, at midnight, I ordered a cab. Henry hadn't organised a motel that night; with no vacancies at his normal hotel; calling my motel, with a vacancy. What a dump!!!! It was cheap, dirty and I was there for two nights. Suck it up princess. I said good night to Henry and Nikki and went straight to bed, as it had been a very long day.

In the morning I'd just woken up when Henry and Nikki called in to say goodbye. Still in my jarmies; they were heading for breakfast to meet Alison, Henrys wife. I should've gone with them, but needed to get my rental car picked up, to explore the country-side. *(I did catch up with Henry and Nikki in Chapter 21)*

AN INCREDIBLE DAY

A cab dropped me off at the rental-car-business; costing me twenty-four-dollars for twenty-four-hours, with unlimited mileage. As I had no plans, the rental car guy mentioned a resort would be a good place to start. I followed the signs along the highway, for probably sixty minutes, taking in as much of the country side, as possible; while driving. My Dad and I travelled through here, on our tour, but nothing looked familiar.

I arrived at the resort with a young man, standing in the middle of the road, directing traffic. I wound down the window, as he asked me "Are you here for the concert".

I asked "what concert".

He replied "Ryan Jones' free concert".

I replied "yes" and turned into the car park.

I had an awestruck look on my face OMG. What were the chances of me being here, at this time, with one of my most favourite actors Ryan Jones? What were the chances? OMG I can't believe it; do you think I was excited? Hell Yeah!! The universe was certainly looking after me today; still shaking my head five hours later, waiting for the concert to begin.

What could I possibly do for five hours; obviously a perfect opportunity to explore the resort? The resort had many shops, stocked full of gifts and sporting gear. My biggest 'bug bare' for wasting time was window shopping. A mixture of bars, small cafes and restaurants; plus street food vendors were setting up for a busy afternoon.

I paid eighteen-dollars for a lift pass, to explore the resort; a very popular ski resort in winter, and during summer, the whole mountain was full of BMX bike riders and hikers exploring the lush green landscape. Every second chair, on the lift, was changed out for a bike rack, with the riders travelling in the first car; their bikes follow behind.

As I hopped off at the top of the chairlift, the temperature was quite warm. I started walking towards the restaurant; closed for the summer, with no refreshments available, or a place to sit to chill out, while having a coffee. I didn't go off exploring, without any water, so I only stayed for an hour, looking out over the resort and taking in the activity of the walkers and bikers. I rode the lift three times, during the afternoon, travelling up and back without getting off. That morning at the motel, a thick haze sat in the valley; as the day progressed, the haze became thicker, and by late afternoon, the view of the valley was obscured. Apparently the large fires burning in Colorado; the southern winds carried the haze into Canada.

Near the resort a parked flat-bed-semi-trailer was constructed as the stage. The slopes, during winter, were the downhill run; now transformed into an outdoor theatre. People placed chairs and blankets, on the ground, reserving their spot for the concert. Other bands entertained the crowds during the afternoon, listening from one of the restaurants, enjoying a late lunch.

As the afternoon progressed, I found a spot up on the bank; with the afternoon sun creating a little heat wave; people watching; chilling out and enjoying the atmosphere. The mozzies were bad as the afternoon progressed; offered free bug spray, from a booth near the resort.

Finally, Ryan Jones made an appearance, graciously walking through the crowds, on his way to the stage. The band was thoroughly entertaining with their country rock sounds.

At one point a couple of girls were introduced to the stage, who'd won a radio competition to meet Ryan and stay at the resort. The girls had written a rap song, detailing all the movies Ryan had appeared in. Ryan was so impressed, with their private performance; he invited them, to perform on stage. I understand why, the girls won the competition, they were gorgeous and thoroughly entertaining. The song lasted for a few minutes; with each movie title mentioned, my mind flashed back momentarily, to that movie. Ryan had certainly starred in many movies over the last thirty-years.

After the concert Ryan walked back down through the crowds, shaking hands with the fans. I was able to stand four metres away from him to take a photo. The whole day turned out so much better, than I'd ever hoped for or dreamed of. *(Remember Judy's quote: about finding more than you dreamed of – in Chapter 2.)*

I was definitely on a high, heading back down into town, along with the other few thousand cars heading in the same direction. I can't believe I found my way back, to the motel, without any problems, U turns and no GPS. A late snack of fries with a hot chocolate were enjoyed, as I relived the last twelve hours. I woke up early, checked out of the motel, found breakfast, before returning my rental car. It cost me eight-dollars to refill the fuel tank, with the guys at the rental place, driving me down the road, to the bus terminal.

ON THE ROAD AGAIN

I arrived at the Ploomaks bus terminal; proceeding to the check in counter with my luggage, placing the bags on the scales, with the cost of forty-five dollars. I offered the lady my credit card to pay for the charges; cash only was accepted for the payment.

I didn't have enough Canadian cash; offering US currency, instead an ATM was available in the café; however the machine was out of order, so the lady said she couldn't charge me. I thanked the lady, as she handed me the luggage tags. Whooa!!!

Being a Sunday, the direct bus services weren't in service, travelling via a few towns, waiting for connecting buses. The morning trip was ok; then waiting around for ages, before the next bus arrived. The bus had air conditioning problems; the only option of staying cool, was opening all of windows and the roof hatches.

My energy was being zapped, with the temperature of the bus soaring. I felt like I'd been travelling for days, as I started drifting off to sleep. Suddenly a little voice, in my head, told me to wake up and grab the camera. I excitedly grabbed my camera, looking around, what was I supposed to be looking at? What was I missing?

My first thought was that my dream house was located here. My dream was about a house, with green and cream siding, nice tidy gardens and neatly mowed lawns. An older man came from around the side of the house, with a friendly smile and welcoming look on his face.

As the bus drove around the little towns I didn't see the house from my dreams. *I did mention this situation to someone, and they thought, maybe my little voice was saying I just needed to wake up, to see the area I was travelling in. If you're sleeping, then you miss whatever opportunities are presented. You're a long time dead and life just passes you by if you don't make the most of every moment. But I knew, deep down, this area was the location of the dream house, which I discovered in Chapter 21 with the Dream Sequence.*

Chapter 8

HOST NO. 4 THE SUSTAINABLE FAMILY – JULY

THE ARRIVAL

At the bus depot in Nonverlone, I collected my luggage, with no sign of my host. It'd be easier and cooler if I waited inside the depot, with air conditioning. The bus ride had been shockingly hot; almost like a sauna, with very little fresh air coming into the bus. I'd just finished struggling with the door into the depot, when I spotted a lady, walking across the road heading in my direction. We had had miscommunications about the arrival time of 4:00pm instead of 2:00pm. Joanna and I walked over to a café for a cold drink, after I loaded my luggage into the car. I needed something to cool me down; with no air conditioning in the car either, on the drive back to the farm.

Joanna's sister, who lived upstate, had recently lost her husband, so Joanna spent this last week supporting her. We were both full of questions about the farm and my duties, filling Joanna in with details, about my journey so far, at the other volunteer places.

THE FAMILY

The family consisted of Joanna, her husband Brad, three daughters and one son. All three daughters were attending university in the east; with their son, living in the Yukon, who was about to get married, which was why I was there.

Peta one of the daughters, had committed herself, for the entire summer, helping her parents out with the vegetable patch, looking after 'things' while they were away. Peta's main job was to make jams out of the fresh fruit, selling them at the locals markets. Peta had had her own agenda of what she was going to do with her time; which I discovered involved, mostly entertaining her friends. Peta wasn't my boss, as Joanna gave instructions of my duties while they were gone.

The family were very musically talented, with the entire lounge room, filled with musical instruments. Brad and his brothers had been playing in bands for many years.

Joanna looks forward to the winters where she cross-country skiers, around the property, when the whole valley was covered in white powder and minus twenty degrees.

THE PROPERTY AND SURROUND AREAS

The fifty acres farm was located near a lake, thirty minutes drive from Grosvenor, the nearest town. The back of the property were set up with large paddocks suitable for raising cattle. A deer fence, erected around the orchard and vegetable garden, protects the crops from any four legged intruders. Brad loves driving the tractor, slashing the sides of the roads; including the vacant area of land between the veggie patch and the orchard. I liked the fact he slashed the long grass, because I wanted to be able to see any snakes, on the path, as I was walking to and from the patch.

The farm was located in a valley, where summer crops, were grown, with at least a million acres of hay. I'd hear the tractors, during the night, driving around the fields, turning the hay. I'm not sure why they do this, because I thought they'd just cut the crop and bale it. I will have to find out *WHY*.

THE HOUSE

I was pleasantly surprised when I arrived at the farm. The house was exactly what I envisaged it to be, when I thought about this rural farm house. The house was old, but was not run down, like my previous host. An exterior set of stairs lead down into the basement, as I was guided through this entrance, to access my room. Three bedrooms were located downstairs, along with a shower and toilet. The basement area housed storage shelves; washer and dryer; freezers; workshop benches and the heating system. A door, leads to a cool storage room where preserves and any long storage fruit and vegetables were stored. The room was cool, but was not a cold area during summer. This cool room was located under the deck accessed from the main floor.

The main floor had an open plan kitchen; dining and lounge room; together with two bedrooms and bathroom, with an interior staircase, linking the basement, to the main floor. Joanna and Brad bedroom, the computer room and bathroom were located at one end of the floor. A wide south facing deck, off the front of the house, (*above the cold room*) was where the family spent a lot of time each day, before and after work. The deck was beautifully cool and peaceful in the mornings, before the sun rose above the mountains to the east. I'd sit there eating my yoghurt and fresh fruit; and in the afternoon, if the mosquitoes weren't bad, I enjoyed the afternoon view over the orchard and valley.

The dial-up internet was available only via an old computer, located in the computer room. This was my only option to connect to anyone.

SPECIAL HOUSE GUEST

An extra house guest, Vincent, a summer intern, worked at the business of the farm owners. Vincent's room in the basement; was next to mine. One night I heard all of this commotion, and later found out a large nest of ants had moved in. After a couple of days and a few cans of spray the problem was solved with Vincent moving back into his room.

Vincent's Italian migrant family were from Vancouver, and some weekends he headed home and other times he hung around the house. Vincent had purchased an inflatable canoe to try his hand at fishing. Vincent drove to the lake, in the afternoons after work, taking a chance on catching dinner, with sadly no luck, while I was there.

ACCOMMODATION

Initially I'd been offered the cottage; located away from the house, but this was now occupied by Peta, for the entire summer. My room belonged to Ellen, one of the other daughters, returning after the wedding, but for now it's mine. The basement was the perfect choice for me; having restorative sleep each night, with the temperature ten degrees cooler, than up on the main floor.

I read a comment, on the volunteer's website about the mosquitoes, at the property over summer, so I brought electric mozzie zappers with me. The small window in my room had an insect screen covering the opening; the window was open all of the time, with my bedroom door closed. I had the mozzie zapper plugged in 24/7, insuring no mosquitoes were in my room. I have a reaction to mosquitoes when they bite me, which causes my skin to form large welts, gets infected and the skin takes ages to repair itself.

The house was very quiet most of the time with no television or radio. I spent most of my spare time, in my room, as it was the coolest part of the house. With Peta staying over at her cabin, Vincent having his own agenda, I had a lot of time to myself, reading books and meditating.

MOSQUITO REPELLENT

Now I'm being honest. *I HATE MOSQUITOES WITH A PASSION*. I hate them. I hate them. I hate them. Vince and Peta were commenting on how much mozzie spray, I used each time I went down into the patch. I just couldn't stop the mosquitoes, from biting me, all throughout the day. I also got sick and tired of Vince and Peta's comments about 'toughening up, princess'. One afternoon I turned on the computer; researching for hours, natural remedies for mosquito repellent. Surely someone had come up with a natural product, instead of the chemical based products, I was currently using.

I found a solution; giving Peta money, with the list of ingredients to purchase. Peta arrived home with the two ingredients I required. Vince was beside himself with laughter, the two ingredients which were; vodka and lemon eucalyptus oil. "What are you going to do with these" was his first question.

I answered "drink the vodka becoming so drunk, I wouldn't know I was being eaten alive by the mosquitoes". Ha!! Not such a bad idea, except it's only a very small bottle.

The recipe used vodka as the base, adding the eucalyptus oil, until it blended. So that's what I did. I emptied almost a half the bottle of the oil into a spray bottle with the vodka. Guess what? It did work, reapplying the solution more often, was definitely better for my health, if not my pocket, costing forty-dollars for the ingredients. I still had oil, only needing to buy more vodka, when I ran out.

ALL IN A DAY'S WORK

For the first couple of days on the farm, Joanna showed me around the property, detailing all of the chores; I'd be doing while they're away. In the lower part of the property, via a steep path; barns, hen and pig houses and a building which stored the chickens and pigs supplies.

My job, both morning and night, was feeding the chickens and pigs; collect eggs and keep the garden alive and weeded. Strawberries and raspberries were picked for jams, sold at the local markets or sold fresh to local customers. The vegetables were grown for our own delicious enjoyment. A cat, an older dog and young puppy, all needed love and attention with Peta, Vince and I attending to their needs. Sheep and bullocks were roaming free in the paddocks, not needing any attention, except to make sure, they're still there and had water to drink.

This was an organic farm, so no sprays, and heaps of weeds. I believe in weeding every day, so they don't have a chance to grow. I love the Dutch weeder with its long handle, with several different types to choose from. I used two types; one shaped like a triangle made out of a flat piece of steel; the other one was like a double edged rectangular shaped piece of steel; set like a double action razor. Running the blades, through the ground, this action cuts the stems from the roots. With small weeds, it was easy work, raking them up into a pile.

Peta would kneel down on her knees; weeding and then take the weeds over to the compost pile. These weeds had seed heads on them; disposed of, out of the garden. One morning I'd spent a good two hours, cleaning up the potato patch. Exhausted and dehydrated; hiding out, in the shade of the raspberry patch, cooling off. Peta yelled at me 'that I wasn't supposed to leave, the pile of weeds, in the garden, as they belonged over at the compost pile'.

I wasn't impressed by her attitude, and I cannot believe how quick witted I was. I replied back, like a venomous snake, telling Peta "the wheelbarrow was just there". If stares could kill, I would've been struck down like lightning. Peta had no concept; of the fact that I was only having a rest, before I would've collected the wheelbarrow. I wasn't telling Peta that, as she picked up the weeds, stomping past me, wheeling the barrow full of weeds; I could see she wasn't happy. Neither was I, because this wasn't a concentration camp; and she was definitely not my ruler. I was doing a bloody good job, as the veggie garden, was almost 'weed' free before I started on the raspberries full time. I had a regiment of duties; weeding the area before I watered, to avoid the mud; all the plants receiving attention on a regular basis.

I loved the fact Brad had corn growing, planted in a spiral formation. As the corn grew higher I wasn't able to fit in between the rows to take out the weeds. I bet the corn would have looked a picture, had I been tall enough to get an aerial photo. A few fresh sprigs of asparagus, I chomped on when I walked past, to sustain my hunger.

Another job was thinning the apple trees, loaded with fruit, with each cluster of apples, being reduced to one or two apples. I completed the job over a few days, because it was hard on my wrists, twisting off the apples.

When I was weeding around the vegetable patch, I noticed a strange looking crop of four or five plants, growing inside a mesh cage with hessian wrapped around it. I asked Peta what the plants were, she replied "an experiment of her Dads" and left it at that. The plants obviously had been planted the previous year, with the hessian used to protect them from the snow. I knew exactly what the crop was, growing in full view, of all of the visitors arriving at the property. The parents were away for over three weeks; the watering and hot temperatures; the crop was looking mighty healthy, nearly five-feet high. I noticed the first morning, after their return home, the plants had been laid over on the ground. Not sure why; probably for vertical shoots to grow off the main stem.

Raspberries were my favourite fruit, along with blue berries, and when the raspberries started ripening my job changed. One raspberry for the bucket, one for me! Instead of spending all day doing weeding and watering, I basically became the raspberry picker. Bucket after bucket with Peta using the strawberries and raspberries to make jams, for sale at the local markets each weekend.

Each morning I waited for the morning's sun, to dry off the dew, before we started picking the raspberries. These weren't early starts; but by the time I fed the chickens, pigs and *ME*, the raspberries were ready. The day time temperature in the patch was high; luckily, I worked in the shade of the plants, transferring buckets, up to the house, when they were full.

At the beginning of my stay, I recorded what hours I worked, along with any other events, on the farm; like the dead chickens and pig. Mainly for the parents information, if they wanted to know. I had a piece of paper at the computer; Peta commented, one afternoon, I didn't have to work such long hours. Peta obviously wasn't there to work a full day, spending days with her friends. I just kept seeing, all of the ripe raspberries that needed picking, with nine hours being my longest day, not including the chicken/pig feeding. Who else was going to pick the fruit if I didn't? I decided if Peta doesn't care about the raspberries; then why should I, so I'd stop at my six hours a day, which were long enough, when I had to handle the animals as well.

One of the most tedious jobs was picking currents one by one. At the beginning *OMG* it was so slow picking one current at a time; before they all started ripening up and you could just grab a handful at once. Currents were Joanna's favourite fruit; Peta placing the ripe currents in the top of a double boiler, with the juice draining into the bottom of the pan. The skins remain in the strainer and Peta bottled up the juice in the canner.

Brad received a gift of a beautiful leather-bound-book to record weather details, over the next five-years. The journal was located in the lounge room, where I recorded storms, rain and the daily temperature. I recorded the hot weather, storms, and even northern lights; I didn't wake up for. OMG what was I missing.

Brad had left instructions not to water the garlic, but how can you not water the garlic when it was next to the potatoes. I asked Joanna, and she said to keep watering the potatoes. When Brad arrived home after the holiday, a little note appeared on the breakfast table, *NOT* to water *ANYTHING* that day. Oh dear, I don't sit at the breakfast table; so I was in trouble*^&)#<>*% as Peta came down later to turn off the sprinklers. The main concern was the garlic which was ready to be harvested, it needed to dry out.

I passed through the apple orchard, each time on my way down to the veggie patch. One morning discovering a bird's nest with three, dusky blue coloured eggs. The mother flew away each time I came near her, so that's how I could see the eggs. It wasn't long before the new little babies, were hiding under their mother's wings, and then basically the next day, they were all gone.

THE PIG CHASE

The baby pigs arrived, who were very scared, of being taken away, from their mother. The first morning checking on the pigs, one had died, trying to escape through the square wire fence. I helped Peta remove the dead pig; disposing of it down a disused well. Peta arranged to have a replacement pig, and when the lady delivered the pig, she forgot to close the gate properly. Peta and her friends were sitting on the deck, when Vince arrived home, mentioning he saw a pig on the driveway. I went down to the pen, and sure enough, the gate was open. We now had a pig escapee, and luckily Vince was there to help, spending an hour chasing the pig; dealing with the dogs, having a wonderful time, chasing the pig around the property. I think the dogs were more of a hindrance, but finally there was success.

The pigs were small, when they arrived, and sadly would become, food for the freezer. They had their own pen, with lots of ground to root around, plus a small shed, where they're fed. A small nozzle on a tap; the pigs learnt pretty quickly, how to suck, to get the water out. Their pellet mix diet; fed twice a day, and as the pigs got stronger, their trough would be in different positions, as they rooted for every piece of food.

I knew something was up, with the pigs, for a few days; spending a lot of more time down near the bottom fence. On the day before the parents arrived back, the pigs managed to make a hole under the log fence and escaped. Luckily Vincent came to the rescue again; the fence repaired, and the pigs were returned to their pen. The next morning, the pigs had almost escaped again; temporarily fixing the fence, and hopefully they'd all remained safe and sound, when the family arrived home, that afternoon.

THE CHICKENS

One hen house was the home of the meat chickens; locked in a small room, to grow as quickly as possible, before they're slaughtered, for the freezer. The other chickens were the laying hens, laying their eggs all over the place. It's funny each day, climbing up onto the hay stack, in the barn, searching for places where I might find the eggs. Laying boxes; in their house would be so much easier, but no they had to be difficult; my daily adventure was sort of like, Easter egg hunting.

Finding dead animals was part and parcel, of having a farm; but still wasn't a pleasant thing. Peta would take the carcass, up behind the house, throwing them down an unused well; to avoid attracting any wild animals, like cougars, bears or anything else roaming the mountains.

WHAT'S IN THE MIX?

I was concerned about, what I was feeding the animals; which in turn I was eating. I ripped off the tags from the packets and looked on the web.

The chicken pellets ingredients are: wheat, barley, wheat mill run, canola meal, soya bean meal, corn, limestone, multiphos, vegetable oil, salt, lysine hydrochloride, methionine, pellet binder, choline chloride, vitamin A premix, vitamin D premix, vitamin E premix, riboflavin, niacinamide, calcium pantothenate, folacin, biotin, thiamine hydrochloride.

The ingredients for the pigs were: barley, wheat mill run, wheat, ground corn, canola meal and/or soya bean meal, vegetable oil, pellet binder, multiphos, limestone, lysine, methionine, vitamin A premix, vitamin D premix, vitamin E premix, copper sulphate, manganese oxide, zinc oxide, ferrous sulphate, calcium iodate, sodium selenate.

The farm was basically organic, but the ingredients being fed to the animals were *NOT*. The taste of the chickens and pork, were definitely better, than supermarket meat, but a long way from being a true organic product. The laying hens roamed the paddocks eating worms and grass; consumed the mixed ingredients, making their eggs not truly organic as well. The beef and sheep were a different matter, grazing in the open fields. In the end, Joanna and Brad were doing the best they could, being self-sufficient, raising their own animals and growing food as naturally as possible.

HOUSE GUESTS

The house was getting fuller, by the minute, with the arrival of Joslyn, a friend of Peta's. Joslyn was heading east to Manitoba; but was stranded, until she found a car to buy. The neighbours down the road were fixing up a couple of cars; to sell, with Joslyn looking at buying one of them. Joslyn's work involved planting seedling trees, into forested areas, harvested of wood. The work was mainly during spring and autumn, with Joslyn planting up to eight-hundred trees in one day. The trees are placed, in bundles, on their back, carried from the supply truck, and planted. Joslyn was very fit and she enjoyed her job, working only six-months-a-year.

I went upstairs for breakfast, one morning, noticing a different car, parked out in the driveway, and Peta's car was missing. I didn't think anything of it and went down into the raspberry patch, to start work. I heard a car approaching, looking up to see a car, stop at the house; then another car arrived, then another.

I needed to investigate; collecting my full buckets of raspberries, returning to the house to find ten people in the kitchen, raiding the fridge. Peta told them, to come over, for breakfast of bacon and eggs.

It wasn't my place to say anything, as I walked back down to the patch, continuing to pick raspberries. The group stayed at the house, for the entire day, before going to a rave party at a local hall, that night. The group had showers, ate whatever they wanted, from the cupboards or fridge, as Peta eventually returned home.

I was a little disappointed I wasn't invited to the rave party. But then again; was it a real 'rave party' or just a pretend one? The parents were obviously into pot, but that's different from the other drugs, usually available at rave parties. Hey I do read the newspapers and see the news occasionally! I was obviously thirty-five-years too old to attend this party. But the thought was there; but I believe they thought me as their grandmother, as I was definitely old enough. The following morning; a repeat performance, when the friends, came back for breakfast, spending the day recovering; before heading back, to wherever they came from.

NORTHERN LIGHTS AND THE MOON

Darcy the dog, spent most of the night barking, which had bothered me, but there's no way I was going outside, to see what he was barking at. The thought, there could be, a cougar or even a bear, kept me firmly, tucked up in my bed, all night long. The young friends told me how spectacular the northern lights were; while they camped under the stars, and I slept through the whole lot of it.

The next night, I kept one eye open, and went upstairs to look out, but there was nothing there. The northern lights are one of my bucket list items, and the reason why I travelled to Churchill and Alaska; to experience this phenomenon.

The full moon was always my favourite time of the lunar cycle, with the moon not visible in the sky, until after midnight, when she rose high above, the mountain range, to the east of the property. Making a special effort, on the night of the full moon, I stood outside on the deck paying my respects, for a glorious night, in another part of Canada.

FOOD

While the parents were at the farm Joanna prepared the dinner and I couldn't believe how small their meal portions were. One night I cut up one potato per person (they were only small) roasting them in the oven. When dinner was dished up, Brad had asked why, there were so many potatoes.

I like to have my main meal for dinner, so breakfast was fresh fruit and yoghurt. Lunch was usually an omelette or sandwiches; and dinner was a choice between chicken, pork or lamb out of their well stocked freezer. My favourite meal was smoked pork, cooked up with fresh garden vegetables.

Peta, Vincent and I all shared cooking dinner, with one person choosing the meat; preparing some or all of the meal. The others collected fresh veggie from the patch, or gathered the extras needed to make a meal. When Joslyn arrived she shared the roster for our dinner preparations.

Making ice cream; the old fashion way, was a delight, but I'm not sure of the ingredients. Placing a frozen bowl, into the ice-cream-maker-machine; add your ingredients; close the lid and turn the handle (about 1,000 times). Magically turning into ice cream; usually served with fresh raspberries. Yummy!!

EXPLORING

I had a riveting experience, driving the car, for the first time. I was doing really well, until I reached the end of the driveway. Indicating to turn left but turning on the windscreen wipers instead. Then I forgot the car was a manual; the engine stalled while sliding to a stop, in the middle of the road. I looked up, to see a car approaching from the right; quickly starting the car and pulled over onto the side of the road, with the wipers still going. The man in the car was a neighbour, who stopped to ask if I was ok and I said "yes". I'm not sure what he was thinking, as he drove off, while the wipers were still going. Finally I got my act together. I had to remember how to get to Grosvenor; with my biggest concern, was finding my way back to the farm.

One afternoon Joslyn and Peta were going to the lake for a couple of hours, and asked if I'd like come along. I said "Yes"; taking the opportunity to have some time off, and explore the area. The road we were travelling on, had recently been re-gravelled, and widened in places, as the valley's timber was currently being harvested. Luckily for us the logging trucks weren't operating today, enjoying the peace and serenity of the lake. The contractors were moving closer to the farm, eventually the entire valley, would be harvested. Joslyn would then come through replanting; so in another twenty years they'll do it all over again. Sustainable living was what it's called, these days.

Peta parked the pick-up, as we climbed down the embankment, to her favourite spot; arriving to find a group of people were already there; who'd pulled into shore, on a boat, enjoying a picnic. It wasn't long before they left and we made ourselves at home. Both of the dogs enjoyed the outing, with Peta and Joslyn continually throwing sticks into the lake, with the dogs fetching them back. Peta and Joslyn swam, while I just made myself at home, on a towel, attempting to read a book, but instead fell asleep.

After delivering raspberries, I went exploring finding a cheese factory selling, what do you think, different styles and flavours of cheese? I purchased a small piece to enjoy with my meals. Another day a charity event was held in Grosvenor, with live music; so I stayed and listened to the local bands for a few hours. The weather was really hot; sitting outside the fenced area, under shady trees, reading a book and relaxing. I paid for my ticket, purchasing Mexican food for dinner. The event wasn't very well supported, by the time I left, but it would continue on into the night; hopefully more people arrived, as the temperature dropped.

I had to share the car with Peta and if I wanted to go somewhere, I'd check with her. One day I wanted to go to the movies in Nonverlone; with a list of items to purchase from the supermarket. I purchased all of our necessities and a young man, from the shop, carried the big bag of dog food. We walked over, to where I thought the car was parked, and it wasn't there. I went around in circles, for about five minutes; how embarrassing, for me, finding the car three rows away from where I thought I'd parked it.

On the day I drove to the airport in Poomlah, to pick up the parents, I left early so I could enjoy driving through new territory, especially along the amazing Namangan Lake. The sky was clear with its reflection making the lake an unbelievable colour of royal blue. Every time I'd a chance to look over at the lake, I did. When I reached the airport, I continued driving towards the township itself. I was looking for a mall, to grab a quick lunch, before I headed back to the airport. I kept on driving and couldn't see anything looking remotely like a mall or even a standalone restaurant.

Finally I spotted a complex with different shops, and found a nice restaurant for lunch. I hadn't dined out for ages; and this was a high class restaurant, with fresh salmon my target. On the menu, the salmon was labelled as sustainable. I cannot believe, this high class restaurant chain, served farmed fish; I can tell you I wasn't impressed in the slightest. I ended up having a steak, with the total cost of the meal plus a tip was forty-two-dollars. OMG how expensive was that!

When I arrived at the airport OMG was it hot, with the flight being delayed for one hour. I grabbed a coffee and my book to read, to fill in the extra time. Brad and Joanna arrived, dressed in layers; as the Yukon weather was a lot colder. Leaving the airport building, the layers of clothes, came off at a rapid pace.

On the way home from the airport, Brad was driving, so I was able to look around. Brad made diversions around the towns, and before I knew it, we were back in Grosvenor. I refused to tell Brad and Joanna anything about the farm, until I got back to the house. However, Vince opened his big mouth and told them basically everything; when they dropped into the office quickly, to check on things. Joanna and I called into the supermarket to get a few essentials before we all headed back to the farm.

When we arrived home I gave Joanna the docket to reimburse me for the groceries I had purchased. She said I could buy anything I needed, while she was gone and that was what I did. I didn't lash out at anything extravagant, except for cherries and dog food. I got confused by the prices between pounds and kilograms. I thought the price was five-dollars-per-kilogram NOT five-dollars-per-pound; so ten-dollars for a tiny bag of cherries I purchased. *(Which I thoroughly enjoyed)*. The dog food was also expensive, and Peta should've purchased it, from the local produce store, along with the pig and chicken feeds.

When I handed Joanna the docket for the groceries, I thought the eftpos receipt, was from the grocery store; instead it was the receipt from lunch that day. Joanna looked at the docket; asking what it was for, as I apologised for giving her the wrong receipt. Joanna was shocked at the cost of the lunch, asking if I expected her, to reimburse me, for the lunch as well. I said *NO* as it was my treat for myself.

Only one main job had to be handled immediately, after their return, which was fixing the pig fence; then we drove down to the river, to swim. The whole area had had major floods; from the snow melt this year, with a swift current still flowing in the river. Joanna dove into the water upstream and half swum and half floated down past us. I wasn't interested in swimming in mucky rivers, but I put my feet in and cooled off that way. Vince, Joanna, Peta and Brad along with the dogs enjoyed the outing.

SPEAKERS

I was supposed to have days off; but I still had the responsibility, of looking after the animals each morning and night; however, the time in between, was mine. I arranged one day to attend a club meeting, scheduled for lunch time. Two amazing speeches were delivered; the first speech was from a lady, who had devoted her life, to creating art work. As part of her delivery she wore a paint stained shirt and told us about her passion for creating. The most incredible part, of her story, was being able to support herself financially, as a full time artist. How many people would love to be successful? I also believe if you love your job, then it wasn't work.

I had an opportunity to make hat boxes for the local markets. But after working for a few years I lost my enthusiasm for being creative; because I had to do it for money, not for the love and enjoyment.

The second speaker told us about her encounter, with a pack of wolves; working in a remote area of Canada. The job was a new location; for the lady ranger, deciding one morning to take a short cut to work, from her cabin via a trail through a forest. Not long after entering the forest she encountered a wolf, blocking the path, in front of her. She immediately made eye contact with him, calling him 'blue eyes'; having the most intense blue eyes, as she looked deep into his eyes, for the longest time. The lady wasn't alarmed or felt any fear, while standing there, alone in the forest, with the wild animal.

When the trance was broken, the lady realised they weren't alone. Surrounding her was the rest of the pack of wolves; in a position to attack her, at the whim of their blue eyed leader. Her heart was beating at a rapid pace, as she kept eye contact with blue eyes. It felt like hours, but was more like one minute; while the lady stood there, waiting for the pack to pounce on her, but they never did. The pack wandered off back, to wherever they'd come from; once again she was alone with 'blue eyes'. She continued to look into his magical blue eyes, thanking him, for allowing her, to continue walking, on her path to work. Blue eyes also slinked off; disappearing back into the foliage of the forest.

The audience, listening to her speech were spell bound, by her technique, of retelling the story.

This was the reason, why I love Speakers so much; as people share with you, their incredible life's journey. I thoroughly enjoyed my visit to the local club.

SPECIAL DINNER INVITATION

Neighbours, Claudette and Hans; close friends of the family, invited Joslyn, Peta and I over for dinner. The family originally from Europe, had built this multi-storey house, perched high up on the side of a hill, with incredible views over the valley. The family hosted volunteers, who stayed at the house, down near the road. The established farm had hot houses; fields with crops; the pigs; bees; chickens and a variety of fruit trees. There were many helpers selling their produce each week at the markets. Joanna purchased, from Claudette, a twenty litre bucket of honey and the new piglets I was feeding.

Joslyn, Peta and I walked up to the house, enjoying an amazing afternoon, as the family made supper for twenty people. Peta had baked a chocolate brownie slice for dessert, shared with everyone. As part of the meal, branches off a cherry tree, laid on the table, with the ripe cherries still attached.

One young volunteer from Europe had visited this farm, on previous years. There were lots of joking about his naked tractor driving; with Claudette giving him strict instructions, this year he had to be appropriately dressed, as her young teenage daughter was working on the farm.

SPECIAL VISITORS

I had a visit from the Steve and Lauren, the house sitters from Benton, arriving for lunch, so we could meet each other. I had to pay to stay at their house, which was a little different, as usually the home owners paid you. Working it out, it cost thirty-five-dollars-per-week, including internet, heating, gas etc. It's a bargain, if I eat relatively cheaply, and get a great deal on a rental car.

Steve and Lauren wanted a security deposit; refundable, if the house was clean and tidy. I arranged a bank cheque, and couldn't believe the process, supplying enough information and identification, for withdrawing a million dollars; not depositing three-hundred-and-fifty.

GARLIC LOVERS BEWARE

One of my favourite vegetables was garlic; with a huge crop, currently growing in the garden. While waiting for the new garlic to ripen, the cold store had a good supply, from last year's crop, cooking up gloves every night for dinner. The old garlic wouldn't last too much longer, as they're sprouting.

Peta left home to attend the wedding; with Joslyn finally organising her car and departed for Manitoba. Vince and I were alone in the house for a week; and on the final weekend before the family returned, we decided our final dinner, would be extravaganza. Both of us have worked our arses off; over the last few weeks, me with the garden and Vince at the office. We chose the perfect size lamb roast, for the two of us, gathered all of the vegetables from the garden including *ONE WHOLE GARLIC* each to have with our dinner. We had wine and sat on the deck savouring every last mouthful. Cheers to wonderful memories of a month at the lake.

I've discovered recently, garlic's an aphrodisiac. No wonder all Italian and Greek men, or probably ALL men (maybe women too) are so sexual. Something to think about if you enjoy garlic and definitely explains the urges I have on a regular basis☺.

CHANGE OF PLANS

Before I left the farm I opened my emails; noticing an email from the car rental company, informing me, the car was available for pick-up before 12 noon *TODAY*, because Monday was a public holiday. What the :{+#)!@. Ringing the company, I told them, I wasn't in a position to pick up the car, as I was in the next province. Why had it taken this amount of time, to advise me of the changes, when I booked the car four-weeks ago.

The lady and I had verbal debates; for her to understand my position, for the plans I'd already made for my trip. The ladies unprofessionalism was the cause of this misunderstanding, and she wasn't aware of that. We finally agreed to meet at her offices at 6:00pm Sunday night, to pick up my car.

FAREWELL

The last night at the farm I was left home alone, as the parents went out, to a party. I was upset they didn't think I might have liked to have joined them.

Sunday morning Joanna and I loaded up the car and headed to the bus station in Nonverlone. Our goodbyes were at the same bus terminal, I was picked up from a few weeks earlier.

I booked the bus directly to the Poomlah Airport, to continue onto my next adventure. Arriving at the airport desk, to discover my ticket had been cancelled; as the ticket was for the 6:00am flight. Jeremy my travel agent had booked the wrong flight. I hadn't checked my ticket as I thought it was the same as my instructions. It'd cost me fifty-dollars for a new ticket, which also secured the flights I had booked in the middle of September. I emailed Jeremy and he apologised, refunding me the fifty-dollars, for the inconvenience.

The airline attendant spent a long time rearranging my travel plans, before finally getting my bags through the system. *THEN* there was another problem; having to pay for the excess weight; directed to a different counter, for the payment. What do you know? There was a problem with his machine, and after numerous attempts, he said "it's your lucky day, the machine was down and you don't have to pay anything".

Going through security, I was told my jars of jam, I'd purchased from Peta that morning, were not allowed, as they were considered liquid. I didn't want to lose the jams, so I ended up checking through my back pack, as well. I repacked the backpack, so the jams were all in the middle, however my crystal box got damaged on one corner; but I was thankful there wasn't a huge mess of raspberry jam.

Finally I could relax and celebrate, the fact I'd just finished my fourth work place; with three days off, before I started at the next one. I enjoyed the ambience of the airport, with the flight east being only one hour – *OR SO I THOUGHT!!!*

THE REASON FOR THE VISIT

I still haven't worked out why I was chosen to stay there; so Joanna, Brad and the family, had the privilege, of attending their son's wedding together? Joanna and Brad spent ten days on a kayak trip, before the wedding. Did the family really appreciate all of my hard work? I felt they tolerated me, with no real thanks of appreciation.

What did I learn? I still hate mosquitoes. I love, love, love raspberries, fresh garlic and vegetables. Having the field filled with fresh produce was a blessing. When I was down in the patch, I could sustain my hunger; by picking peas, strawberries, asparagus or another other crop; ready to be eaten straight off the plant.

Just maybe the reason was to sustain my body with the amazing produce and the grace of time to reconnect with myself in solitude and peace.

Wildflower fields

Chapter 9

IN TRANSIT BY PLANE AND CAR - AUGUST

THE ARRIVAL

As soon as the plane landed in Garland I quickly grabbed my luggage and a cab; rushing to the bus terminal, before the 4:00pm north-bound bus left. The transit Centre clock said 4.15pm and the bus had already departed. I didn't take into account the time change of one hour, and once again I hadn't looked at the booking for my airline ticket, so the day was just getting worse.

I approached the ticketing counter, with a new ticket issued for the next bus at 6:00pm. I texted the rental car lady, saying I was delayed, and she told me 'Tough' as she was only there at 6:00pm, and wouldn't be able to help me any further. I went into the café, grabbed a table and opened my laptop to search for a rental car; an option of returning to the airport, which had already cost me sixty-dollars for the taxi 'one way'; to pick up a new car. All the enquiries, for a new rental car were unsuccessful.

In the process of trying to find a car, I missed the 6:00pm bus, now having to wait now until the 8:00pm bus. The bus trip was certainly a weird experience, with an African lady sitting in the second row, in the window seat. Half-way through the journey, the lady started to chant and sob; the sobbing and chanting becoming louder and louder; the wails becoming very scary. When we reached the outskirts of Banks, the bus driver asked, if anyone was travelling with the lady, as he might have to detour via the hospital, to take her off the bus. I'm not sure what happened, as I didn't see her when I hopped off the bus.

Once I collected my luggage, found a taxi, and booked into the motel, it was 10.30pm. There weren't any restaurants open, as I ended up ordering fish and chips, from a pizza delivery place, eating dinner at 11.30pm.

With access to the internet, I found a new rental car, to pick up the next morning *(which was already here as it was 12:00am)*. The problem was paying three times the price, of the first rental car company. What was I, supposed to do, when I had these plans? Looking back; I should've looked at all the road blocks, and stayed in Banks for the weekend. I should've listened to my intuition, and asked myself 'what's this all about'.

Why I am so dead set, on this stubborn; don't interfere with me attitude; of stand clear, I'm coming through, no matter what; nothing's going to stop me. Had I listened to myself, then maybe I would've rang the next hosts; to advise them, I was here a little early, and stop the domino effect of my actions.

The next morning I was up reasonably early; organised a taxi for a ride to the rental car place, picking up my car. I returned to the motel, collecting my luggage and found a place for breakfast. I've never seen a restaurant like this before, with an amazing and truly unique menu. I ordered a fruit platter big enough for four people, with plenty left over for my snacks for the next couple of days. The amazing thing about their food was how they presented the fruit on your platter. All of the fruit was cut out and designed like flowers and placed so carefully on the plate, it was a shame to disturb the display.

I asked the wait staff for directions to the highway; following the signs, for an easy exit from Banks. Still upset and frustrated about the course of events, of the last couple of days, when Lincoln Lake came into view. I pulled the car over; into the parking lot, along the edge of the lake; hopping out of the car, my jaw dropped looking at the turquoise blue colour of the water.

The heavy weight of the frustrations, of the last couple of days fell away, as I felt the energy of the mountains start to consume me. Oh how I've missed being in Canada, as this was home for me; I just know it. I hopped back into my car and continued to drive, but it wasn't long before, I stopped again. As the car climbed up around a bend, the lake was visible, from an elevated position, with fir trees framing the view. I walked across the highway to take the photo which I believe was 'picture postcard perfect'. *This photo was in the top ten out of the thousands of photos I took during my trip.*

Now this time when I got back into my car, my enthusiasm for the trip, had magnified, as I felt more like my 'normal' self. I was once again excited about my trip back to the wildflower fields, staying at the hostel in the mountains. Yes finally the trip was looking more appealing; turning on the radio, to listen to some music.

A LIFE HAS BEEN TAKEN

After only five minutes; I rounded a corner, and noticed the traffic, ahead of me, had stopped. A man was standing, in the middle, of the road directing traffic, and as I approached him, I realised there'd been an accident. Passing the man, I got my first glimpse, of the accident, where a black SUV had a huge indentation in the front, where the motor should be. I slowly acknowledged what'd happened; driving through the crash site, with debris from the motor bike, and items of clothing, scattered all over the road.

OMG behind the black car, a man was kneeling, beside what appeared to be, a body underneath a blanket. Driving past, I made eye contact, with a young man, aged in his early twenties. I put my hand on my heart; as the grief and despair on his face; was too much to bear. I drove past slowly, as the tears, welling up at the back of my eyes; started rolling down my cheeks, a large gasp was released from my throat. What had I just witnessed? The evidence on the road revealed the rider had been female; as the whole scene, registered in my senses; I acknowledged a life has been lost, and the lives of many, had been changed forever.

A small voice in my head told me to stop the car, to comfort the young man, whom I'd made eye contact with. His eyes begged and pleaded with me for help. I should've stopped and helped, but this exact scenario; I'd always dreaded. My fear was; I'd be the first person on the scene, to witness the carnage of a road accident.

I COULD NOT STOP. There's no way, I could've stopped; to help that young man. I was already emotionally scarred, by what I'd witnessed; and to subject myself to more grief, I just couldn't do it. The young man's eyes, pierced into my memory, for the next fifteen minutes while I kept driving, as I contemplated turning around numerous times.

LIVES CHANGED FOREVER

I didn't turn around; arriving at the entrance to the park, paying my entrance fees, and continued towards Greensboro. I stopped for a break at a resort with a shop, petrol station and accommodation complex.

Stepping out of the car, I looked around the car park, noticing a few people crying; mostly the motorbike riders, who were travelling along the same highway as me. One motorbike rider, with a pillion passenger, had stopped at the Lincoln Lake car park with me; I was travelling behind them, when we came across the accident. I noticed, the man had comforted, his lady passenger, by patting her leg, as they drove through the accident site. How caring, was the man, to know what she was feeling. I'm sure his gesture was to comfort his lady and assure her, everything would be ok.

I grabbed an ice cream; texting Ricky, (the ex) to ride carefully, while travelling around the States on his motorbike. On our 2011 trip with the family, he pushed the speed limit at any opportunity. I think, he thinks, he's bulletproof and nothing can harm him. Instances, like this accident, make you realise, the risks are not worth taking. What do you save? Just sit back and enjoy the ride; if you don't enjoy the journey, then why bother travelling.

I finished the ice cream, regaining some of my strength; completing a three-sixty-degrees-turn-around to look at the scenery. The stark, grey colour of the bare mountains; towering above the resort; were majestic against the clear blue sky. I had to remind myself, this trip was about *ME*. I needed to take time-out from my volunteer work, to enjoy the adventure.

I had left the farm early; to travel back to the wildflower fields. This was my time to go exploring; giving myself permission, for some time-out, from everything. The last few months had already been a life changing adventure; having learnt so much about myself, and who I am. I'm definitely living the dream.

STOP AND SMELL THE ROSES

My little rental car and I continue to explore the mountain ranges; with the most incredible lake waters, the colours of gem stones, sparkling in the sunshine. I always stop at the same view point, travelling through a mountain pass. The road, travels along the valley floor, before snaking its way up, around the switchback road. Standing at the view point, looking straight ahead, towards the south; your eyes are drawn to a large three-thousand-meters high rock formation, which appears to have been sliced apart, by a carving knife. Your mind is studying, the layers of the rocks, as the patterns, are revealed.

Heading further north, my next item on the adventure, was looking at the horizon; glacier spotting. Reaching the main glacier area, you are surrounded by this incredible sight. I'd already climbed the glacier, in 2008, and wanted to see the changes. The car park was very busy, as I found a tiny spot to pull over to park the car.

I dressed a little warmer; leaving the car and started hiking up, to the edge of the glacier. When my mum and dad were here, in 1975, they didn't have far to walk, from the main road; now the glacier had receded, about two kilometers from the road.

From the car park you can't see where the glacier starts, and the anticipation was always high as you wonder what awaits you over the crest. On the walk along the road, different markers have been placed to record the recession, over the last fifty, seventy and nearly one-hundred-years since the glaciers were discovered. Informational plaques were placed, to read about, the different aspects of the area.

Looking at the glacier itself; was beyond comprehension, with the crevices the most amazing deep dusky blue colour. Once you reach the viewing platform, the glacier was located a couple of hundred meters away; with the surface covered in a snow, sand and gravel compound.

Four years previously, I was here walking up the glacier on a guided walk. We followed the guide, basically step for step, knowing, we'd be safe. The walk lasted over three hours; travelling one kilometer up the glacier. At one point our group stopped, at a viewing point, where the guide had made a brace in the ice, for his foot, at the edge of a vertical shaft. The guide supported everyone by leaning back and locking our arms, as we leaned over the hole. I held my camera out over the edge, as far as I could, and pressed the shutter, to record the view down into the glacier.

If I happened to fall into the glacier, there'd be no survival or body retrieval. The movement of the glacier ice melt, made it impossible for a body to remain in one piece. Like; I needed to hear that! Apparently, in Europe, a body recovered from a glacier, had been preserved perfectly for hundreds of years; locked in behind a ledge. The movement of the glacier and ice melt had gone around the ledge, until the body was recently discovered.

Back to the present time, today, standing here at the glacier I noticed a small difference in the size of the lake, formed at the edge of glacier. I took a few minutes to enjoy the energy of the glaciers before I headed back down to the car to continue on with my journey.

Driving along the highway; individual mountain marker signs were erected, like a finger pointing. The finger points out the biggest mountains, mentioning their height. I spotted my mountain's finger sign; I'm almost there.

THE WILDFLOWER FIELDS

The hostel was located, outside the township of Greensboro; making a quick trip up to the glacier, before I checked in. It felt surreal, walking along the high track, leading to the viewing point, looking up onto the glacier.

When I was here in September 2008 the lake area at the base of the glacier had less water; I stood below the glacier, capturing the sun setting directly behind the glacier. Even with the extra water, and the sun in a different position, I was still able to capture the glacier with a golden glow behind it.

With the summer sun setting at 10:00pm, I checked into the hostel, before going into Greensboro for dinner and supplies. When I arrived back at the hostel, a few people had booked into my dorm room, with the ladies from Europe, starting the fire in the cabin. I left my window open wide, all night long; didn't even have a sheet covering me, because the room was so hot.

The hostel had mixed-dorm-rooms, sleeping twenty people and Monday night there were five of us in the room; with no power points and only minimum lighting. In the kitchen, a gas stove was available, to cook and heat up water for washing up. Bio toilets were used, without any lighting, to see what you are doing. Bears were active, in the vicinity, but luckily I didn't come face to face with them, in the dark, as I ducked to the loo.

I forgot about charging my camera battery, with the manager kindly recharging them up for me. Unfortunately, I had to wait until 8:00am, to collect the batteries, which meant I didn't get an early start to my day. The weather was overcast, packing my cold weather gear into my back pack, as I prepared for my day's hiking.

READY SET GO! I was off exploring, a wonderland full of wildflowers, and creatures that lived in this extreme climate, year round. A marmot was very friendly, performing for me, by laying down, sitting up and then slinking off, when he heard other people approaching.

There were lots of minor tracks, to explore, and since it was my intention, to spend the whole day on the mountain, I checked out some of these tracks; with snow visible on the ground, sheltered from the sun. I also spotted ground squirrels, and a few different bird varieties; whispering their thoughts, on the tune of a song.

I was happiest when I didn't encounter any bears, so when no other people were around, I sang the Aussie theme song 'I come from a land down under'. I'd hear people approaching, as you were supposed to be, as noisy as possible, to ward off the bears. I did encounter, one man from France, visiting with his family. The man was wearing a bear bell and carrying a can of bear spray.

I am sorry, but the bear spray just wouldn't work for me; as you have to be within three-meters of the bear for the spray to hit him☺. Or, do you throw the can, at the bear, to knock him out. How funny?

I climbed to the height, of the lookout marker, at 2910 metres. The thin air was a little hard on my lungs, so I rested quite regularly, sitting on rocks, connecting with mother earth, becoming one with the mountains. For the last one-hundred metres, the track consisted of shale, as I climbed up on all fours, to reach the marker. This adventure was four-year's worth of anticipation; spending five hours exploring; making every gasping breath and aching muscles worth the effort.

I climbed down the track, back to the car park, and headed into Greensboro for a shower and dinner. I spent an hour or so at the Laundromat; recharging my phone, camera and computer. I checked my emails, and downloaded photos, while enjoying a cappuccino. While sitting in the laundromat, I recognised some familiar faces, from my day on the mountain.

After dinner I headed back to the hostel, where seven people were sharing the dorm room tonight. A group were booked into the other dorm building; cooking their dinner at 11:00pm and sitting around the camp fire, outside our dorm room until 1:30am. One thing I enjoyed about staying at the hostel; the stars were shining brightly, and the moon was watching over me, with her beams re-energising, me during the night.

I didn't sleep very well, and had packed the car and left by 7:00am; headed for one more look at the glacier. The crisp, clear morning air was a surprise, to my lungs, staying just long enough, to witness a trillion tiny ice crystals, glistening in the sunlight. As I cruised my way down the mountain, I felt like a rally car driver, driving around the sharp curves and bends. About half way down the mountain, I had a wonderful encounter, with a mama bear and her cub. This was how I like to encounter bears, when I am safely in a car and they're wandering in their own natural environment. The bears continued walking on the road, for a little while, before they wandered off into bush land, as I continued on my way.

ON THE ROAD AGAIN

I stopped at the first road side restaurant, for a breakfast that would sustain me, for my day's travel, heading towards Banks, and my next host family.

Heading east, towards Lincoln Lake, my thoughts were with, the family of the young woman, who had died in the motorbike accident. Reaching the accident scene; only a patch of oil, where the impact occurred, marked the tragic event, from two days ago.

This day the weather was perfectly clear, and the reflections on the water, almost perfect, even though there's a slight breeze. I spotted a track off the main road, leading down to the edge of the lake; I cleansed my new crystals in the pure glacier waters. I arrived early in Banks, parking the car, and slept, while I waited for my new host to pick me up.

WHY WAS I HERE

The decision, to come to this area, was not one I anticipated; basically the decision was forced on me. Planning my trip, I tried to book places in order, to maximise the opportunities to see as much as possible. I planned the trip from the Island, to Alaska, back to Canada travelling from one province onto another. I had no intention of back-tracking, with the decision making, a bizarre flow of events.

My original trip plan was to travel from Canada to Montana; then head east. As I kept contacting hosts in Montana, I wasn't able to find anyone, besides one lady; deciding I wouldn't travel over one-thousand-kilometers, for just one week's worth of work.

I started looking back in Canada. The computer mouse picked up host's locations, on the volunteer map, as it glided over the different areas. Every time the screen mentioned this area, I kept saying to myself, I didn't want to go there.

Eventually I had to listen to my intuition, as I sent Grace an email, to check on availability. Grace wrote back to say, she didn't have a vacancy, but her neighbour next door, did. Wanda and I started emailing each other, as we worked out, I could stay with Grace in her van for one week, before arriving at Wanda's.

So that was why I travelled back to this area. The *BIG* question was *WHY*?

Chapter 10

HOST NO 5 - ALPACA PROPERTY - AUGUST

FIRST ENCOUNTERS

Entering the city limits of Banks, I got totally lost, with my new hosts directing me back to the rental car place. While I filled in the paper work, Derek unloaded the rental car, placing my gear in their car. Grace and Derek had a quick stop at the supermarket, before we were on our way home.

My trip was going too fast; I'm already half way through my hosts.

ACCOMMODATION

My home for the next week was Grace and Derek's trailer (caravan). I slept very well each night in a queen size bed all to myself. A bit different, from the single beds, I've been sleeping in for the last few months. The bed was located, at the front of the caravan, in an alcove, like a 'stairway to heaven', as I climbed into bed each night. Most nights were peaceful, except for some oil rig drilling, at a nearby property.

THE FARM AND ANIMALS

The farm had twenty-five alpacas, but only the females (*I like to call them girls*) were there, as the males (*the boys*) were staying with a friend, nearby. Grace and Derek keep them separated, during summer, because, the boys wanted to mate, all the time – sounds familiar!!!! Ha.

Grace, Derek, Anya (the Japanese volunteer) and I, visited Christine and Brian, for a fire pit; to say hello to the boys. Grace and Derek haven't had a very successful breeding season over the last couple of years, with no new babies. A couple of years ago, a wild cat killed a few of their breeder, during the winter, while they were living, in the barn. The cougar was tracked, with a shooter, collecting the bounty. It's sad the cougar, had to be killed, because of its instincts for survival. Grace and Derek were hoping for a more successful season, this next year, with the gestation period, for a baby, being eleven months. The alpacas were very nervous animals; losing their baby with stress, or even in extreme weather.

We visited another alpaca farm; to cuddle and feel the new babies. In Peru, baby alpacas don't have a high success rate, and die quite young. The young alpaca skins were used for teddies, and Grace has these teddies, for sale in her tea room.

During the summer months, the local farms are a hive of activity, as crops are grown, for harvesting and bailing. Most farmers have large storage sheds, for supplying their animals with hay, during the winter months. With the temperatures of between minus twenty to forty, not all animals are housed inside, during the winter months.

Grace and Derek keep the alpacas in a shed during winter, so they need lots of hay, as well as their normal feed to sustain them. A nearby neighbour grows a natural grass; the alpacas like, with Grace and Derek arranging to buy the bales from them.

The alpacas are guarded by marimba dogs, such a beautiful animal. Grace and Derek had just brought home a new puppy, Lucy. Sophie one of their older dogs, had to be put her down, because she'd a bad hip. Sophie wasn't able to do her job properly, and they couldn't successfully prolong her life. Life on a farm was full of comings and goings with animals and events. It was a tough life sometimes?

Anya was in charge of looking after the alpacas, so I didn't get to feed them. When visitors were at the farm, they could feed and pat the alpacas. One hot day, I was refilling their water trough; using the hose, I sprayed a fine mist in the direction, of the alpacas. The alpacas enjoyed the treat, while pushing and shoving, each other, out of the way, to get to the water.

SHEARING TIME

Grace enlisted friends to help her shear the alpacas, each year. Grace sends the fleeces, to a company, processing the wool, into large scions; then creating one-hundred gram size balls of wool, for resale. A hundred-gram, ball-of-wool was worth anywhere between twelve and eighteen dollars. One of the many jobs, I enjoyed; was turning the handle, on the wool winder, creating the balls; for customers to buy in the tea rooms or at the markets.

WORK AND LEARNING NEW SKILLS

Grace liked her mornings to herself, so breakfast was at 9:00am, a rather late start for me, but it's ok for just this week. *(Working in Australia, in my garden, I'd start work some mornings at 4:00am or 5:00am, as the summers were so hot. I stopped working at about 8:00am until late afternoon, unless I could work in the shade of the established trees, and I'd finish at 8:00pm. So starting work at 9:00am and working through the hot parts of the day, weren't the ideal situation.)* When we finished breakfast, the mornings were spent outside completing tasks around the garden, including raking the grass areas, weeding, picking up branches and chopping fire wood.

The afternoons were the fun times, inside with creativity and productivity. Anya was staying for three months, and Grace had taught her, so far, to crochet and knit. Anya was creating a few beanies and head-bands each day.

Anya was then learning how to make scarves on the loom. The process was very time consuming with measuring, cutting and threading the yarns onto the loom. Grace uses bamboo fibre for the main threads in the scarf; depending on how warm you want the scarf, was reliant on what fibre you used for the cross threads. For the warmest scarf possible, use only alpaca wool; for a warm scarf you use more bamboo and less alpaca; and for a scarf with a little warmth; use only bamboo.

The bamboo fibre colours; Grace used, were very vibrant, some with variegated colours, whereas the alpaca wool had a natural colour. You might think, wool from alpacas, might be boring and bland, but seeing the wide range of colours together, they're all quite different. The wool, from Grace's alpacas, range from different shades of brown, creams, whites and grey based. Each year the fibres from the alpacas were different, in texture and colour.

Anya had chosen her bamboo colours, with the lengths measured and cut, as I helped her thread the loom. Once the loom was threaded; the design chosen; the colour of the wool, to run across the pattern. It was time to start work; as Anya spent a couple of days, working on her first scarves.

Once Anya had finished her first scarf, it was my turn, to create mine. The measured length of the wool, allows three scarves, to be created, at the same time, using the same thread. The first scarf was ours to keep, and the other two were sold in Grace's shop or at markets. *(Basically we make all the mistakes on our scarf, as we learnt what to do, AND WHAT NOT TO DO and by the time we start the second scarf, we have sorted out all the problems).*

Did I have any problems? OMG did I have problems with my first design. Something wasn't right with the design, as I kept losing stitches at the edges. I unpicked several times, because the last stitch, didn't get locked into the design. It took ages for Grace to work out a solution.

(Grace marked the card, never to be used again, because there was a big mistake in the instructions). Meanwhile, it was very frustrating for me, not really knowing, what I was doing wrong. Needing to watch your tension; with the right pressure; perfect tension, not too loose or tight.

After we worked out the problem, my first scarf came off the loom. Whooooooooa!!! Time for a second colour and a new design, and by the end of the second day, I had all three of my scarves off the loom; ready for finishing off. Each scarf, I tidied up any loose threads; creating a fringe. Many decisions were needed, when creating a scarf, and the last decision, was the length of the fringe; short, medium or long length, to suit your individual tastes. Grace had a hand tool that twists the fibre, to make a nice fringe, and then you were finally finished. Wallah!!!

Initially it took one day to measure and load the fibres, onto the loom; one day to make the scarves; then another day to finish. Anya fell in love with the loom; creating a new set of scarves every two days. Anya had a beautiful eye for textures and combinations, with Grace selling the scarves upwards from sixty-dollars, depending on the amount of alpaca wool was used.

FIRE PITS

The second night at Grace's, was a fire pit night; and a nice way to meet Wanda, before I went over to stay with her. The rest of the neighbourhood, turned up, for the pot luck dinner. What usually happens, everyone brings their own meat and a salad or dish to share. The host puts on the fire pit, and everyone cooks up their meal, while socialising. This event occurs almost every week or so, during the warmer months.

REST AND RELAXATION

The closest town was Romberg, as Grace, Anya I enjoyed a trip to town. Together with a rubbish dump run; grocery shopping; and Grace had to visit the dentist for a checkup. For lunch I ordered a green salad and Grace and Anya ordered a roll. While driving around town, Grace pointed out different places, to visit when I was in town. While Grace was at the dentist Anya and I wandered around the streets.

PETS

Grace was a cat lover, with her cats living, inside the house. Grace's daughter, Jodi was on holidays, with the house full of her cats as well. The cats were quite demanding; as Grace let them in and out of the house, all day long. One day after lunch, we found one of Jodi's cats, had died in the garden. Grace was distraught, as Jodi had had the cat for a long time.

THIS WAS THE REASON I WAS HERE

I took the cat up in my arms, stroking its fur and whispered loving thoughts into his ear. Anya grabbed a towel, placing the cat, in the towel; wrapping him up safe and sound. This was the most beloved thing; I've ever done for someone, whose pet had died. I felt this calming energy flowing throughout my body, as I knew *THIS WAS WHY I WAS HERE*. Grace was beside herself with grief, as I truly believe, she wouldn't have coped, if I wasn't there. We placed the cat in the freezer, with Jodi due home in three days; deciding the best thing, was have the cat cremated. Wanda delivered the cat to the vet, as we continued, on with our day, with sadness in our hearts.

Fire Pits

Chapter 11

HOST NO. 6 – CATTLE PROPERTY – AUGUST/SEPTEMBER

THE PROPERTY

Wanda purchased the property twenty-years-ago; wanting a private place to retire to, after she finished working. Events took a turn, for the worse, when Wanda's partner passed away, before they made the move together.

Wanda built the house, sheds and established the one-hundred-and-sixty-acre property, before she met Kim. Wanda raised cattle, using a 'managed grazing system' from spring to autumn. The cattle were a business venture; shared with her friend Paul, who breeds the cattle. Wanda looks after them and 'finishes' them off, before they're sent to the market, with Paul and Wanda splitting the profits.

Wanda moves the cattle, every few days, depending on the size of the paddock; taking four to five months, to utilise the entire property. The property was divided into several large paddocks; set up with permanent fences; water pipe connections, along the main lanes; where water troughs are set up. Wanda uses an electric fence system, to divide the bigger paddocks, for the managed grazing.

Over the last twenty-years Wanda had re-seeded the property, with natural grasses, to establish the cattle feed. These grasses continue to come back, each year, after the snow melt. Wanda sets up a large metal structure, in the shape of a cow, constructed with a dish to hold loose salt, seeds and a face cloth; keeping the cattle's faces clean. This portable structure was placed in the paddock where the cattle are grazing. When the cattle, approach the structure, to lick the salt, the fabric; acting like a curtain, attached on the front of the structure. This fabric has a damp solution, rubs onto the face of the cattle, preventing flies, infecting their eyes.

In spring Wanda places grass seeds, in with the salt mixture; and when the cattle lick up the loose salt, they pick up grass seeds as well. The cattle remain in the same pasture paddock, for maybe three or four days. During that period of time, they walk their urine and deposits back into the ground. During the summer, these seeds germinate, and this was how Wanda has established her grasses. The natural grasses, I walked through; were over five feet tall, and sometimes you couldn't see the cattle, unless they stuck their heads up.

This was a fantastic set up, sharing her ideas, with anyone interested, in how Wanda achieves huge success with her cattle.

Wanda installed solar panels on her property to help with running costs. The government had a solar rebate scheme, subsidized one-hundred-percent.

THE FAMILY

Wanda was a very talented artist/painter/potter, spending many years living in the States. She was actually in hospital and witnessed one of America's most tragic events herself. The hospital prepared for the survivors, but unfortunately, not many people, made it to the hospital. Wanda said it was a bazaar feeling, losing many friends during this tragedy. It was a very touching, personal account, suggesting I visit the memorial, if I have the chance.

Kim was previously married, with three children; meeting Kenneth and Conrad, up at the farm. Kenneth worked as a supermarket checkout operator; paying off his condo, where he lives alone. He was twenty-six-years old, and definitely a success story for his family, supporting himself, even though he was mentally challenged. Conrad was the eldest son, living in a supported lifestyle home. One weekend Conrad came to visit the farm with Kim, challenging each other in a game of chess. Sarah was Kim's only daughter, and a twin sister of Kenneth. I didn't meet Sarah, who was working at a resort, over the summer holidays, away from her studies of becoming a registered nurse.

Kim has a house in Garland, working for the education system, travelling up to the farm each weekend. During the warmer months, Kim helps Wanda with the vegetable garden, as they reap the fruits of their labour.

Kim was a very talented musician and each weekend she played the flute, in the art studio, where the acoustics were excellent.

THE ANIMALS AND PETS

Jackson was a ten-month-old puppy; with blankets and toys, just like a baby. You'd see him dragging his blanket, around the yard; then lie on his back, with the toys in his mouth. Wanda trained him during doggie obedience school; he was a very intelligent, obedient, cute and placid puppy. Jackson was taller than me, when he puts his feet on my shoulders, which I discouraged him from doing, as he was just too strong.

Quincy was older corgi, with his only thoughts being food; and how long before feeds. One afternoon it was cold and wet, and I was sitting in my cabin, finishing off my scarves, when Quincy and Jackson came for a visit. I looked up, to see them, both staring through the window, at me, with their front feet, placed on the bench seat, outside the window. Both of them were looking, in through the window, to see what I was doing. It was only 3:00pm and still three hours before dinner time. I could see Quincy, questioning what I was doing, and why wasn't I feeding him yet.

There was a ritual for the dogs at feed time, with Quincy locked inside the front foyer area. Quincy had to be instructed to sit, shake hands, with you, on both front feet, while telling him to wait, until he was calm enough to eat his food. He was impatient; just wanting to eat. I had to make sure he was drinking enough water, so I placed a few dry biscuits into his water bowl, as he lapped up the biscuits; he drank at the same time.

Jackson was the complete opposite with his food; having to hand feed him. Jackson was fed out on the back deck, near the hot tub; while I sat on the chair, next to the feed bowl. Jackson would wander over, as I placed a few biscuits, in my hand, for the first mouthful, to taste the food. I had to sit with Jackson, until he finished the entire bowl; otherwise Quincy would run around to finish it.

Earlier in the summer Wanda had spotted, close to the house, a young coyote pup that didn't seem scared at all. Jackson's job was to protect the house, so some nights he'd bark all night, as the coyotes roamed around. Poor baby boy, some days I'm sure his throat must have been so sore from all the barking. Even birds weren't allowed, to fly over the paddocks, as Jackson barked at them, if they came too close to his territory.

Wanda was building Jackson, his own little house, with insulated walls and a heated bowl, so his water didn't freeze. The dog house was attached, to the front of the house, to access electricity for the connections. Last winter Jackson was only a puppy, so this will be his permanent home, even during the winter months.

Wanda had a family of feral cats, living in the barn. They were fed with dry food placed in their dishes; checking the water and food levels, every few days to ensure they were full. The cats roamed the property, entering the barn, via cat doors. Occasionally I'd see them, out on the cattle rails, sunning themselves.

ACCOMMODATION

Derek and Grace kept mentioning the cabin; commenting on how great it was, compared with their trailer. Grace dropped me off, at my own private log cabin, complete with bathroom and kitchen. The design was open plan; a small horizontal dividing wall, at the back of the little kitchen, hid the claw-foot bath tub and toilet. A large queen bed, with kitchenette, a small table and chairs, and rocking chair made the cabin all cosy. A gas heater was installed to keep the room, at whatever temperature I needed or wanted; with storage under the bed, for my suitcases, making myself at home, for the next five weeks.

The cottage's location, in a grove of trees, away from the main house, with all of the privacy I needed. Double glazed windows, meant I kept the blinds open, for views of the surrounding forest of trees.

The bathroom window faced east, catching the morning rays, through a crystal ball; I'd hung in the window. During the night, the moon entered the room, shining her beams into the cabin.

The cabin was my sanctuary, spending most of my time, when I wasn't working. Wanda also liked her mornings to herself, with work starting at 9:00am. Toast with creamed cheese and jam; and a couple of cups of coffee, before I started work. I set up the cabin with my crystals, and tarot cards, using my time for meditation and journal writing. I purchased some new books to read, from the second-hand-book store, spending my nights reading stories, before exhaustion took over, as I closed my eyes for sleep.

WORK

I house/cattle/dog/cat/veggie garden sat the farm, for five days, while Wanda and Kim were away. I was thankful the cattle and dogs behaved themselves, and didn't need to dial 911 or the vet to attend to any emergencies. I checked the cattle, fences and water twice a day, with Jackson; my protector, protecting me from any possible danger. Wanda had trained him to walk beside her, as she walked down to check the cattle. Once I arrived at the cattle pen, Jackson sat at the gate, until I was finished; then he walked beside me, back to the house. How cute was that!!!

Over the weekend I moved the cattle with Brett, a friend of Wanda's, who'd came over to help. I would've handled the job on my own, since I was used to electric fences. It wouldn't have been, the first time I got zapped by, an electric fence wire. The cattle behaved themselves and the whole process only lasted twenty minutes to complete.

Wanda had a list of jobs, she was hopeful of me completing; painting the front entrance gates was one of them. One morning the weather was super hot, driving the ATV up to the front gates; managing two coats of paint, in the space of two hours. As I finished painting the second gate, the first gate was ready to repaint. Had I been given the choice; I'd have chosen a nice bright *PINK* or even purple or an ordinary blue, but no, Wanda chose the normal boring, forest green.

My main job was processing all the veggies in the garden, as I picked, washed, blanched, bagged, and froze them. The huge freezers were full of veggies from beans, peas, beetroots, carrots, onions, chard and spinach. When Kenneth was at the farm, we worked as a team, outside in the fresh air. Kim purchased a few large carry bags; excellent for carrying and storing the different vegetables, into sections of the freezer.

I love being in the kitchen, and Wanda asked if I wanted to cook up some relishes. What do you think I said? Of course I said *YES*, searching the internet for some new recipes, to add to their favourite ones. I had my own recipe, for caramelised onion jam, and this recipe turned out to be a crowd pleaser.

The main ingredients from the garden were beets, onions, green tomatoes, carrots, zucchini, and beans, so that's what I used. My day would start out in the garden; weighing all of the ingredients I needed. I washed, trimmed and processed as much as I could, outside at the wash station, before transferring everything inside. Once inside, I grated or sliced the ingredients in the food processor. Wanda had large pots, big enough to make a few batches, at a time.

I spent many days in the kitchen, standing at the stove stirring the ingredients. We ended up shopping for more ingredients; such as sugar, vinegars and more preserving jars. I loved my time in the kitchen, with the music playing, dancing to the beat, of whatever tune was playing. In the afternoons, I sipped my liqueur, as I cleaned up my mess.

I processed about one hundred and fifty jars of relishes, chutneys, salsas and onion jam. Hopefully, they'd remember me, each time they opened, a new jar.

Another big job was processing the potatoes, placed in Grace's cold store room. Most Canadian houses have a cold store room; however Wanda didn't, so we used Grace's basement, as an experiment. Wanda and Kim were not big potato eaters, with the gift of potatoes for Grace. *Talking with Kim, the potatoes were always so successful, and I wondered why they grew them if they weren't part of their diet.*

Onions were the next item on the job list, finding an article online; storing your onions in panty hose, separated by a knot, hung from the ceiling, like a rope. I spent one day trimming up the onions, before placing them in the sun to dry. I joined all of the onions together in pantyhose and transported them over to Grace's; very optimist they'd store well over the winter. *Grace's cold room wasn't cold enough, and the result wasn't pretty. Oh well, it was worth a try, so next year the safest way to store them, was in the freezer.*

JOB SHARING

Grace asked if I could help her friend Christine; look after the tea rooms, while she visited her daughter. Christine had helped out previously; familiar with its operation and where everything was located, and how to work the machines.

Anya looked after the alpacas and continued making scarves, back at the house, watching television while she worked.

Christine and I just chatted, while using the wool winder, for the two days, creating balls of wool. We had a lot in common; chatting about crystals, inspirational people, the planets and all of those exciting subjects, I loved discussing with people. There were only a couple of customers; with little interruption, enjoying lunch and sampled heaps of different teas.

HAY PICKUP

Wanda with her pickup truck and flat bed trailer, headed up to a neighbouring property; to load hay for the alpacas. Betty and George joined Grace, Anya, Derek and Wanda to load the hay onto the trailer. The bales weighed sixty pounds each and I couldn't lift one off the ground, so I opted for the driver's job. It was a cushy job, driving the truck, around the paddock, as the rest of the crew ran behind the truck. The runners hauled the hay onto the trailer; Grace and Anya placed them in position, as one-hundred-and-forty bales were loaded over two afternoons. The job was double ended; as the trailer was reversed to the door, of the shed. I tumbled the bale down from the stack; dragging it along the trailer, as Grace grabbed the hay to stack into the shed. It was hard yakka, with grateful appreciation from Grace, for getting the job done quickly.

The whole region was a huge hay production area, with nearly every farm growing crops. Along the verges on all the roads and highways, the native grasses were mowed and baled. I think it's a fantastic idea, of 'waste not, want not' utilizing the hay during winter.

CHUCK WAGON RACES

Derek invited Anya, Kenneth and I for a night out; at the chuck wagon races. We enjoyed all of the excitement of the evening, each picking our team, at the beginning, of each race; cheering them on. The funniest and most entertaining race was the junior riders, with their little ponies. The boys and girls, aged about five or six years old, worked as a group, to tie up their pony. One of the boys had a hold of the rope; refusing to let go, as the pony dragged him the entire length of the arena. The whole crowd were standing, clapping, cheering and in hysterical laughter at the performance. *I know I was*☺

After the chuck wagon races finished, we waited at the bar area, sampling a few drinks, waiting for the fireworks. Kenneth and I shouted each other drinks, throughout the night with maybe four drinks, which I thought was ok, over a five hour period. The next day, talking with Kim and Derek, about our night out, and what Kenneth had to drink. Kenneth should have known better, than to have more than two beers. I apologized to Kim, as I didn't realise Kenneth couldn't handle alcohol. Kim should've mentioned the situation, so I could've acted differently. I didn't need alcohol to have a good time, and thought differently about my consumption level. *There aren't many occasions where SOMEONE else was driving; so I was able to have a few drinks. When you live in rural areas, you had no choice, with drinking, if you wanted to sleep in your own bed that night.*

Kim was also angry, with Derek, because he subjected Kenneth to chatter about cheer leaders and sex. *I have the same problem with my older brother who's mentally challenged. Kenneth may look an adult, but in reality he has a child's mind.*

Derek invited Anya and I along to the movies a couple of times; enjoying the treat of an ice cream on the way home.

REST, PLAY AND BIRTHDAYS

My birthday was on the 27th August, the day Wanda came back to the property, from her time away. I mentioned to Wanda we should have a special dinner; visiting the golf club and enjoying dinner outside on the deck. Wanda organised a meringue with cream, fresh fruit and a candle in the top for dessert. It was a lovely gesture, arriving back at the farm, before sunset. The northern summers, with such long days, were something to get used to.

Wanda organised with a few friends, to play a round of golf, on one of my days off. I hadn't played golf for quite a few years; hiring a buggy to go around the course. The course was very busy that day, as we constantly waited for people, in front of us, to play on. At one stage the group behind us kept catching up, so we let them go in front, as they seemed to be in hurry. I was surprised to discover wash rooms, placed around the course, which I was very grateful for, during the game. After the game we relaxed over lunch, on the outside deck, at the restaurant, enjoying the day out, meeting new people.

The rest and relaxation was something I struggled to find time to fit in. When Wanda was away, there was no rest, as I had to be up early to let Quincy out of the house, feed the dogs, and staying up late, each night, to place Quincy back in the house. With the cattle to look after, and helping at the Tea House, my weekend of house sitting, was a full time job.

I did end up reading a few books, I had purchased at the second-hand-book shop; finding a café with an exchange book system. I thoroughly enjoyed working, my way through, some amazing books from my favourite author.

FIRE PIT DAYS

You should know; Aussies love to go camping with an open fire; well the locals here, like their fire pits each weekend. On a Saturday or Sunday night each week, during summer, the neighbours get together, bringing their own food, to share, with a cook up. The fire pits were usually at Grace's or Wanda's place, as I enjoyed meeting new people each week. I don't know why, the food tasted so much better, when it's grilled on a BBQ plate. The afternoons spent at the fire pit were perfect for watching the sun set in another part of Canada.

George and Betty's son, Jeff entertained us each week, with little ditties, on his guitar or harmonica. Jeff sang us a song he'd written, for a competition for a new national song based on the early settlers.

ROLLER DERBY

I had a really exciting time with Christine and Brian, attending a roller derby game in Banks. We left home early, having dinner at a food court, near the stadium. For some reason, I received a free ticket to the game, which I wasn't complaining about.

The roller derby game was similar to the 1970's TV programme; except the track was flat, and used for basketball games; apparently, the fastest growing sport, across the world. The players had their own nick name; wore really bright fluorescent costumes, with mixed gender teams. I thoroughly enjoyed watching the heats with the tag team efforts, a special thrill. Christine and Brian's son and his wife; had to maintain super fitness, to continue competing. If I was thirty-years younger; I might even consider giving the game a go. Yeah, hell no!! I remember when I was twelve; going to the skating rink, wearing roller skates and it was fun, as you rounded the bends while listening to all of your favourite songs. Butt (get it, but) boy did it hurt, when you landed, on your arse, on the concrete.

MY CRYSTALS

Just in case you didn't know I have a fascination and interest in crystals, for their healing properties. I started my collection, a few months before this trip, adding on, while travelling; carrying them in a divided box, wrapping each crystal in silk, to protect them. The case was hand luggage, on the planes, and so far security hasn't commented on them; I'm sure they see, many strange things, people carry onto the planes.

I have a good story to share with you all. On the full moon in September I decided to place my crystals in the veggie patch, protected by an electric fence, keeping the dogs and deer out. I carefully placed my case, full of crystals on a stool, knowing they'd be safe for the night. The crystals would enjoy the evening, under the rays, of the full moon; and in the morning enjoy a new sunrise. This activity energizes the crystals, each month, travelling to different locations.

This particular night Wanda sent Kim a text, warning her, to be prepared for a sight when she arrived at the farm; as I maybe dancing, naked, around my crystals, under the full moon. Of course I waited until the stroke of midnight to participate in such a magical ceremony. *Believe it or not? You be the judge: did she or didn't she. Ha!!*

THE SPECIAL VISITORS

Well the physic network was certainly, switched on, with a few interesting occasions, while staying at the farm. The first one's mentioned, later in this chapter, under 'The reason I am here".

The second event occurred while I was sleeping; and in my dream, I was in this same cabin. I was saying to someone, I had to go to the bathroom, but I couldn't go, because there's a man sitting, in the corner of the room, watching me. I was unable, to get out of bed, because I didn't have any clothes on.

When I woke up to go to the bathroom; the same man was actually sitting there, in my room watching me, and I was unable to go to the bathroom, because he was there. I went back to sleep; waking up later, to go to the bathroom, and the man was gone. The next morning, after I had woken up, I realised what had happened.

I didn't recognise the man, at the time, but now believe he was the man I met through my dream back in January, while I was still at home in Australia. He lived in the green house; I was searching for, near my third host (in Chapter 7) in July. This bathroom event happened in September and it wasn't until March, the following year, I found his house and left the note. See Dream Sequence in Chapter 21.

The third event happened one day, out in the veggie patch with Kenneth, processing the vegetables. Wanda and Kim were looking, at the new solar panels that had, just been installed.

I heard my name being called "Bella"; looking up, I couldn't see Wanda or Kim, so I went back to work. "Bella" was heard again, and it wasn't just me; as Kenneth heard it as well. Taking off my gloves, I headed in the direction of the solar panels, calling out, asking what they wanted. They were confused, as neither of them, had called out my name. We all went back to Kenneth, as he told Wanda and Kim; he'd heard my name being called out as well.

WHY?? Who knows? But it happened again over at Grace's place when I attended a fire pit. Everyone had left the fire, and I was clearing up, the remaining items, to take back into the house. Someone called out my name. "Bella" "Bella". The tone of voice, wasn't urgent, but was more like, I should pay attention; like stop for a moment to see this. Was I so busy; I wasn't taking the time, to breathe, and realise I was in *CANADA*.

This reminds me of a story about Dominic, my youngest son's best friend, who committed suicide in the May. In July/August that year, while my family, were touring around the USA and Canada, my daughter, Nicole suggested, we should all find the highest mountain, and call out Dominic's name. She told me, she called out his name, as she rode on the back of the Harley, with her father.

Had someone, called out my name, and this was when it caught up with me? I felt at the time, it was a significant message; someone wanted me to do 'something'. When I heard the voice at Grace's, I was alone, but I had a feeling that I was being watched, even protected, by those who have passed to the other side. Who knows maybe the pieces of this puzzle will come together to form a wonderful picture that's my life? There's more of this story in Road Trips North, Chapter 21.

THE CRAFT MARKET

I took the wool and winder over to Wanda's, to fill in time, if or when I was bored, which wasn't very often. An opportunity presented itself, with a few rainy days, where I spent most of my time in my cabin, finishing off my scarf and winding wool.

Derek, Grace and Anya spent the Friday, loading up the trailer and car, with all of the necessary gear for the markets. I borrowed the old truck from Wanda, arriving at Grace's on the Saturday morning at 7:00am. Grace had purchased new self-supporting shelving racks; and when the shelving was in place, we set up all of the alpaca products. It's a big job, but before we knew it, the whole centre was filled with different crafts and products.

Most craft markets are nearly the same worldwide; with the exception of a few unique products. Grace's stall area was not very big, so the three of us took turns, at being there. I spent a lot of time walking around, and talking to other stall holders; and visited a farmers market, located in the adjacent building.

We had such an early start, with the markets, making it a very long day; with Grace buying lunch for us all. The markets for Grace were reasonably successful, including the sale of two scarves; Anya and I had recently made. I was so pleased, as obviously someone else, has the same fantastic taste as me. Who could ever; have believed that? Ha!

I scored a pair of alpaca socks and a thermos, for helping Grace with the markets, and these are still a memento of my time with them. (*The socks are so warm*)

PLAYING LADIES

One afternoon, during my last week at the farm; Wanda invited Grace and Anya over for afternoon tea, creating a beautiful memory. I prepared a taste-test sample, of all the preserves I had created; served with cheese and crackers. Grace and Anya were amazed at the wonderful tastes and textures, picking a favourite one or maybe two. It was lovely afternoon, spending time with the girls, as we've all been so busy, over the last few weeks.

THE REASON FOR THE VISIT

At the end of my transit notes *(Chapter 9)*, I mentioned visiting this province again; not knowing why the signs were directing me come back here? Within a couple of days, of arriving at the cattle farm, I heard a voice clearly state to me, one morning "the man you're going to meet, was seventeen-years younger than you". The message was crystal clear; my first reaction was I didn't want a boyfriend, that young.

Over the following few days Wanda started mentioning her friend Brett, who she'd known for twenty years. Brett was sixteen-years-old when he called in, to see her one day, with his friends. The rumours going around town were, Wanda was an artist, and Brett wanted to meet her. The group of friends had been drinking; Wanda suggesting, he come back another time. That was the start; as they say, 'of a beautiful friendship'.

Brett was still at high school when Wanda wrote a reference letter; helping Brett secure a place, in an arts programme at university. Brett finished university, but knew he wouldn't be able to support himself being an artist; pursuing a different line of work. Over the years Wanda had been there, as a friend and mentor, continuing to support each other, on many levels.

Wanda currently had been guiding Brett with investments, as he visited Wanda regularly for a breakfast meeting, to check out the stock exchange. Their regular breakfast meeting was coming up and Wanda said we could all have breakfast together, so I could meet Brett.

The more Wanda talked about Brett, the more I was convinced; he was the man I was here to meet. The final piece of the puzzle came, when Wanda said, Brett was thirty-six-years-old. *WHAM BAM* this was it.

From the moment I received the message about this man I started sending out messages of peace, love and understanding. Along with my eyes, from him to recognize me, knowing I was waiting for him.

On the morning of our first meeting, I was very nervous, because I didn't know exactly why we were meeting; and how I was supposed, to help him. Wanda thought Brett was attractive; now this opinion was from a gay woman, aged in her sixties; do you think I believed her? NO. Brett was handsome, in his own way; not what I'd call a hunky young man.

We had a nice breakfast together and then Brett left; but there was this constant reminder. Brett had been injured in an accident at work; when a bolt of electricity travelled through his hand, up into his head, down through his body and out his feet. Brett had problems with light; focusing and seeing out of his right eye; constant headaches and problems with his heart.

Brett kept coming into my mind, with reminders I needed to help. One day while in Romberg, on my day off, I stopped at a gift shop, Grace had suggested. The shop was decorated with absolutely everything you needed or wanted to decorate your house with. As I entered through the main door, the first items I saw; was a stand, filled with journals, and the first book I looked at had the word 'courage' on the binding.

As my thoughts clicked over; what else could I do to help Brett? On my computer I had a poem called 'courage'. I visited a book store, purchasing a book on healing. Back at the farm I had the quartz crystal, I purchased in Alaska. These items formed the contents of the gifts I'd present to Brett. Wanda printed out the poem, and Grace laminated it, sealing the poem forever more.

I told Wanda about the messages; she was dumbfounded as to *WHY* I was helping a stranger. For some unknown and unexplained reason; this felt right, with the financial cost being thirty- five dollars. During my last week at the farm, Wanda invited Brett over for dinner, suggesting he bring along, some of his art work. Brett's father had died; leaving him a large property, filled with old farm equipment and car bodies. Brett used parts of the machinery, as the base for his art work; using acids, cutting out designs, adding objects, to create amazing masks and wall hangings.

I'd spent the afternoon, preparing a lovely meal and afterwards I gave Brett my parting gifts. He was very humbled by my gifts; presenting them, one at a time. The book 'courage' could be used for his doodles, or a journal, as there weren't any lines on the pages. Brett was aware of the author, of the book, I'd given him on healing; and the crystal had a loop, to wear it, around his neck, on a chain.

Brett gave me a thank you hug, and left with his presents; feeling my work here was complete. I was blessed and proud to help Brett on his journey.

Did I make a difference to his life? In 2014 Wanda told me, whenever she had visited Brett, he still had the poem 'courage' on his refrigerator. Brett had changed careers; almost finishing his training, as a cranial sacral therapy healing professional.

TIME IN GARLAND

So my month with Wanda was over, leaving with Kim, heading to Garland. Kim lived in her family home, in an affluent area, on the outskirts of the city. The house was very elegantly decorated; built on multi levels, connected via many sets of stairs. I decided to leave my huge suitcase in the front music room, as I had two lots of stairs to climb, to get to the top floor. The stairs were constructed of polished wood, and I wouldn't have been able to carry the bags up the stairs.

The first night, I showered and went straight to bed; and Kim had left for work, before I got out of bed. I was allocated a few jobs to complete over my four day visit. I had breakfast before Kenneth arrived, as we were cleaning out the garage; ready for the delivery of a freezer full of meat on Thursday. After the garage cleanup we swept the front verandahs and tidied up the front entrance to the house.

Tuesday morning I spent time in the kitchen tidying up cupboards, while I had my music pumping out; enjoying my action moves, as I vacuumed the polished wood floors.

Kim and I went to the theatre; on Kenneth's recommendation, saying the play was a comedy. Instead it was a dark comedy/drama about suicide, death of a child and how the family implodes in the aftermath. We didn't realise the show was a musical, until we sat down and looked at the programme. *The show was toooooooo close to home for me, spending the first half of the performance, in tears.*

Wednesday I spent the day in the kitchen, baking twenty loaves of zucchini bread, with different flavours added to the mix including bananas, oranges, cinnamon, chocolate and chocolate chip. The music was playing, as I enjoyed, the freedom of dancing around the kitchen. Kim arrived home, just as I finished baking, snapping a nice photo, before the breads found their way into the freezer.

Tuesday, Wednesday and Thursday when I had any spare time, I created two publisher documents, with photos, for Grace and Wanda to add to their respective volunteer books.

Thursday I baked lasagnes, using the large zucchini's from the garden at the farm. Thursday afternoon Wanda arrived with a refrigerated truck, with the meat from the butchers. These were the bullocks she 'finished off' each year; feeding them a special diet for thirty-days before they're slaughtered. Wanda finished off a certain amount of cattle each year, to distribute to her friends, for their consumption. Wanda decided, next year she wasn't going to spend her precious time, during summer, finishing off the cattle.

Wanda also made a special delivery, to a homeless shelter, in downtown Garland. The donation was a tax deduction for Wanda; but that wasn't her main reason to donate. Who wouldn't be grateful for a whole bullock, cut up and packaged, delivered to your door, for free?

Wanda had been on the road for most of the day; exhausted when she arrived at Kim's. The first thing she sampled was a tea, and a slice of zucchini loaf. I got a double 'thumbs up'.

After the friend's orders had been picked up, we loaded the rest of the meat, into the freezers in the garage. *AND THEN WE WERE FINISHED FINALLY!!!!*

Susie, the daughter of a close friend, arrived to help with the orders and stayed for dinner. During dinner (*of freshly baked lasagne*) I presented a beautifully carved, oval-shaped-glass crystal to Wanda and Kim. As soon as I saw the crystal, I immediately knew I should buy it for Wanda, as a token of my appreciation. I had beautiful cards and gifts, I presented to each of my hosts, as a token of my appreciation.

It had been a long week, and the lateness that night started to take effect; preparing my bags to hit the road, *AGAIN*. Friday morning Wanda plans were to return the rental truck; pick up her truck and head back to the farm. Wanda's long time friend, Lori, would keep her company for the day, while she travelled. Lori planned to spend the weekend at the farm with her husband driving up to the farm later.

I said a sad goodbye to Kim, as my gear was loaded into the truck. Wanda, Lori and I headed towards a fuel station, before returning the rental truck. After the vehicles were swopped over, we headed to the airport, to deliver *ME*. With a heartfelt goodbye, I thanked Wanda for this wonderful opportunity to experience Canada with them.

I was hoping every time, they opened one of my jars of preserves, or tasted one of the zucchini breads or lasagna's they'd think of me; their wonderful Aussie volunteer. I heard from Grace; that the prized jars of preserves, were only served up, on special occasions. Grace received a special jar for her birthday. Everything worked out well, as when I revisited in 2014, I restocked the pantry again, with another one-hundred-and-fifty jars of preserves.

Chapter 12

IN TRANSIT EAST - SEPTEMBER

FRIDAY

I said a sad goodbye to Wanda and Lori, as I checked into my flight, to continue my travels east. By the time I checked in and security processed; there wasn't much time to find something to eat, before boarding the flight to Ville Lauer.

I had a window seat, in the plane; however I slept most of the flight. Approaching the airport, I gazed out of the window, to see whether the maple trees had a 'show'. Hoping the landscape would display a range of autumn colours; unfortunately, most of the trees were still green, which meant my plans for tomorrow had changed. Planning to travel by train through Quebec to see the colours only IF there was a display.

One bucket list item was to travel to Eastern Canada or USA to see the autumn colours. I've previously travelled to Quebec in late September before, but the colours were only just starting to change. Lucky for me, I'm staying until the end of October.

Due to the time difference between the provinces it was 6:00pm by the time I arrived at the hostel. I checked into my accommodation, with a mammoth job carrying my luggage from reception, up a large flight of stairs, over the roof top of three buildings, before arriving in my private room. Luckily the staff at the hostel had a young man, who helped.

This part of the hostel had its own exit stairs, leading directly down into the street. Every time I wanted to leave the complex, it's easier and safer, to go down my exit stairs. My room was nice and freshly decorated, with a shared bathroom just around the corner, which serviced the four rooms located on this level. A small kitchen was located near my room, which I didn't use. The main kitchen, located near reception, served the complimentary breakfast each morning.

I dumped all of my gear in my room, before heading out for dinner, at a Chinese restaurant, a couple of blocks away. As I headed back to the hostel, the heavens opened up, getting drenched to the skin. *Maybe I should've looked at the weather forecast, but I didn't have an umbrella anyway.*

Arriving back at the main entrance, to the hostel, a group of people were hanging around, the front foyer entrance. I stopped to talk to them, for a few minutes, as they continued to smoke in the foyer. Most of the guests I spoke to were from France, plus an Australian, chatting about our experiences in Canada.

SATURDAY

I ate a banana and coffee for breakfast before, walking twenty blocks to the water front. A wonderful surprise was waiting for me, with a large gathering of tall ships, docked, at the marina for a weekend of festivities. An admission charge applied for entry onto the ships; deciding just to photograph a few of them and enjoy the festivities; spending the morning listening to musicians singing *(in French which I didn't understand)* and entertaining the crowds who were gathering on the waterfront.

Dad and I went for a river cruise here, back in 2005. I also remember coming here in 2008, walking around, the cobblestone paths that linked, all of the old buildings.

For lunch I found an outdoor café; located in a courtyard surrounded by landscaped gardens; with each building a multi-leveled café in itself; opening up to this courtyard. Individual elevated terraces had seating; overlooking the whole courtyard area. A collection of magnificent large trees formed a canopy, over the entire area, creating a truly magical atmosphere. *I could image the nights here, with ambient lighting and fairy lights, wrapped around the tree trunks and branches.* The weather was pleasant, even though gas heaters were working above each table. A jazz band entertained the guests; obviously a popular place for diners; as the length of the queues were long. I stayed for almost two-hours writing in my journal, enjoying a cocktail or two, a nice brunch and of course a fabulous dessert.

As I left the café, plenty of tourists were roaming the streets, with buskers and street performers entertaining the crowds. I stopped to watch magicians entertaining the crowds; with a hat placed in the centre, for donations, which I gladly contributed to. Walking through Chinatown, I realised something was wrong; spotting a person dressed in a costume. I noticed more people, dressed up in costumes; following the costumed people, into a large civic centre, discovering, a comic book convention, was taking place today. I was totally mesmerised by the exhibition of characters, spending time watching everyone go in and out of the exhibition hall. I even got a few people to pose for a picture for me. Crazy time – what a blast!!!

As I started to walk back to the hostel, I was concerned, about how *FAR* I'd walked that morning; I calculated a pretty good guess; walking two blocks too many and then just had to walk one block over. *This, of course, was without a map. I must be getting better with 'where my true north was'.* I'd been thinking of going back down town, for the nightly laser show, instead I found dinner a little closer.

THE DREAM SEQUENCE

I had a dream, I walked into this bar one night and ……………..

The bar was a low level dwelling, situated on a corner block; where the building was constructed along an embankment. The front entrance was located, along the side street; where the embankment stopped, to allow access to the building. Glass windows, running the length of the building, were at street level, on the main road. As you passed the windows, you could see down into the room; lit with soft down lights, and bright neon signs; advertising different products, highlighting different areas. High tables with bar stool, were placed along the windows; and cozy booths along the other wall.

The bar was located in the centre of the room; with a large collection of bottles, placed on shelves, in front of a mirrored wall. A couple of wait staff were tending the bar; and a few customers relaxing on the stools.

I stood in the doorway of the bar, waiting; for my eyes, to adjust, to the low light, of the room. Soft music was playing; a small crowd of people were placed around the room; in a relaxed atmosphere.

My eyes were drawn to a group of men; aged around the forty-year mark. One of the men was speaking, with the whole group, listening to his story. I couldn't take my eyes off one man, standing in the group; facing my direction; looking up; his eyes immediately connected with mine. With a dark complexion, longish dark hair, with sparkling mischief in his eyes, his lips were shaped in a smile. The next minute, I was standing beside him, as he reached out to take my hand.

The bar, from this dream, was located on the street I just walked past, on my way to dinner. Eating my dinner, I thought about that dream; whether I should call in, to meet this amazing man.

Believe it or not? Did she go into the bar???

OH, OH BAD NEWS

With all of the happenings with my life at my last host, I had not given any thought about writing to my next host to confirm she still wanted me? *AFTER* I arrived in the Ville Lauer, I sent Pam an email to confirm my arrival. I was shocked to receive a reply back, to say she didn't plan on me turning up. *WHAT THE%$&(:?* Pam's email stated I had to agree to her terms, before she would commit. Agreeing to stay in her cabin, with a pit toilet and a camp shower located in the barn. I'd have to collect, my own water, from a hose near the house. The hours of work were six hours a day, I replied to her with a YES. I agreed to these terms; as I didn't really have a choice.

Thinking about this situation with Pam; I decided to contact my next hosts to make sure everything was 'ok' with my visit to them, in the middle of October. I was so pissed off when they replied *"NO"*. The next host weren't taking any more volunteers this year, because it'd cost more money to have the workers, than they had made out of the garden. *WHAT THE*…… What was I supposed to do now?

SUNDAY

Sunday morning I was up early, ordering a cab to the train station. When I arrived, the office wasn't yet open; waiting to check in; only to receive a message, about a schedule change, for my trip tomorrow. I phoned the train ticketing people; advising me, the train was replaced with a bus, and I'd be reimbursed, the difference in my ticket.

When a porter came along I gave him my luggage, including my pillow and carryon bag to place on the train. I went to a café for breakfast; preparing for the day's travel, by purchasing fruit salad and munchies.

My heart was heavy; with another sad goodbye to Canada. The train stopping just inside the state line; boarded by Immigration officials. Everyone was asked, to show their passports; as I was directed back into the dining car; set up as a temporary office. I handed over my passport; as a young officer asked questions, about my plans for my visit to the States. He asked where I was visiting; I planned to stay with a friend, who'd an interest in gardening; meeting online. I had to buy a new visa, costing six-dollars; luckily I had cash, left over, from my time in Alaska. After thirty minutes, of interrogation, my passport was stamped. The officer placed a huge green notice, in my passport; for departure from the country by the twelfth-of-December.

What was that all about? What was I: a middle aged woman travelling alone? Surely I was the latest terrorist threat entering the country.

I returned to my seat as the train proceeded, on its journey southbound. I just love train travel and after about twenty minutes of sulking, I went down into the dining car for coffee and see what's on the menu. I'd purchased some fruit salad and yoghurt from the train station, but it always nice to have a warm lunch. We're on the train for five hours; I needed to find people, to talk to. A group of men, had just completed, a bike ride (pedal bike), raising money for local charities. The distance was over six-hundred-kilometers, taking seven days to complete; visiting attractions and point of interest, along the way.

I also met a lovely lady from Montreal; listening to her talk, about her life. I told her about my island, I'd visited, on both my previous trips to Quebec. The island had an old flour mill, converted into a restaurant; dining there, on both my previous trips. There's something familiar about the island; forcing me to spend hours searching the internet to locate it, name it and want to spend more time there; if I'd an opportunity to visit again.

I thoroughly enjoyed the day, travelling past lakes and beautiful country side; before I knew it, the train arrived at Esperance, my destination for today. I grabbed a cab to my motel; spending the afternoon exploring the area; finding a nice little Italian restaurant, ordering my favourite dish; veal scaloppini. The standard was nowhere near the same, set by my favourite restaurant, in my home town.

MONDAY

I had an early night, sleeping very well, with the morning to chill out, with a late checkout; catching up on emails, my journal and just enjoyed doing *NOTHING*. I had left over fruit salad for breakfast.

I checked out of the motel at midday, with a shuttle bus, going over to the train station. The train station was full of activity; with passengers coming and going, with two buses travelling to Stonebridge that afternoon. Grabbing a hot soup for brunch; I found a comfy chair, while I waited.

The buses were jammed packed with passengers with a group of us chatting for the three-hour trip. Most of them commenting; they're sick and tired, of the train tracks being closed, with the bus alternative, being normal for them.

By the time the bus arrived in Stonebridge, it was dark, and I was busting to go to the bathroom. The bus pulled up, outside the train station, as I dashed to find a bathroom. When I got back to the bus, I had to find my luggage receipts, before the guard allowed me, to take my luggage. I found a cab costing me forty-five-dollars, for the one way ticket to my motel room; costing me one-hundred-and-eighty-dollars for the night. Boy oh boy, I felt like I was being ripped off, as apparently, this was the cheapest accommodation I'd find in town. The cabbie talked during the trip over to the motel; about the economy and how the town was doing it tough, with vacant buildings and unemployment.

When I arrived at the motel my room was very nice; but so over priced; 'suck it up princess'. Next time, I'll know better, to avoid staying in Stonebridge. It was 9:00pm when I walked next door to a buffet style restaurant; enjoying freshly cooked pork with salads. I'm not a big fan of buffets, and it was too late in the night, to be eating dinner. I try to only have two meals a day when I'm not working. Buffet meals where expensive, if you only ate a little, so I paid for the meal and went back to the motel. I went straight to bed; as tomorrow I continue my journey from a different train station.

Trying to find reasonable accommodation, near the train stations; seems near impossible, when you're unfamiliar with a city. Maybe, the alternative; of sitting on a bus, for twenty-four hours, and travelling by road from Quebec, south into the States; was a better option.

The next morning the cabbie charged sixty-five dollars, for the peak-hour-traffic trip, to the north bound train station. At the train station, I waited for the departure; while dragging my luggage around, lining up for coffee. With just a hint of colour in the trees; I enjoyed moving around the train, admiring the small towns and scenery, before reaching my destination. I grabbed a cab, to meet my new host, at her offices, near the waterfront, in Crescent Heads.

Chapter 13

HOST NO. 7 THE COTTAGE GARDEN - SEPTEMBER

MEETING THE HOST AND MY FIRST DAY TUESDAY

I arrived at the office suite, waiting for Pam to finish with a client before she came down to greet me. Pam had appointments until four o'clock; so I explored the waterfront while I waited. I left my luggage with the receptionist; ordering some deep fried vegetables, from a Japanese Restaurant. I browsed the shops, discovering a row of seafood restaurants, along the water front. I should've walked a little furtherer; having lobster for lunch, instead of the vegetables. A cruise ship was docked; with tourists, looking at market stalls, set up for their benefit.

I went back up to Pam's for a cup of tea, before she attended another meeting. I waited in a café, for her to reappear again. Pam then held a meditation session, with the option of waiting downstairs or joining in. I like to experience, how different people, lead the mediation sessions, so that's what I did.

After the session, we finally started heading, to where we're staying the night. Pam had other plans; since she hadn't expected me, to turn up. I tagged along, calling into a supermarket to purchase food. I asked Pam what she was doing for dinner; telling me, she had dinner at the meeting. *Well thank you very much for that information. Alert No.1.* I looked for bread and cheese for dinner, with some yoghurt and fruit for breakfast.

Pam's brother had just placed, their mother, into an aged care facility, that night we stayed at her mum's house. Pam and I spent a little time, talking to the brother, before we made plans to retire for the night. I had a mattress, on the floor, in the lounge room, as my bed for the night. A foot pump was needed to inflate the mattress; with the bedding was filthy, and full of grass seeds. *She expected me to sleep on that. Alert No.2.* The bedding material was polyester; dirty and itchy. What was I supposed to do? I had a shower, taking forever, falling asleep, with Pam sleeping on the couch in the same room.

I had to take off my watch, which had an alarm that beeped, every hour, on the hour. I had to place the watch in a kitchen drawer, close the kitchen door so *NO ONE* would be disturbed by the beep. *WHAT THE &^%$?$%*. Pam also barricaded the kitchen door, so her brother didn't come into our part of the house. *Alert No. 3. AGAIN, WHAT THE HELL WAS GOING ON IN THIS HOUSE?*

SECOND DAY WEDNESDAY

Breakfast was the same as dinner, toast and cheese, as I placed my yoghurt in Pam's cooler.

Pam and I travelled to the nursing home, to visit her mother, to make sure everything was ok. We inspected her room, with Pam smelling the crutch of her mother's pants; making sure they were being washed. Her mum was sharing a room with another lady, so we met her as well.

The nursing home had a schedule of activities; the residents participated in each day. Each morning after breakfast, was the time they sit in the lounges reading the paper. Each resident has to order and pay for their own newspaper; then it's time for some exercise, before morning tea was served.

We spent about an hour at the nursing home, with Pam talking to one of the duty managers; about her mum. Pam made an appointment, for the following week, for her mum to visit the doctors, so they could check her condition.

We left the nursing home stopping at a library with internet services; Pam checked her emails, while I did the same. In the afternoon we arrived at a little town; where Pam had an ongoing night class. While Pam was conducting the mindfulness class, I organised her documentation that supported the class. There were lots of pieces of papers, on different subjects; most of these were just photocopies of photocopies. I thought I'd spend; some of my time, at Pam's retyping the information, to look more professional.

When the class was finished, we travelled over to a friend's place, where we're spending the night. Pam told me, the family wasn't wealthy; don't to expect too much from them. We had a lovely dinner with Lea and Charles and their ten-year-old daughter. The couple were involved in higher education; with their adopted daughter, having the perfect parents, to teach her. Pam stayed with them, on a regular basis, when she had classes nearby and I enjoyed listening to the family talk about their lives.

Lea asked if I wanted to have a shower and Pam answered for me "No, she was fine". *Alert No. 4*. I was astounded, amazed and shocked; Pam thought she had the right, to speak for me. I freshened up in the bathroom, before I went to bed on a mattress, and thankfully this time the bedding was clean.

DAY THREE THURSDAY

The next morning we were all up early for school. I enjoyed a lovely breakfast before I thanked Lea and Charles for their hospitality, and Pam and I continued on with our journey.

There was a little hint of colour, in the foliage of the trees, lining the motorways. While we were driving, Pam informed me, she would be travelling, over the next two weeks; I'd have to look after myself. I mentioned I'd like to stay for six-weeks, and Pam said that'd be great.

When we arrived in Huston, Pam dropped me off at the grocery store to shop for supplies, while she went to do other chores. As I hopped out of the car, I wondered where the agreement was; about being supplied food and board, in exchange for the work. I started filling my trolley with groceries, I thought, I would eat in the two weeks. I didn't know how big the fridge was, so I purchased cans and packets that stored well. When Pam came back, she didn't offer to pay for my food (plus a bottle of liqueur), which totalled one-hundred-and-eighty-dollars. We loaded the food into the car, and drove to an organic shop, with a café. I enjoyed a coffee while I looked at their groceries and notice board. Again, Pam didn't offer to pay for my purchases.

As we got closer to home Pam pointed out different property owners, who also had volunteers; I could visit, if I wanted to. Pam pointed down a road, to the beach; with these, the only directions she gave me, as we pulled into the property.

THE CABIN AND FACILITIES

Pam's showed me to the cabin, located along the tree line, at the back of the property. My initial impression of the cabin was positive; knowing it'd be lovely to sleep there; being far enough away, from the main house for privacy; with a beautiful expanse of green lawn stretching across the entire back yard area.

I carried all of my bags up to the landing, at the side of the cottage; before I moved into the cottage, I had to clean it. Pam come up to the cabin, and didn't even apologise for the state it was in. Pam just accepted; if I wanted to stay in the cabin, I'd clean it or not. Her attitude was; it wasn't her concern, either way. *Alert No. 5.*

Pam guided me for a walk, into the forest' joining the back of the property, to find the pit toilet. The last volunteers had dug a new hole, to be used for my bathroom. Yes, a pit toilet was exactly that, a hole in the ground; with no evidence of a seat or even a building. I stood facing the pit; my eyes roamed around, the surrounding area; discovering the neighbours, would've full view of me, hovering over the pit, to deliver my number twos.

I had a pee bucket, to use with the contents added, to the pit toilet. *But please don't tip the contents of the pee bucket over the lawn near the cabin, as lichens and mosses were growing under the trees.*

The cabin hadn't been used for a long time, with mice poo throughout the cupboards. I washed up every item of cookware including pots, plates, knives and forks etc. The bed was an inflatable air mattress, with its own frame; but there's a problem, it wasn't inflated fully. Placed on top of the airbed, was a mattress, as I found sheets and blankets, in a plastic bag in the loft.

After an hour I had the cabin clean, with my suitcases unpacked and my groceries stored away in cupboard and fridge.

When I toured the shed, Pam showed me the shower system; a solar shower, was a plastic bag, filled with water; placed in the sun, during the day the water heats up. There were a few problems with this system:

1. You needed the sun to heat up the water, and if there's no sun, then there's no hot water.

2. You have to be super human, to hang the bag, high enough to stand under the nozzle.

3. The hook, where the bag hangs up, was located in the hot house; lined with opaque glass; facing the neighbours, on that side of the property; with a clear glass door facing the road. *All together you had to be strong and an exhibitionist to shower in the hot house.*

I had no access to the internet or a telephone; Pam didn't provide me with, any phone numbers, of friends I could ring, if I needed help.

THE HOUSE AND GARDEN

The size of the whole property was about half an acre; including the main house, a small work shed with the hot house attached. At the back of the shed, was a partially fenced veggie garden, full of produce. Behind the house, next to the veggie patch; a sunken fire pit area, with seating, constructed in elevated rows, on the natural incline, of the back yard; with the fire pit in the middle. The back of the house had a hedge row, nicely clipped. The large set of beautifully constructed stone entrance stairs, located near the garage, had large pots filled with herbs. Along the road, a row of tall hedged trees, gave the house privacy; and the front gardens, were filled with mixed perennial plants.

THE WORK

The first couple of hours; at this new location, were the same emotions I usually felt; as my expectations and initial impressions were raw; still processing the details about the bathroom situation; taking a deep breath. I finished setting up the cottage; walking back down to the main house, where Pam had wooden boards, needing to be primed; for a builder, arriving the following morning. I found a brush, the paint and started working. All of the boards needed two coats, which was an easy job. When I finished the boards, Pam discussed the jobs, which needed completing or maybe just attempted, while I stayed there.

Pam asked me to tidy the barn; a mammoth job; with piles of different materials, scattered all over the place. A few plants needed to be transplanted, into the hot house; plus some weeding in the veggie and perennial garden.

That night Pam had purchased fish for dinner; which I prepared, while Pam had an appointment. After dinner I helped clean up, and then went to my cabin. I wasn't allowed to use her toilet, shower or washing machine during my stay. This was the agreement I'd said '*YES*' to via the emails. *WHAT THE FREAKING HELL WAS I THINKING*? This situation was a lot worse than I'd anticipated, and this wasn't an ideal situation, I found myself in.

FRIDAY

Pam left that morning, as I started my second day of work; working three hours yesterday, painting the boards and cleaning the cottage. I had made the executive decision, if I'd paid for my own food, I'd only work three-hours-each-day; a fair decision; based on my own principles. Deciding the shed was the biggest job; I started organising that. When I'd finished my three hours work I had a coffee; found a book to read and snuggled up on the lounge in the barn. The worker, fixing the roof; was at the house, using the boards I'd primed. The weather was cold, with the barn not very warm; having nowhere to sit up in the cabin. I found a blanket and spent a few hours reading, with a nana nap, as well.

My last shower was on Tuesday; and now day two at the property, still without any hot water. Pam had said "privy in the barn', with absolutely no privacy; especially with the builder working here, I couldn't have a shower, even if I wanted to.

For breakfast, lunch and dinner I cooked up a storm; using all of the fantastic ingredients I'd purchased. I was tired and went to bed early.

SATURDAY

I had a lot more energy today; cleaning up more of the shed, and moving a few plants into the hot house. I worked for three hours only, and spent the rest of the day reading and resting in the lounge area of the barn.

Pam sent me a text, to see how I was going, telling her, all was well. Day four; there's still no sunshine, to warm up, the shower water. Deciding I was brave enough; to use the back corner of the shed; hoisting the hot water bag, up on a rope, over the beams. This allowed enough height, so I could've a decent shower. The water was warmish; stripping down and standing in a large plastic tub; which collected the water. Did I say the water was warmish? NOOO it was freaking freezing! The water cleansed my skin for about ten seconds☺, having to wait for a better 'warm' before I tried it again.

Once again I cooked up some lovely meals, using all of my fresh ingredients first; so I didn't have to worry about them spoiling. In the cabin, as I lay in bed each night; I could see the clouds, the moon and the stars hovering overhead. The cabin was perfect for star gazing, as I drifted off to sleep.

SUNDAY

My sleep, last night was terrible, as the bed was getting flatter and flatter, waking up early because I couldn't get comfortable.

By lunchtime I had finished the barn and since I could see a glimmer of blue skies, I decided I would go exploring, to find the ocean. I set off down this huge hill; quickly realising I would have to walk back up it, to return home. At the bottom of the hill, was a culvert showing glimpses of an inlet, just on the other side of some tall sedge grasses.

I continued my walk uphill this time, as I passed some other people walking on the road, as I said a quick hello. The road, I had been walking on, was rather quiet, with very little traffic, as I enjoyed the peacefulness of the area. I spotted some houses, located off the road, hiding behind natural timberland. I came to a 'T' intersection, with a sign indicating the location of a boat jetty, a good indication; I was on the right road. I must have walked at least one-and-half-hours before I actually spotted any water.

I continued walking until I came across a lobster shack, set up on the side of the road way, with huge water tanks, filled with live lobsters. I was the only customers, at 2.30pm on a Sunday afternoon. I made myself comfortable, at the table and chairs, set up on the jetty, as a few other diners arrived, to enjoy the ambience of a beautiful autumn's afternoon. A couple of men were working on a boat, moored at the end of the dock. I wondered whether they'd been out on the water for the weekend or getting ready for their next adventure.

Ordering 'the special of the day' lobster tail with coleslaw and a cool drink, as I watched the changes on the bay. It was certainly a beautiful afternoon, with the sun lowering in the western skies, and the tides had changed. I stayed nearly two hours reading a book, to escape into another reality, before I started to walk back home.

On the walk back I enjoyed the changing of the day with more people out walking. I reckon I spent at least four hours walking this afternoon. When I reached the road, near the house, I noticed Pam's car, was parked in the driveway. Pam had texted me, she would heading home, but I didn't look at my phone until after I arrived back at the cabin.

As I walked past the house, I didn't see anyone about, and that night, no lights were on in the house so I didn't disturb Pam at all.

I wasn't hungry; drinking a coffee for dinner, needing sleep, as it'd been a long day. Trying to get comfortable; even thinking about deflating the air bed, and just using the mattress.

MONDAY

Awake at 2:00am because I couldn't sleep, needing more support for my back, than this air mattress. I went to the bathroom; stretching my back, before going back to bed, to try for some more sleep. I heard my phone 'ping' with a new message, as Ricky had sent me a message about my phone bill. Apparently it was very high; asking if I could be more conservative with the use. I wrote back, mentioning its only high, because of all of the birthday calls for my children, my birthday plus father's day.

Ricky was now commenting 'don't worry'; as he'd just been to a weekend conference, 'to find his centre', spending a lot more than my phone bill. We texted back a few more times, before realising this situation, was ridiculous.

Here I am at 4:00am in the morning not being able to sleep at a place where

1. I had to clean the whole place up because of the mice poo everywhere
2. I had to buy my own food
3. I was denied the use of a toilet, shower and washing machine
4. I have to pee and poop in a bucket, and take my own waste out into the forest to dispose of, in a pit toilet; I am supposed to use, in full view of the neighbours next door.
5. I have to shower in a barn with cold water with absolutely no privacy.
6. I currently smell like a dead person, because my skin hasn't been cleansed properly, for five days.
7. I had to sleep on a bed that wasn't acceptable, on any level.
8. There's been no respect, shown to me, on any level, for who I am, and what I'm offering.

As I starting thinking about the last week, I realised, I needed to pack my bags, and leave here ASAP. I'd promised myself, before I left Australia, if I wasn't being treated the right way or appreciated for what I was offering; then I 'owed it to myself' to leave. I felt Pam didn't appreciate what I was offering her; because there's absolutely no respect, otherwise she wouldn't have treated me this way. I felt like a slave and fortunately, slavery disappeared, from this country, about a hundred-years-ago; but obviously Pam missed getting that email.

In the next couple of hours I'd packed all of my things, emptied the fridge and taken the linen off the bed. I kept looking out for Pam, but she wasn't to be seen. At 9:00am I carried my luggage down to the barn; placed my dirty washing, in the wash basket in the barn, and made sure the cabin was empty and *CLEAN*.

I knocked on Pam's door and when she answered it I told her I was leaving. She asked why and I told her it was a multitude of reasons, starting with not being able to sleep in the bed. Pam informed me, she was just about ready to leave as well, but there's no room in her car for me. At that moment, the phone rang and it was Peter, her neighbour, who was calling in shortly to drop off his volunteer, for Pam to take to a doctor's appointment in Crescent Heads. Pam asked Peter, if I could catch a lift with him, and he said yes.

Pam was definitely not prepared for my departure, becoming flustered, trying to get some jobs done right there and then. I wasn't prepared to help her with the jobs. She asked me 'who helped me with the barn', as I replied "no one. I did it all on my own". Pam was shocked and taken back with my reply; as if I wasn't telling her the truth.

Peter arrived, with the workers exchanged; I quickly loaded my stuff into his car. I had all of my groceries to pack up as well as my luggage. I said goodbye to Pam; relieved to be out of there, however I did feel sorry for Pam; in one way, because she'd counted on me to help her. Then reality kicked in *DO NOT* feel sorry for her.

Peter worked in the education department; on his way to work that morning. We pulled into a coffee place; shouting him a coffee for helping me out. *(Yeah $1)*. As we travelled closer to his work; I asked him to drop me off, at the first not tooooo expensive motel; having just spent over $1000 travelling in the last week.

I was lucky to find a motel at 10:00am to check into, and you won't believe the first thing I did, when I got to my room. *I WENT TO THE BATHROOM*. There's absolutely, not a chance in hell, was I pooping in a bucket, one more time.

EMERGENCY TRANSMISSIONS

The motel was costing me ninety-five-dollars-per-night; I needed to find a new host quickly. The second thing, I did, was secure my WWOOF website, on my computer. I thought I'd travel anywhere, within a two bus ride, from here. Two hours north, would take me almost back into Canada; studying the farms, appropriate for what I wanted to do. I was desperate, for a place to stay, but still needed to be true to myself, for what I offered the new host, as well as what they're offering me.

Within an hour I'd found, six different suitable hosts that looked interesting; sending off emails enquiring about vacancies. Within the next hour, I had a reply from Betty and Roger, who operated a B&B. They asked me to phone them; which I did; Roger saying I was welcome, to come stay with them. Roger gave me details of the bus service, leaving first thing the next morning.

By that afternoon, I had six replies, all saying *YES*. This morning; at the beginning of my search, I decided, I'd choose the first host to reply. Even though some of the farms looked amazing, I couldn't be fussy; at this point of time, waiting for the best offer.

I was so happy, relieved and excited I found a new place to stay. I sent Peter an email, telling him I was *OK;* thanking him for his generosity. A shower was the next activity on my list, then sleep in a BIG queen size bed that didn't sink. I ate my fresh food, as there weren't any cooking facilities, in my room. I repacked my groceries into my bags, leaving most of the fresh fruit and vegetables, at the motel, as there's only so much luggage, I can physically manage, at one time.

I booked a cab to the bus station; purchased my ticket, jumping aboard the bus. I really enjoyed the trip along the coastline; with the little sea side towns, offering so much character. Driving through one town; I felt like yelling, "stop" to the bus driver. I felt, I should've been staying here; with a strange and familiar sensation, I'd been in this area before.

The towns, I travelled through, had tunnels of golden splendour, with the deciduous trees starting to colour. The canopies, of the trees, were highlighted, by the rays of the sun, in stark contrast with the glimpses of bright blue skies. The structures, of the trees were evident, with their intertwining branches, visible from the bus; travelling along roads, resembling golden magic carpet.

One of my favourite sunsets

Chapter 14

TAKE TWO HOST NO. 8 B&B
– SEPTEMBER/OCTOBER

THE ARRIVAL

When I arrived at the bus station, Roger was waiting for me. My bags were loaded into the car, before heading home; the historical home of a former governor. Betty greeted me, setting up the guest's fridge, for all of my food.

During lunch, I filled them in with details of my last host; retelling what I've been doing on my adventure. Usually Roger and Betty don't have any volunteers; from the end of August until May, but they took this opportunity, as a gift *(as I did as well)*. After lunch, I helped Roger prepare an order, for a delivery to the food bank that afternoon.

THE AREA

I didn't know, until recently, eastern America and Canada were settled back in the sixteen- hundreds. On a tour of Nova Scotia in Canada I learnt about the history of the French invasion and why there were forts built along the Eastern coastline. This part of the country had a wealth of historical areas, becoming interested in hearing stories about the local places.

THE PROPERTY

The original house was built, in the early nineteen-twenties; extensions added on, over the years. The original house area included the kitchen, laundry, the lounge area, and Roger and Betty's bedroom upstairs. Many years ago, a fire destroyed the section, where the parlour and downstairs guest's rooms, were now located. When the lower rooms were rebuilt, the second story was added, with three bedrooms all with private ensuites. A sunken area was built, onto the front of the house; used as the breakfast room, with a toilet, and a large settee, placed in front of an open fire place; where you can snuggle up, in this room, to watch all of the activities outside. Located on the northern side of the house were storage and change rooms, toilets and access to the indoor pool area. Above the pool area; a self-contained unit, with fully equipped kitchen, five bedrooms; sleeps eighteen people, with all the comforts of home.

The size of the property was four-and-a-half-acres, with the majority of the property, landscaped and divided into various garden rooms. The property was consisted of a long and narrow shaped block; with the house placed in the centre, on the highest part of the block. The immediate house yard was level, achieved by constructing a rock wall, on the western boundary. My first impression of the rock wall was admiration; admiring how skillfully the stone masons, had constructed the wall. Inside the wall; a sunken garden, used for growing herbs; had a view point along the entire creek bed. A stone path, running along the bottom of the wall; on the outside, had broken up, from the strength of the roots, of the trees lining the path.

The grounds were beautifully designed and landscaped with sweeping gardens, filled with trees, shrubs and perennial flowers forming perfectly balanced vistas.

On the southern side directly in front of the house; a large sweeping perennial garden filled with all types of flowers, shrubs and small trees. The whole area was visible from inside; through the large glass windows, creating a wonderful display, through all seasons.

Using a clock as a reference, travelling clock wise around the house; the area directly west of the house, was the raspberry patch. This area takes advantage of the slope of the land, towards the creek bed, at the edge of the property. On the northern-western side of the house, the land contours to a lower level, where the intern's summer house was located. The house features bunk beds for the workers, with open spaces available. On the same level as the house, on the western side; another large perennial garden, had a pathway, leading from the car park, to the self contained unit.

Located on the northern-side of the house; the circular driveway, with a large grove of mature trees, planted in the middle of the drive, greets the guests. The front door was located here, with parking for guests in the driveway. Further out, from the house, on the northern-side; a large lawn area, with flower gardens and large established trees, lined the boundary. To the west of this lawn area; the land falls down, onto the same level, as the intern's summer house. This area has large hot houses; and open garden beds, worked by a young man, named Steve. Steve uses the land to grow organic vegetables, for his market garden stall. With Steve using parcels of land, Roger and Betty were able to keep their property manageable and sustainable. Steve has a huge compost area, using the 'hot compost method'; keeping a tarpaulin over the heap, to generate heat, to speed up the decomposition, of the green matter.

Running parallel to the roadway, the eastern boundary of the property; planted with a large forested hedge, gives privacy to the house and reduces the traffic noise. On the road side of the boundary, a terraced rock wall was constructed; massed planted with a mixture of plantings, highlighting a magnificent display of colours, shapes and sizes, for all passing traffic to enjoy.

On the southern side of the house further afield from the sweeping garden in from of the breakfast room; a network of worked gardens beds, with paths connecting to other areas. Directly in front of the house, in the middle of the lawn area; Betty created a love heart garden, planted with strawberries, with the shape of the heart, more clearly defined, from the second floor.

At the southern end of the property, on the lowest part of the block, a swimming pool was constructed. Back in its 'hay' day, the pool house had a change room on each end, with the middle part open to the pool. When the governor had pool parties, the building was set up to serve Devonshire teas.

This area was protected by the surrounding forested trees, and a large earth bank above it. When Roger and Betty bought the property seventeen-years ago; the pool was not repairable, placing a layer of soil in the bottom, and erecting a hot house at one end. This area has its own micro-climate where Roger grows the summer veggies; requiring a hotter temperature including peppers, eggplant and tomatoes. Beans, peas and other climbing plants are grown in the open ended part of the pool.

ACCOMMODATION

I carried my heavy suitcases, up the stairs, to the second floor. Boy of boy! Roger wasn't able to help me, because of his health and bad back. Happiness entered my whole body, when I opened the door to my room; overwhelmed that it's decorated in a pink floral, shabby-chic design, with a huge, wrought iron queen size bed. I had my own bathroom with a claw bath, toilet plus a shower. My room was located, on the northern side of the house, with a view out of the windows, over the circular driveway.

The internet signal worked in my room; spending a lot of time in my room and still be connected to everyone. I enjoyed watching movies, downloaded from the internet.

Enjoying my own space; especially as I was left alone most nights to read, meditate or talk online or catch up on emails. Whatever my little heart desired, was on the cards. I took every opportunity to listen to online meditation programmes; study my crystal books; and ask for guidance from the universe. I asked my guides for direction, to help me become stronger, confirming I'm on the right path, for my life's purpose.

THE WORK

The interns help with ALL of the garden work. I don't think I'll ever recover from my time here. The work was hard work, six hours each day, full on for six days each week, for the entire six weeks I stayed. You have to realise, I'm a woman aged in my fifties, not very fit and not very strong. What I lacked in size, I made up for, in determination and hard work.

Some days, I wished for really bad weather, and forced to stop working. But work went on regardless of the weather conditions. I was like an ever-ready battery; keep on soldiering on. If the weather was too wet, I worked inside, so I had a couple of easy days, tidying up the house. With the B&B guests, I helped with breakfast, servicing the rooms; changing the sheets etc. These were easy days, meeting lovely people, and enjoying the conversations.

One morning, I discovered, Roger was tackling a big job, that spelt T.R.O.U.B.L.E. for me. Roger was up a ladder, with a hand saw, cutting down branches off an old apple tree. Looking at Roger; working up the ladder, I couldn't believe he's aged in his mid seventies. I exhaled a big sigh, as I realised what my job tomorrow would be. I'd asked Roger about how we would dispose of the branches. He told me I'd carry them up, via the stairs, onto the driveway. Years ago Roger had access to a road, to this part of the garden; but when the property next door changed hands, the new owners asked Roger, not to use the road anymore. The road was public access, and I would've contacted the owners, about using the road, for a couple of days, while we removed the rubbish. But NO, I carried all of the branches, up the stairs, while avoiding other trees and plants, before placing the limbs on the bed of the truck.

Day one; the tree removal job, was started and finished, on the same day; managing to carry all of the small branches, up onto the back of the truck. The remainder of the tree needed a chain saw to complete the job; with Steve offering his services. Day two; I woke at 2:30am in extreme pain, with spasms going up and down my arm and back. Carrying about forty loads of branches wasn't such a good idea, spending the morning resting, with pain killers and a heat pack. By that afternoon I was doing light jobs, like pruning. *NO MORE TREE BRANCHES* for this little black duckie.

COMPOSTING

A massive list of jobs, were listed for me to complete, or at least attempt; and when I get sick of one job I'd moved to another. Most of the work involved trimming plants; composting every piece of garden waste. Roger had compost piles, located in every section of the garden; easily accessed, so I didn't have far to carry the waste. Roger and I were both layering the compost heaps, with different materials, like a Danish pastry: layer, upon layer, upon layer.

I have to tell you, Roger's passionate about compost, and the 'cold compost method' was his choice; for the green waste on the property. The compost beds take a couple of years, before they're ready, to be used on the garden beds. With the amount of work I was doing, we were starting fresh heaps; some of them five-feet tall. The next process was to wait, wait and wait; until the organic matter starting breaking down. The pile of compost was then moved, over onto the ground beside the original heap, creating a new one. The materials, from the top, were now on the bottom, of the new heap. Any big twigs or tree limbs were taken out, with Roger rotating the piles, until the material was ready to use.

Roger didn't want any items that wouldn't decompose quickly; avoiding self seeded plants, which spread into the garden, via the compost. If you're lucky enough; finding a vine growing, out of the compost pile and ending up with amazing pumpkins. The most beneficial reason, for using the hot compost method, was it killed all the seeds.

THE FLOWER GARDENS

Established gardens covered the majority of the four acre garden; full of my favourites, such as stocks, hostas, rhoderdendrums, dahlias, mays, roses and hydrangeas. I believe a gazillion bulbs, were spread throughout the garden, for spring and summer delights. The colours of the trees were changing; waking up each morning, anticipating a wonderful day full of colour.

One huge job was the removal of the flower heads only, leaving the 1.5 metres stems, to protect the gardens during the winter. The stems act as a vertical barrier; during snow storms when the snow hits the stems and stops. In spring Betty spends a couple of days stomping all the stems flat, while waiting for the new growth; to start the process all over again. Did I mention this area received a lot of snow, and temperatures can be around -15 or -20 Celsius.

THE VEGGIE GARDENS

Three 'veggie patch' people, worked on the property; Betty has her own beds, growing food for the house, and the school students who visit the garden.

Roger has his own individual vegetable garden beds, growing the plants he loves to grow and eat. Roger has a second garden; growing food exclusively, for donations to the food bank/soup kitchen in the local community.

Steve was allocated a large number of garden beds, and hot houses spread throughout the property, growing vegetables for his road-side market stall.

SOUP KITCHEN GARDEN

Roger had acquired an acre of ground, belonging to a neighbour, with exclusive use of this area, for his charity and community contributions. The garden was surrounded by, a six-foot-high deer fence, protecting the vegetable beds. Roger's magic hands, have turned over, fifty-thousand-pounds of produce, in the last fifteen years.

The volunteers (interns) worked extensively in this garden. While I was there, the entire area was cleared of all produce and foliage; with the waste material, creating new compost piles. New garden beds were created with fresh compost; and when Roger and I were finished, we locked the gates until spring, when the process would start all over again.

Roger records into a book, the weight and product processed each week. Roger's biggest year to date; was a whopping five-thousand-pounds of vegetables; he's contributed to the local community. Roger you're a legend.

THE SUNKEN HERB GARDEN

On the western side of the front lawn area; through a hedge; an arch and stone steps leads into the sunken garden. When I first looked into this area, I could only see two-metre-high weeds covering the entire area. Walking down the steps, the first time; I noticed stepping stones on the ground. At the edge of this area, a four-foot-high, beautifully constructed, stone wall, enclosed the garden; forming the boundary of the property. Just inside the stone wall, a large section of self-seeded trees, had taken over the area.

Ready for the challenge, I took a deep breath and went like a maniac; at one-hundred-miles-an-hour through the garden, taking away, wheelbarrows full of the rubbish. By the end of the morning, the structure of the garden was visible, unearthing the interconnecting stone paths; shaped like a sundial.

The self seeded plants I had identified; but I didn't want to touch others, especially if they're treasured plants. Betty was away visiting her son and grand children; as I wanted to surprise her. Two exhausting days later, the jungle had been turned into a beautifully sunny area; the stone wall exposed; interlocking paths created a sundial; playing hop scotch on them☺. The lover's seat was placed, under the shade, of the large tree, and Betty was very grateful, I had saved, some of her prized possessions.

STRAWBERRY FIELDS FOREVER

Betty loved strawberries, designing a love-heart-garden; created entirely of strawberries. One morning, looking down from Betty's bedroom window; both of us agreed, the love heart was a little 'twisted'. I tidied up and reformed the rows, trimmed the strawberries; transplanting the extra plants, down at the school. Betty sprinkles human hair, over the strawberries, to keep the deer away. I was amazed the deer didn't destroy more of the gardens, as Roger's food bank garden was the only fenced garden.

THE SMILE GARDEN

Betty was excited she'd 'done a deal' with Steve; regaining control over the 'smile garden' again. The smile garden consisted of three, large-round-shaped beds, looking like a smile. I'd been working near that area; where a large crop of corn, needed to be cut down, before I could begin work. Betty had picked the corn, Roger had cut off the stems, and I just had to dig up all of the roots, which wasn't a small task. Once the stems were removed, I spread and dug the new compost, into the newly created garden beds. It was a big job, taking me, the best part of one day to complete, and you know what? *IT MADE ME SMILE,* when I walked away from another completed job☺

B&B DUTIES

A continuous flow of guests stayed in the B&B; helping Betty with breakfast and the housekeeping. One weekend, the entire house was booked out, which was a very busy time. When Betty was sick or away visiting family; I made breakfast, then handled house duties on my own. When the weather was cold and wet, I had easy days with only having to help with breakfast, and servicing the rooms. When the weather was fine, we used the clothes line to dry the bedding; to save electricity. I became handy with a vacuum cleaner and love that scene from the movies. I laugh out loud, whenever I find the same vacuum and try to imitate the moves; which just cracks me up☺.

I especially enjoyed meeting the guests, especially one couple from Vermont, who'd regularly travelled to the Caribbean, spending time at the resorts. They shared travel tips, on what to see and left me a cd of reggae music, which I was very grateful for.

VOLUNTEERING

Each week Betty conducts lessons about gardening; with children from the local primary school. Every Tuesday Betty travels to the school, where an organic garden had been established, to show the children how plants grow; by seed, bulb etc. In spring, Betty helps the children plant their crops; over summer the garden looks after itself; and in the fall, the crops are harvested. The children, aged between eight and twelve, were enthusiastic students learning about plants and gardening.

The Thursday class was at Betty's house; with the school bus, dropping them off. The children explore Betty's garden; picking items to prepare for their afternoon tea; one afternoon cooking hot soup, and another time; pizzas. Betty had the patience of a saint, to work with children, as after two hours, my head was spinning. When the children were at the house, I'd help out, and talk to the children, about their interests and their families.

One of Betty's projects was a stall at the school festival in December. The children were sanding down and repainting, old wooden chairs, with bright colours and designs. I enjoyed that project, as I loved being creative. One afternoon, at the house, the weather was very cold; the children gathered things from the garden, creating collages, to take home. Betty was a real 'go getter'; you'd never guess, she was turning seventy soon. My hat goes off to Betty and Roger, for contributing to the community; needing to be congratulated, for the work, they continue to do.

A working bee had been planned at the school, but with wet and cold the weather, and Betty wasn't feeling very well. The working bee would involve volunteers from a nearby penitentiary; definitely giving me, some real muscle, to help with the jobs, around the garden, which I was struggling with. The group comes once-a-year, completing their community service. Unfortunately, the working bee was cancelled, as Betty was the only supervisor, for the gardens and workers.

Another day Betty arranged, for a load of compost, to be picked up, in the truck. *(This was when I needed the muscle workers)* Betty backed the truck; up to the edge, of the garden beds, and I was the delivery person. Betty shovelled the compost off the truck into the barrow, which I dumped onto the different beds. Boy oh boy, I felt like a slave; definitely enjoying a soak in the tub that night. You have to remember I'm in my fifties, and not some young-spring-chicken.

There was one successful working bee at the school, where some parents (mainly mother's) arrived to help clean up the garden. A sign was attached to the fence, advertising 'mulch was needed', for anyone dropping off leaves. Over a few weeks, the pile of compost, was getting larger and larger, each time we drove past.

SEAWEED DUTY

In the mornings, while eating breakfast; I'd shudder as Roger would stop by to mention he had a new job for me. I'd follow him to the location; where Roger would describe the 'new job' listening to him intently, nodding in agreement.

This particular day, we hopped in the truck, driving towards the golf club; a new part of town I hadn't seen before. We drove through the golf club grounds; stopping, in front of a row of houses; with their backyard bordering the golf greens, and the front view was a little cove.

Our job, or I should rephrase it, *MY* job, was to load, the seaweed, into the back of the truck. As I jumped out of the truck; I looked around the cove, discovering thousands-of-tonnes of the sea weed, washed up onto the beach. Roger had an agreement, with the golf club; collecting the sea weed, for free, so the beaches remained clear for visitors and guests. I was just lucky; Roger didn't have a bigger truck.

Roger and I worked well as a team, with Roger raking the seaweed, to within my reach. Then with a large pitch fork, I'd throw the seaweed up, into the back of the truck. Now the truck's floor was almost to my shoulders; working out a system, loading the truck in thirty minutes. Just like the 'horse poo shovelling episode' at the horse stud; I definitely know how to shovel shit. *See The Garden Work in Chapter 6.* Boy oh boy did the seaweed stink, and of course the job was only half over, as it needed to be unloaded back at the farm.

I can remember looking at this farm, when I was researching places to stay; never thinking I'd be doing this job.

After a morning tea break, we unloaded the seaweed, onto some new compost beds. Roger had been using seaweed, for many years; and you only have, to look at the garden, to know this practice definitely works.

FLY AWAY SOUTH FOR WINTER

Do you remember a true story; about a girl, who led geese, in a motorised hang glider? The girl acted as mummy to the geese, as they all flew south for winter. I'm staying in an area where I experienced, a true magical experience; of the migrating birds. During the night, I'd hear the birds squawking in the night skies. During the day, I'd hear them, off in the distance, searching the skies to locate them. Parts of the eastern coastline were protected, allowing the migratory birds to nest and rest.

I found it amazing, the bird life that's present, here in the gardens; with some of these birds staying here, for the winter, before going *SOMEWHERE* else for summer. Hummingbirds were present here, only during the summer months; they'd already departed, before I arrived.

LOBSTER DINNER ANYONE

Lobsters are one of my favourite meals; enjoying a couple of lobster dinners, while I was on the east coast. The first one, on the wharf near Pam's, and the second one was when Roger and Betty bought me one. I could've gone to the local lobster shack; dining in for twenty-five dollars. Or dine-in at the B&B, for six-dollars; killing and cooking the lobster myself. Roger returned home from shopping with three live lobsters, which he placed in the fridge. I found a large pot in the cupboard, boiling the water; saying thank you to the lobster, as I lowered him into the water. Thirty minutes later, I was sitting at the table, enjoying fresh lobster with salad. Yummo I loved the lobster, along with the blueberries and raspberries from the garden.

FOOD GLORIOUS FOOD

Betty was an amazing cook and gluten intolerant as well; preparing food I could eat, including pancakes and waffles. On the counter top in the kitchen; Betty had jars full of the mixtures, containing only the dry mixtures of pancakes and waffles. Reading the directions; adding the wet ingredients such as eggs and milk and mix together. This system, worked well, when you have a crowd to cook for.

The main thing about the food, at the B&B; everything was organically grown, including items they purchased. Meal times were strange; with breakfast I'd have oats, fruit and a yoghurt mix usually with coffee. Lunch, two or three times a week; Roger would cook the meal with meat. On the other days I cooked an omelette or toasted sandwiches. Dinner was usually whatever I wanted to prepare, usually something easy; one night I had yoghurt and fruit.

There were plenty of vegetables in the garden, with the freezer full of raspberries, strawberries and blueberries. Each morning, I'd check out the raspberry patch, to discover berries for my morning tea.

A LITTLE BIT OF CULTURE

Betty was a friend of the local college; receiving invitations to various events, during the year. Betty received an invitation, for a musical performance, involving new students giving their first performance; coinciding with the open weekend for parents.

The teachers spoke, first about their performances, with Latin American and Middle Eastern music represented. The students had three weeks to rehearse; noticing how nervous some of the students were, with signs of stage fright amongst the groups. The performance was only forty-minutes long; with Betty deciding coffee and cake, at a restored factory on the river front, was an ideal way to finish off our night. We enjoyed the ambience of the old building, relaxing in the lounge chairs, scattered around the premises, where a good crowd filled the factory.

One Saturday afternoon I joined Betty at an art exhibition, again at the college. The artist uses dogs, wearing clothes, in a murder-mystery-type-scenario movie solving crimes. The movie was twenty minutes in length, and hilariously entertaining.

The man was also a painter, with his paintings, so simple in some aspects, while others were quite extraordinary. What I liked most about his work; were the paintings where he placed a postcard on the canvas, painting a scene around it. 1. Paint the scene, in real life or 2. Paint whatever you thought the scene should be. I thought it a brilliant and clever idea, especially now my new hobby was, water colour painting. I purchased a 'guide to painting' text book, paper, paints and brushes. I will add 'artist' to my list of accomplishments in life☺

Roger, Betty and I along, with a couple of their friends, attended a short film festival in Thanes. We travelled in one car, arriving early, to enjoy dinner at the restaurant, before the film festival started. The agenda was to watch ten short films, then choose our top three. A fifteen minute break, after the first five films; to grab another drink and/or a restroom break. At the end of the night we placed our ballots, into the voting box. Later that week I checked, on line, to see which movie had won the award. My top three movies were there, not in the same winning order, proving I had excellent tastes in movies☺.

I was grateful for Roger and Betty, for including me in their social life; attending the concert at a local church, where supper was provided. A young couple performed a mixture of little ditties, including their four-year-old son, William who had 'charisma plus' playing the banjo, wearing dark sunglasses, a cute black hat, and a mischievous smile, while singing along with his parents.

EARTHQUAKES

Seven-thirty one evening, in early October, a large rattling sound, accompanied a little shaking of the building. I thought Roger must've been doing something, somewhere, only to find out it was a 4.2 magnitude earthquake. I only gave the situation about five seconds of my attention, before I continued watching my movie. However one of the children, from the school, was thrown from his chair, hitting his head on a cupboard; rushed to the emergency department with a black eye, needing stitches to the side of his head. Talking to Roger, the next morning, he confirmed the house didn't suffer any structural damage.

SUNSETS

For my last week on the peninsular I had the best weather of my stay. One afternoon, after another, I witnessed beautiful clear days and fantastic sunsets. I borrowed the car to visit a local historical site, located nearby, at the mouth of the river. The fort was built in the early eighteen-hundreds; and today was still a rather impressive structure. I stood in the middle of the road, looking left; to see the sun setting, then looking right; as the moon rose over the inlet.

With an almost full tide; the sheltered waters, showed a perfect reflection of the buildings and landscape, surrounding the fort. Standing on the ocean side of the point; I noticed the scenery change around me, as a constant flow of waves were delivered onto the shore. A lighthouse, located off in the distance, continued to revolve around on its axis, glimpsing the light; warning ships of the nearby dangers. On the beach, drift wood was scattered about, with the native grasses bending, in the light breeze. Boats were not found, out on the water tonight, but I did hear some rowdy noises coming from a lobster shack nearby.

I spent an hour near the fort being mesmerized. After the sun had set in the west; the eastern horizon turned a beautiful array of soft blues and pinks, creating an amazing backdrop, for a perfect photo, highlighting the full moon, in all its glory.

Towards the end of October, Betty mentioned wearing a bright orange safety vest, when walking to the beach; because shooters were active, at this time of the year. I opted to wear the vest, rather than risk being target practice.

My favourite spot, an outcrop of rocks was located at the northern end of the beach. I found this spot to be magical, capturing reflections over the water, with the setting sun, disappearing on the horizon. This day was a beautiful afternoon; with a nip in the air, as the temperature dropped. With the sun setting earlier and earlier each day, I arrived at my favourite spot, with only about twenty minutes to spare. The clouds were lining up on the horizon, creating a wonderful image; with a lobster boat returning into the harbour. I waited patiently, for the boat to line up, with the lowering sun. *CLICK.* The boat moved slowly, through the waters, capturing several photos, of the boat, silhouetted against the golden sky.

Just then, my camera battery died; returning my camera to the carry case, mesmerized by the scene in front of me. The lobster boat disappeared around the river's bend, the golden globe inched its way below the horizon, as clouds were highlighted; continuing to change as the light faded. *I thought to myself, what a pity I wasn't sharing, this moment, with a special someone. I immediately corrected myself. I was, sharing this moment, with the most, important person, in the world. ME. Nothing could make this moment, any more special.*

SUN DOGS

Betty and I were driving back from the school working bee, when Betty looked up, and said "there's a sun dog". Looking out the window of the car; the light had caught my attention. I'd never even heard of a sun dog; excited to learn more. A sundog was a rainbow, around the sun; of course, during the day, usually appearing before a storm. The bigger the circle, the bigger the predicted storm; this was the Sunday afternoon, before Hurricane Sandy hit the east coast, on the Monday night.

At the beach, the sundog was still visible, through a mass of dark clouds. The sundog rainbow, I noticed, was located at four points surrounding the sun, like a clock at twelve, three, six and nine o'clock. I walked along the beach, spending a couple of hours taking photos; the storm clouds rolled in, taking over the entire sky; with a tiny hint of what's behind them?

I'd noticed over the last twenty-four-hours; the houses along the beach front, had their windows all boarded up, and furniture was removed from the verandahs. This beach front area, was for summer holidays accommodation, hopefully, all safe during the storm.

HURRICANE SANDY

The whole east coast was on alert, for strong winds and torrential rain. Betty, Roger and I spent Monday morning, storing away the outside furniture, and cleaning up anything that might be a danger, if it became airborne. *(I've lived in Australia in a cyclone area, so this chore wasn't new to me)*.

After dinner, I was hanging out in my room; when Betty yelled out, from the bottom of the stairs, to run water in the bath, in case we lost electricity. Laying upside-down on my bed; looking directly out of the window, watching all of the trees, out in the garden. The wind was making their limbs go crazy; like one of those funny balloon men, you see in car yards that go crazy, as air, was pumped into them.

It was still daylight, as I stood at the window, watching how amazing the wind controlled all of the leaves, lying on the lawn area, in front of my bedroom window. There were thousands of leaves on the lawn, with the wind controlling them, like a dance floor full of couples; dressed in swirling ball gowns, doing the waltz. After thirty-minutes, the leaves were all placed on the right-hand-side of the lawn, in the garden beds. The wind raked them up; in such a fine and spectacular manner, in a matter of minutes. Even Roger commented, the next morning, how amazingly the leaves had all ended up in the garden bed, without any effort on our part.

As darkness fell upon us, the power was cut, but I didn't mind, as I snuggled up in my bed. I was aroused from my sleep, periodically, during the night, hearing the effects of the strong winds, lightning and thunder battering the house; praying we'd all be safe.

The next morning, I woke up to dull skies, as Betty and Roger were very grateful they didn't sustain any damage, to the house; and relieved no big trees, had fallen in the garden. Roger, Betty and I went for a drive; as you do, to the beach to check out the ocean. We noticed where the high tide level had peaked; with the ocean wild and scary. Driving around the peninsular, we noticed a few trees had been blown over, but basically there wasn't much damage to be reported.

When we returned to the house, we turned on the television, to see all of the damage in the southern states. A friend of mine had sent me an email, asking how I was, since she knew I was staying on the east coast. I sent her a reply back, telling her, the media knows how to exaggerate, as it wasn't that bad. I sent this email *BEFORE* I watched the news cast. Well it really was not bad here☺; very fortunate to come through, this storm, almost unscathed.

FALL EXPEDITIONS

Roger showed me the area, with a tourist drive, during my first week; visiting one of the local beaches. Off shore, an island; you could walk to, when the tides were low enough. The area we were in had the biggest tides in the world; just like Seal Bay in Alaska. When we were driving around, Roger mentioned one of my favourite actors, Ryan Jones, had filmed a movie around this area. I will have to watch the movie again, to recognise, the different places, I visited along the coast.

This was now the third time I've had my favourite actor, Ryan Jones, brought into my life during this trip: Alaska with the coast guard movie; seeing him perform with his band in Canada and now this movie. Not to mentioned I visited his casino in 2011. When we were at the casino, I posed for photos on the staircase; filled with posters and items from his movies.

The nature reserve entrance wasn't far from home, and a destination I'd been looking forward to visiting. The beach, via this trail, was a two hour's hike each way; a great way to exercise and explore the area. The first time I walked through the reserve the weather was beautiful, with clear blue skies, a light autumn breeze, making the walk very pleasant. An access road, through the entire property, was restricted to the people, who owned property there. The property had been donated to a conservancy group; to protect the area, as a wildlife reserve and resting place, for migrating birds. A research group, with several buildings, formed a compound, conducting various experiments.

The whole mountain area consisted of walking tracks; through pine forests, open flood plains and marshes. The native landscape contained different types of grasses, shrubs, flowers and trees. The flora was diverse; some with flowers on them, some trees were turning colour and the rest were just stunningly beautiful.

Arriving near the ocean, my first look, at the pristine beaches, had me spellbound. The sand on the beach was a blinding white; removing my shoes, rubbing my toes through the loose sand. I continued to walk in the soft sand, spotting a few other people, walking in the distance. I walked towards the edge of the water; looking out over the bay, towards the horizon. The ocean was as calm as a pond, enhanced by the beautiful blue reflections of the sky. A small yacht, visible on the horizon, had distinctive white sails, standing out against the blue sky. I wondered who was on board? Where were they heading to? Was the yacht on a day trip or planning to go further afield?

The property was strictly protected, available for hikers to walk through, with no picnic tables allowed. The sign mentions, anyone wanting to sit on the beach, in a chair or have a picnic, a public beach was located up the road.

My second visit, to the reserve, was different, instead of walking, through to the beach; I turned along a road, leading to a lookout. A house was built on this magical spot; walking around the boundary fence, to sit outside the property, searching for quiet time. The sun was placed high up, in the clear blue skies, with a slight northerly breeze; rugged up in winter clothes. Looking across the landscape, the sun glistened in the pools of water, along the river system, winding its way, amongst the protected marsh lands.

One afternoon I dropped Betty off at the school; driving to Thanes, exploring the little sea-side town. An organic café, located on a street corner, with large glass windows, gave a view of the actions of the busy afternoon. I spent time writing in my journal, then found a dress shop, with a discounted clothes rack, where I bought two dresses, to wear in the Caribbean.

My expectations, of witnessing the autumn colours; has now been realised, as the late afternoon sun cast a golden glow; on all of the autumn trees, lining the rivers and roads. A magical vista awaited me, where I could've easily stepped, into a photo shoot, for a travel magazine. The reflection on the river water was breathtaking; stopping on a street, to acknowledge the joy of this moment. This part of the country was settled in the sixteen-hundreds; warming my heart, these trees were planted, all of those years ago, now a majestic and empowering presence in these towns.

My next visit to Thanes, the day after Hurricane Sandy, wasn't a pretty sight; even though the impact hadn't been major; vegetation littered the streets, and the sky was grey and bleak. The still waters, from my last visit, were replaced by rough grey waters; the trees were skeletons, stripped of their foliage, standing haunted in their naked splendour.

MISSING JEWELLERY

The night I stayed with Pam, at Lea's house, I left behind my jewellery, as we left in such a rush that morning. *(Chapter 13 – Day 3 Thursday)* I told Pam in the car, on the way back to her house, and she let Lea know. Pam would arrange for the delivery, of my jewellery, to Betty and Roger's, and I'd reimburse her the cost of the postage. After repeated email requests to Pam, I still hadn't received my jewellery. I finally sent a text to say, if I didn't receive the jewellery before the end of the week, I was going to report her to the police. I sent an email to the volunteer group, and they couldn't suggest anything, because I'd left the items behind, and she hadn't stolen them. My biggest concern was she would hock the jewellery, worth about three-thousand-dollars. YES I know that's a lot of money, but I was travelling with my things; and two of the rings were worth over two-thousand-five-hundred-dollars to replace. Finally the post man delivered the parcel; letting out a sigh of relief, because it was causing me so much stress.

After I received my parcel, I sent Pam the cash, plus a hand written letter, explaining how I felt and why I'd left her home. I mentioned all of my concerns, telling her, the property wasn't what I expected. Pam replied to me by email; spending a couple of weeks, exchanging our feelings, to understand each other's point of view.

Pam mentioned; she judged me, sitting in the library, searching the Caribbean and flying back to the west coast. Pam lives a very basic lifestyle and she doesn't know anyone, who'd volunteered, with the resources to fly across the country; to work and fly on a whim, to escape the visa issues. Pam also told me the food she would've provided for me; wouldn't have been up to my standard, so she didn't even offer to pay for what I'd purchased.

I asked Pam to change her volunteer blog, reflecting her true situation at the garden. Pam was considering whether she'd continue; with her membership, as she didn't get very many people staying with her. I took the opportunity to post my comments on Pam's web page, with an honest and very fair opinion of my experiences.

THE NEW LOOK

My volunteer days were almost over, with my hair constantly placed in a band; gathered up high on my head. I love having long hair, *EXCEPT* if you're constantly working. I'd been thinking a lot about dyeing my long and naturally wavy hair, as the chemicals in the dyes, can make you sick. A lot of thoughts were going through my mind, about this decision, to continue growing and colouring it; or get it all cut off and start afresh.

I decided I'd start afresh; ringing Betty's hairdresser, making the appointment, for the day before I started to travel again. I made the appointment, in the afternoon, after I'd finished working, for the day.

The day I chose, to have my hair cut, Hurricane Sandy was due to hit, driving into Thanes and making it home safely. When I arrived at the salon, the hairdresser asked what I wanted to do with my hair. The length, of my hair, was about mid way down to my back, with a natural curl, disappearing with length. I told the lady, I wanted a really short cut; with a natural colour that would easily grow out, if I decided not to colour my hair anymore. The hairdresser and everyone else, in the salon, were shocked; trusting the hairdresser, without any concerns. I had nothing to lose, if I didn't like it; it only takes a few weeks for my hair to grow again.

I braved the scissors, chemicals and relaxed, with magazines and coffee, while being transformed. Examining the long strands of hair, lying on the floor, I was happy with the decision, as I looked up at the mirror, catching the first glimpse, of the new-look Bella Pearce. When I arrived home, Betty was impressed; my hair was almost, as short as hers.

PLANNING AHEAD

With the alarm bells going off, after my cross border incident, I started looking for somewhere else to go after I finished in California. My travel visa expired on the twelfth-day-of-December and I wasn't due back in Canada until the twenty-seventh. I had two weeks to travel, out of America, without having to fly back to Australia; looking at visiting South America and the Caribbean.

I explored the opportunity for a new volunteer place, at the beginning of December. Finally I received an email from Gail; that my application to stay was approved. I'd be arriving at the Island, on the first of December and leaving on the tenth.

As soon as I found out *WHAT I WAS DOING,* I booked the flights, accommodation, rental cars etc. I found a good deal for my flight back to the west coast; arranged my train travel plus motels, shuttles. You name it, I organised it. I now had the next two months planned, with my holiday to the Caribbean; also my flight to Canada for the house sitting job. I love planning trips, just as much as I love taking them. I think it's my triple A, anal retentive, Virgo type personality that gives away the hint; I love to plan ahead.

MORE GOODBYES

Well my time in the east had come to an end, with the adventure definitely working out much better than I had originally planned. I couldn't have stayed at Pam's, for this amount of time, without a shower, bathroom and being treated decently. Roger and Betty were a blessing in disguise, appreciating my help; as much as I appreciated being able to stay, at their beautiful house, I called home for six weeks.

Betty asked me if I was interested in coming back next year, as she'd sponsor me, to help her out over the entire summer. I think, I'd literally die, if I had to work four or so months, at the same pace. Six weeks was definitely enough.

With a sad goodbye to Betty; Roger drove me into Thanes, for the last time. Purchasing my ticket for the bus; hitting the road *AGAIN.*

Chapter 15

IN TRANSIT WEST BOUND – 31ST OCTOBER – 1ST NOVEMBER

CRESCENT HEADS

The bus trip was only a couple of hours long, taking my last opportunity to glimpse the eastern country side. The day was bleak, with very little evidence of the hurricane, as I arrived in Crescent Heads and hailed a cab to my motel. I was shocked (*in a good way*); opening the door of my motel room; the house-maid, had an AAA compulsive, anal retentive personality (just like me). *EVERYTHING* in the entire room was decorated, matching and lined up; with towels and mats folded into designs. I was overwhelmed with absolute delight that the room was *PERFECT,* in every way.

I booked the room on-line, but phoned the motel direct, on Tuesday, to extend for an extra couple of nights, in case the airport departures, from Stonebridge were delayed. After I checked into the motel, I phoned the booking company; confirming the flights would depart as scheduled. In a way, I was disappointed, as I would've loved, to spend, a couple of days exploring.

I grabbed my daypack, spending the afternoon, exploring the area towards the waterfront. I left the motel, following the directions, the motel staff member, had told me. I just kept on walking, until I spotted buildings, resembling the waterfront. I was still a few blocks away, when I asked a security guard; 'I'm almost there'. I'd been walking for over an hour, checking out the architecture of the town, a mix of old and new. Finding a Chinese restaurant for lunch; my stamina was high on fried food☺.

Recognising buildings from my previous visit, as a familiar shop came into view. I entered the shop, containing hundred-percent gluten free products. Yes everything in the shop was gluten free, purchasing a slice of cake for later, as I continued exploring.

At the motel, I checked out the movie guide, choosing the first movie I looked at; exactly what I needed to see; about 'everything' being connected. It's my kind of movie about destiny, soul mates and reconnecting with people; whom you've met, in former lives. I truly believe everything that this movie implies. *Haven't you ever wondered why you have an immediate connection to someone; like you've met them before?* Even though the movie showed a lot of violence, I was thoroughly mesmerised, by the whole concept.

It was Halloween night; with the taxi travelling along a main street, where people were dressed in their costumes, obviously enjoying the night out. I knew Halloween was huge, but I never realised HOW big; until I noticed the houses all decorated and the effort people made with their costumes.

At the motel I rang Brad and Mum to report in; as they were both concerned for my safety, as they hadn't heard from me since before the hurricane. I organised my suitcase, for the plane trip tomorrow; preparing myself, for the next leg of my extraordinary journey.

I just love travelling, especially through airports, finding them exciting and full of life. The shuttle bus had a direct service, to the Stonebridge airport; which was so much easier than how I arrived here the last time. The cost of the motel in Crescent Heads was eighty-five dollars; compared to one-hundred-and-eighty in Stonebridge, and only fifteen dollars for the shuttle. I was so happy, this part of the trip, was *EASY*. Then I checked in at the airline, and ended up paying one-hundred-and-fifty-dollars for luggage. Cheap flights; without luggage included in the price, pay back was a bitch; as they're always going to *GET YOU*.

I had a couple of hours to wait before my flight, boy of boy, it was a big airport; up, down and around elevators and long corridors. I found a shop selling just books (*fancy that*), locating a couple of books written by my favourite author. I had a list, in my wallet of all of his books; ticking them off as I read them. I started reading the first book; waiting for the first flight, continued during both flights, until I arrived at my destination, Salisbury, eight-hours later.

WEST COAST

I didn't even notice the flights from east to west, as I was so engrossed in my book. I had lunch during the stop-over and didn't worry about food, until after I booked into my motel. As a passenger, in the shuttle bus, I had a great tour around the city of Salisbury, before they dropped me off about two hours later. I wasn't really impressed by the motel, as it was dirty and old.

As usual, I put suggestions for accommodation, to be near the railway station, then find I still had to pay forty or fifty dollars to travel by taxi. I seem to be getting robbed blind, by the internet searches; every time I travel to a new place. However, once I visited a town knowing the layout better, for the second visit. I found a place for dinner and finished my book, had a shower and went to bed, after an exhausting day travelling. You would've thought I'd slept well, with the three-hour time difference, as it was 9:00pm local time, but I didn't. The traffic noise, a constant level, all night long, as the motel was located on a main road. Ear plugs work, to a certain extent, before finally the exhaustion takes over. My next travel day would be massive, leaving the motel at 6:00am and not arriving, on the central coast, until about 7:00pm.

I booked a cab, arrived at the train station ahead of schedule; waiting for ages for the transfer bus; struggling with my luggage and a coffee, from the café. This was one of those instances, when I felt uneasy, with my location. I had my bags stacked on top of each other; definitely sure a dodgy looking man, noticed where I'd placed my wallet, after I paid for my coffee. Sitting in a glass-walled room; every time I looked in this man's direction, he was looking at me. When I needed to go to the bathroom, I took everything with me; and when I returned, the man had disappeared. There's no way, in hell I'd leave my luggage, unattended, in a train station. Luckily, the handicapped toilets had enough room, to take your luggage in with you.

The bus arrived and transferred me to the interstate-train-station, connecting passengers, travelling the length of the west coast. The early morning atmosphere, of the city was breathtaking, with the sun coming up over the river system. The city was coming alive at 7:00am on an autumn morning; as the bus drove around the city, calling into the popular hotels for pickups. I enjoyed my tour of the waterfront; with large container ships, as well as smaller craft, heading in all directions. The drive over the bridge was spellbinding, as the sun cast its own golden uniqueness, on the perfect day.

TRAINS AND AUTOMOBILES

I waited an hour for the train connection; the contents of my bags shuffled, as the maximum weight was fifty-pounds. Once on board the train, I place my gear at my seat, as I explored. The first part of the train journey included barren mountain areas, with livestock and an incredible amount of crops. I noticed a sign, on the side, of the rail line that caught my attention. The sign said "it is like you never left"; I *KNOW* I've been here before; I can just sense it.

The west-coast train connects travellers, from Canada to Mexico; with regular stops, for people to get on or off. With a sleeper-cabin, you enjoy all of the benefits of meals and activities, as you spend three-days travelling the entire west-coast. I liked this particular train because the observation car, had windows the entire length of the car, with seats facing out, to enjoy the scenery.

I spent most of my trip, either in the dining or observation cars, chatting to anyone who'd listen; but also found time alone, to catch up on my journal writings. I wasn't sure why, maybe because it felt familiar; I just love being in this part of California. I was on another new adventure, travelling to a new location, new people to meet, and new challenges.

The train pulled in, on time to Merton, as the cab dropped me downtown; for an immediate departure to Simpson, on the local bus. A young man, Tony helped me, with my luggage, and again when we arrived at Simpson; walking over to a supermarket, waiting the three-hours, before the connection bus, continued onto Cantina. I bought Tony, a drink for helping me, as other passengers waited for the connection; we waited together. Other customers came into the café, we all chatted, including a lady, who locked her keys in the car, waiting for her husband to arrive with the spare keys.

When it was time to go back to the bus station, we all went back together; quickly finding a jacket to keep me warm, as the night air, was quite cool. Finally the bus arrived, as I continued my trip to Cantina; with my backpack on, and two suitcases trailing behind me, I reached the intersection, deciding to turn left, in the hope the hostel, was located up this way. The hill was steep, but not like a mountain; I was just exhausted, without one-ounce of energy, left inside me. Finally I spotted a sign; a welcoming front porch light turned on. Finally here; pushing the doors open, releasing my luggage into a pile on the floor.

My favourite sunset destination

Chapter 16

WEST COAST HOST NO. 9 THE HOSTEL - NOVEMBER

THE ARRIVAL

I let go of the handles of my bags; my backpack straps sliding off my shoulders; without any resistance. I felt like a pack horse, at the end of a long and exhausting journey. Tony greeted me; showing me to my room, where I dumped everything; before I left again, to find dinner. I was rather peeved off, there was no welcome dinner; really surprised no effort was made; to make me feel welcomed. The message, I received, was 'get used to it' as the entire month was like that. Each man for himself!

I walked along the dark streets not knowing *WHERE* I was going; until I spotted the signs, for the supermarket. I should've ordered takeout food, but then, what about breakfast or lunch the next day. Purchasing gluten free bread, milk, coffee, jam and cheese; suffice for a few days; then had to carry them back to the hostel.

After a quick shower and toast for dinner, I collapsed; unconsciously on my bed. Tomorrow, I will look, to see, *WHERE I AM*.

CANTINA

The Pacific coastline of California was full of small sea-side towns; relying financially on the tourist dollar to survive. The town of Cantina was your typical sea side town, plus a retirement destination area; the majority of the population, were aged over sixty-five years.

The east and west villages, were the main business areas, of the town; the east side of town was the oldest, with an incredible amount of antique stores. The western side was newer, with more upscale, modern buildings and shops. The art galleries located in the western village; displayed incredible works of art, from amazing artists. I dreamed, one day I may have a little of the talent, displayed.

The beach side area of Cantina was a magical spot, perfect to watch the sunsets, from a large row of resorts, holiday accommodation and restaurants; all with uninterrupted views, of the ocean. At the southern end of the strip, a car park, accesses the beach and board walk area. For two kilometers; walk along the boardwalk, venture around the rock face, or take the stairs leading down onto the beaches below. Strategically placed benches; verandahs of your motel or restaurant; you had a front row seat, to witness the magic of Mother Nature.

EXPEDITIONS WITH TONY

Tony loved to walk and hike; with volunteers encouraged to join him, in a tour around the area. The first morning at the hostel, after the closure at 10.30am, Tony and I drove up along the coast line, to climb an escarpment; jetlagged, and exhausted, this activity was the last thing I wanted to do. The hill we climbed was almost vertical; my time was thirty-minutes, with Tony's record climb, at seventeen-minutes. Boy oh boy, the climb was definitely worth the effort; when I felt like singing 'the hills are alive'; completing a three-sixty-degree spin, to observe the incredible coastline. We continued the tour of the area, including the pier and wild life watching. Tony and I both loved coffee; stopping at the local coffee shop. I walked back to the hostel via some markets, discovering a crystal stall; purchasing an opal; in its raw state, with a beautiful bright centre, you discover, when placed under a light.

The Eldorado Reserve, a five-hundred acres parcel of land, had been donated to the community. This area was a popular destination, with tracks linking all parts of the township, for residents and visitors to hike, bike and explore. On the second morning at the hostel, Tony and I headed out to explore the reserve. I was speechless, when I first discovered the trees in the forests; with lichen growing all over the branches. These trees were a perfect place, to film a scary movie, and not a chance in hell, I'd visit here, after dark. The walk, over to the ocean, was a beautiful way to spend a Sunday, as I walked back to the hostel, via the beach and villages.

The reason for the explorations; was gaining information and insight, to share with guests, about the area. The ocean-front boardwalk links the residences of Barton, on the southern end of the reserve, with the beach. This walk was a popular spot, with the ocean having a calming effect, on anyone who visits. Many seats were placed along the pathway; stopping to watch the ocean swells and listening to the sounds of the waves, crashing onto the rocks, on the shore line below.

When Adelia arrived, Tony led us again on a trip around the area, stopping at a waterfall and exploring the large boulders, forming part of the creek bed. Today the waterfall and creek beds were dry, as they only run during the wet winters. Richard one of the guests, staying over at the hostel, joined us, on our expedition; stopping at the pier café for a late lunch. Ordering a salad with sweet potato fries, there was enough food, left over for my dinner and lunch for the next two days.

HOSTEL

The hostel offers budget accommodation; with six private rooms, and one dorm sleeping four people, also two staff rooms; one doubling as a guest room.

Tony's room was located, in the loft, of the church next door. Tony has been the manager/operator for almost twelve months; using volunteers or interns, for servicing the rooms and helping with the operation of the hostel. Norma, an older lady, travels here on a regular basis as a relief manager, while Tony has time off.

Anne, the owner of the property, converted the old church rectory, into a hostel, many years before. Entering the front foyer; on the ground floor, the dorm room was located on your right; the stair case, on your left, leads up to the second floor. Passing through a narrow hallway, you enter the main living area, consisting of a dining room table, arm chairs and bench seats. This room has two large uncovered windows allowing the sun to shine in and warm up the area. A toilet, snuck in a closet under the stairs, perfect for guests, staying in this area. *I thought it was rather odd, but there you go.*

A private bedroom was located, through an access door, in the corner of this room, also with a large window allowing natural light to enter the room. A large, open plan kitchen was located directly behind, the living room. This room runs the full width of the building, with enough space for many people using the kitchen, at the same time. The kitchen had all of the necessary appliances, such as fridges, freezers, stove, oven, microwave and dishwasher; and heaps of cups, plates, pot and pans.

Directly behind the kitchen, two staff bedrooms and a shower were located. The first volunteer bedroom was to the left; with a single bed, the room, almost the size of a dog box. But you know what? It's private, lots of shelves to store your stuff on; a glass door, accesses the outside world, with a blind; opening to the stars, visible during the night. Oh and the best part was the Wi-Fi device, located on the shelf, above the bed, with no complaints about internet service. If I had a choice; between this tiny space, and the space I shared, with five other girls at the horse farm, this space wins hands down.

The other room, on the right hand side of the corridor; I believed, was the best room in the house. Firstly, the toilet and wash basin, located in the ensuite; secondly, a huge queen size bed; thirdly, the high ceiling, exposed beams, and loft space, located directly above the bed. The south facing room, allows natural light, to shine into the room, through small glass window panes, and a glass door allows direct access, to the outside world.

I spent two weeks, in the single bedroom, before I moved over to this room, appreciating the toilet, and sleeping in a queen size bed.

The shower located, at the back of the ground floor; was created by Anne, out of broken tiles, glass beads; in fact anything, to cover every surface of the room. I loved spending time in this room, hoping some of the creativity, would enter the soles of my feet, to infect me with inspiration. (*Hopefully nothing else!!*).

The second floor comprised three bedrooms and two bathrooms; every room a different size and shape, contouring to the shape of the roof. The smaller bathroom only had a toilet and a hand basin, with the other bathroom having a shower, toilet and hand basin. The toilets had lid-sinks installed, which was; a hand basin placed on the lid of the toilet. Flushing the toilet; clean water comes out of the spout, into the lid-sink, as you wash your hands. The water then runs into the cistern to fill the toilet, with no extra water needed to wash your hands. What a brilliant idea, invented in Japan and installed in all three bathrooms at the hostel.

Two cupboards, located in the hallway, were used for the storage of bedding and towels. My favourite room was number three, with the queen size bed mattress, a meter off the floor, reminding me of the 'grandma's feather bed' song.

The hostel; a former rectory, was located in a quiet street, in the eastern part of town. The large flat parcel of land had a church constructed, on one side of the hostel; and a small cottage was on the other. The cottage was rented out, to a local family; with the church, used by an alternative, religious group. The front area of the cottage was landscaped as a volley ball court, slash yoga space. A neat little garden, bordering the white picket fence, added to the charm of the property. At the front of the hostel a small gate and paved walkway accessing the porch; where a swing seat, sat under a pergola, covered with a flowering vine. A picnic table sat off to the side, of the path, soaking up the warm sunshine. At the back of the hostel, a steep, almost vertical, terraced hill included two buildings. The first building was a storage area; not understanding why, anyone, would store anything up there, as the steps were so dangerous to navigate.

The second building was affectionately known as 'the enchanted tool shed', used as an overflow accommodation for volunteers. The one-room building had French doors, leading onto a small balcony. Glass panels on two, of the other walls, added light into the room. The building was constructed using up-cycled, off-cut recycled boards, metal sheeting and any other available products. A large queen size bed; an eclectic array of furniture; and wall art decorated the space. There's no power or insulation; with the room cold as ice, but in summer, the perfect place to escape the heat.

The stairs, to the enchanted tool shed, were lit up, each night, by a row of fairy lights. I suppose that's why it had claimed that name. Currently the 'shed' was used by Ronan and Kate; a young couple, heading to Hawaii for a holiday. Both Kate and Ronan worked at other jobs, contributing a nominated amount of hours, working at the hostel; in exchange for renting the tool shed. I was replacing Kate and Ronan's shifts, while they were away, for three weeks.

The washing machine was located, behind the single staff room; with the clothes line, set up on a terraced deck behind the church.

THE WORK

After all the hard work, at my previous volunteer homes; do you think I'd earnt a cushy job? Sometimes I really had to question 'what was I thinking'; when I started this adventure. Yes I had to work, in exchange for food and board. Somewhere in the translation, never realising, how hard, the work would be.

My turn had finally arrived, working at the hostel; was nothing like I'd ever experienced before. The work involved sitting at the dining table, between eight and ten-thirty in the morning, and between five and nine at night, checking people in and out of their accommodation. During the opening hours, while you're waiting, for something to happen, you're bored out of your brain.

The deal for volunteering at the hostel involved working four hours per day; in exchange for your bed and breakfast. Payment of thirty-five dollars, each week, helped with other costs. The evening shift started at 4:00pm; with the washing removed from the line, folded and placed in storage. Attending to and action any messages on the phone; check the bathrooms; turn on the lights, close windows and unlock the front door at 5:00pm. With the doors unlocked, wait to greet guests, before processing their registration, using the electronic online system. Each guest has a guided tour; given an explanation of the house rules and regulations; hand them keys and finally show them to their rooms. At 8.30pm, the self-serve breakfast's set up in the kitchen; a quick check around the hostel, making sure it was clean, tidy and secure. 9:00pm on the dot, the front doors are locked. I'd usually collapse from exhaustion or fall into a book.

The morning shift begins at eight o'clock; with a waiting game, for people to have breakfast and check out. The first duty involved checking the complex, for any problems or early check outs. Check out time was ten-thirty, at the latest, with some guests, wearing down my patience, leaving at ten-twenty-nine. The hostel guests, staying longer, weren't able to access the hostel, during the day; otherwise a staff member would've to be present all day. The morning shift finished, whenever all of the rooms had been cleaned, changed the bedding, cleaned the bathrooms and vacuum the entire area. Hanging out the washing, plus clean and tidy the kitchen, empty the dishwasher and put away the dishes. When guests left early, I changed their bedding, with the laundry started *BEFORE* ten-thirty, which helped with my plans for escaping.

I did more than my fair share of split shifts, working both morning and night, which was annoying; with only a few hours off, during the middle of the day. Being at the hostel both morning and night, also added up, to be more than four-hours worked, each day. The main purpose of working each shift, you did whatever was needed. The hostel certainly didn't buck the system, like some of the other places I visited, but rules had to be followed, to be fair for everyone.

The first couple of night shifts drove me insane, as I couldn't leave the living room, because someone had to be there to greet the guests. I'd mentioned to Tony about how slow it was; asking a million questions about how the hostel advertises. For example: whether potential guests booked online or through local organisations. I started googling the hostel, on some websites to see 'where' they're placed. I found one website, where the hostel, was mentioned on page forty; which doesn't work very well, for getting bums in beds. I mentioned to Tony, I'd write a review online; since I was staying here, to see what happens. Over the month of November, over one hundred people viewed my spiel.

Tony's mind opened up to what I was saying, about ways of bumping our statistics; without any financial outlay. For example, I mentioned the local chamber-of-commerce; which Tony was a current member. I couldn't find any reference, to the hostel, on any of their online services.

I could see it, in his eyes; Tony was getting excited, as a new face book account was set up. A competition was created; for anyone booking into the hostel, were being offered a 10% discount. Tony had visited the business centre, with some brochures printed up. The guests could qualify for the discount, in a couple, of different ways. The first idea; if the guest was a published author, had a copy of their book, and in a short video, told us about the book. The second idea; was to perform, recite a poem or sing, with Tony downloading these images; to the face book account. Well I don't know about anyone else, but I *LOVED* this idea. It was a hoot, as the guests performed for us; poets, musicians and even a band from Europe entertained us.

Tony arrived at work one morning; announcing he'd *PAID* for an internet advertisement. I couldn't believe he forked out money, for this service. I was so excited, when two days later, a group of men, travelling north, used the app to find us, paying for two rooms, which covered the cost of the advertising. Whoaooooo!!!

One of my first mornings at the hostel, I decided to give a couple of walls, a wipe over, while waiting for guests to leave. I discovered the wall, was layered with a quarter-of-an- inch of dust, which I believe, equated to about five-years of neglect. I made a commitment, of cleaning every inch of the building; with four-weeks to complete the task. Each day, on the morning shift, I'd pull out all of the furniture, take down the curtains and wash everything from one particular room. Over that four-week period, I was able to clean, ninety-percent, of the interior of the building.

One morning in the living room, Adelia (the other volunteer) and I had a special project, to complete. I asked Tony for a big ladder, to clean the high walls. When Tony walked into the living room, a little while later, he couldn't believe the mess. The problem with doing a 'spring clean' was it all had to be perfect by 5:00pm, when the doors opened again. I had the pictures off the walls; furniture was placed in the middle of the room, as we cleaned *EVERYTHING*.

The stone fire place was covered in a thick layer of dust, placing old towels on the floor. I started at the top of the chimney, with a bucket of water, a wet cloth and a small banister brush. I proceeded to wash down the stones, with the transformation unbelievable; with the centrepiece of the living room, now shining in absolute glory. Tony was so impressed, by our hard work, he drove both Adelia and I to the smokehouse, shouting us a taco.

When Norma, the relief manager, arrived, entering the foyer of the hostel; she 'knew' something had changed. YES 'hurricane Bella' in reverse. Norma had tears in her eyes, when she learnt what I'd accomplished, since I started working here. There was definitely a different aura, when you walked in the front door; actually smelling fresh and clean.

I believe my cleaning washed away the bad energies of people, who've visited here. People leave behind a little piece of themselves, which can make a place toxic. I believe any project or activity, completed with love in your heart, replaces the bad vibes with a loving energy. I enjoyed cleaning up the hostel, with pride and love; my service to Tony and Norma.

The last week of my stay at the hostel, a group of friends, rented out the entire complex; my initial plan, was to have the hostel, spick and span, for their stay. On the day before the group's arrival, I enlisted the help of Adelia and Norma, to finish off the kitchen and down stairs bathroom. The stair well; a height of two storeys; was the only job left to do; by a spider-man and not this little cookie. I believe I gave the job, my utmost attention; proud of actually working during my shifts, instead of just sitting around doing nothing.

Tony, your 'typical' male, didn't see what a mess the place was in. All he wanted was tidy rooms; clean sheets; the bedding 'penny bouncing' straight. That's all good and dandy, if the place was already clean. The part I didn't get, about his roster system; there's no actual cleaning of the building, besides the guest's rooms, washing and vacuuming. The volunteers were there to help; getting them to at least work an hour each day cleaning windows, sweeping paths, cleaning walls etc. If I hadn't put in the extra work; feeling my contribution; by my own standard, wouldn't have been fully recognised and appreciated.

Tony has this over-the-top, anal compulsive obsession, with 'hair' in the bathrooms, especially the showers. I've never seen anyone this obsessed; with Tony ordering us, to collect, even one tiny minuscule hair, still in the shower or on the floor. What the......?

Each volunteer was encouraged, to create something unique, as a memento of their visit. I painted seven little pictures, for the front of each guest's room's door. Painting local spots, like the lighthouse, the historic cemetery, the cliffs, beaches, sunsets and of course the house cat.

I certainly enjoyed my duties as check-in chick; meeting many people, from around the world, bikers and hikers, mostly travelling down the 'one', at this time of year. The guests started their journey in Canada and would finish at the Mexico border; with some guests planning to travel into South America. My favourite guest George, a Canadian man of about thirty-five, chatted after he checked in, telling me about his trip so far. This was his story.

George woke up one morning, deciding he needed a change; deciding to travel by bike to Mexico. He ate breakfast, went shopping; purchasing a bike and all of the necessary gear. By the next morning, George had packed the bike; without any training or preparation, started pedalling. George quickly discovered how unfit he was, with a few challenges during the first week. The biggest challenge, he found was sleeping on a mat, ten millimeters thick; wasn't the most comfortable night's sleep. When accommodation was available, he checked in for a good night's sleep; however, along the 'one', in the isolated places, the thin mat was used, when booking into the camp sites.

The following morning at the hostel, I was up close and personal with George, when he asked me to spray suntan lotion onto him, as he was riding shirtless today. *What THE …. Can I come too? I definitely wanted some of this.* I savoured the moment as any hot blooded woman would. *What was I thinking, he's at least ten years too young for me, but a girl can dream.*

ON THE JOB TRAINING

Offering my services for a job, sometimes a few things needed to be explained; I'm talking about technology, involved with registering guests. Almost having a heart attack when realising, I'd be using an iPad, to register guests, make reservations and take payments. My head started spinning, with Tony leaning over my shoulder, to ensure I was doing it correctly. Well the stress was enough, for anyone to fail miserably, which I did; practice makes perfect; finally working out the system.

Tony traveled to Simpson, to pick up Adelia (the new volunteer) from the bus, unfortunately the bus was late arriving, which left me on my own, to run the show. Of course, a full-house of guests, were arriving that night, and the pressure was on, for me to perform. I completed the check-in procedures, and when Tony arrived, he sorted out the problems, I'd encountered. Lucky for me, the pay was good; otherwise I might get the sack. (There's no paycheck involved - just bed and breakfast☺)

SCARECROWS

I arrived at the beginning of November; with the scarecrows, associated with Halloween, still on display, around the town. I enjoyed walking along the streets taking photos of them. My favourite display appeared in front of the Catholic Church. The scene was a group of nuns and a priest forming a band, playing different instruments. When I captured the scene on my camera the sun's rays added an interesting element to the photo. *I used this photo as inspiration for a painting, for a friend, in Canada over winter. The paper-mache masks of the band were perfect for my cubism project in art class. See Art Group in Chapter 21 for the story.*

HUMMINGBIRDS

On my expeditions through the village, I entered a store, similar to a house and garden shop. This shop formed the front of a collection of shops; creating a little market square, with ten different businesses involved. Once you left the first shop, the area opened up, into an outdoor paved courtyard with seats, fairy lights AND hummingbirds. How amazing are these tiny little creatures. As I wondered around the shops I found a beautiful book about a couple, who'd moved to a new house, discovering a resident hummingbird family, living on their verandah. The couple set up a camera, to record the journey of the mother hummingbird; from building the nest to the final birthing, of the babies and beyond. I thought my mum would enjoy the story, so I purchased the book.

When my mum was in hospital, she took the book with her; to read it properly as it's quite a lengthy book. One morning her doctor noticed the book, when he arrived for his consultation. The doctor picked the book up, took a seat and read the entire book before he placed it back down. He was speechless, by the incredible story, of the hummingbird's journey. I found the book online and my mum gave her doctor his own copy, to thank him for his care.

MY NEW FRIENDS – SHERRY, ADELIA AND DOLLY

During my first couple of days at the hostel, Kate (the other volunteer's) dad Mike was staying at the hostel as a guest. Kate's mum, Sherry, came over with dinner for the family. As soon as Sherry entered the room, I felt an immediate connection; with Sherry's friendly and welcoming aura. We all chatted over dinner, with Sherry suggesting we spend time together.

The next time I met up with Sherry, we stayed out past midnight, drinking cocktails and visiting every bar in town. That night I visited Sherry's home, to discover, her one bedroom house, had amazing views, over the Pacific Ocean; including incredible opportunities, to lose yourself in the night skies.

Sherry was a few years older than me, with three children; Kate was her youngest. Sherry worked with the education department; and after her separation from Mike; found a little house to rent, by the ocean. Initially, Kate and Ronan came up to visit Sherry; loved the town so much, they moved here as well, creating a home at the hostel. Sherry spends most nights having dinner at the Mexican. To catch up, we'd meet there, or she'd come up to the hostel, if I was working. We needed each other's support, as Sherry was bruised; emotionally and mentally hurt, by different people in her life; coping the best she could; doing what we have to, to survive.

Dolly was aged nineteen-years a stunningly, beautiful young woman; tall, slim, with long blonde hair. She's staying in Cantina with her aunty, while studying at college. Dolly was very inexperienced in life; having lived with her parents, in a small country town. That's why, Sherry, became friends with her; as a mother figure, to guide and advise her. Dolly worked at Los Cantinas, as a waitress, and a bartender, at Blanches.

After spending time with Adelia, I now know, why men, love French women. Our nights at the clubs were interesting, because of how many men, wanted to talk and dance with Adelia. She was your typical French woman, even though, she was only aged twenty-one, Adelia had this unique sophistication about her; stunningly beautiful, with a wardrobe of amazing French clothes. Everything about Adelia spelled *FRENCH*.

COUCH SURFING

I mentioned to Sherry, I was moving, into the enchanted tool shed, for one night, as the hostel was booked out. Sherry offered me her couch, if I needed somewhere to stay. Watching the sunset, I rang Sherry about whether her couch was free, as the tool shed was freezing. We enjoyed a lovely dinner, before I went back to the hostel, to collect a couple of things to spend the night, on the couch. Sherry and I spent most of the night talking, and the rest of the night I was spellbound by the stars.

Sherry left for work at 6:00am, dropping me off at the highway intersection. On the walk back to the hostel, I enjoyed looking at the houses, with wild deer, roaming the streets, looking for food. A large set of stairs, linking up with the town centre, were located on an almost vertical embankment, near the Tall Timbers Resort; today glad to be walking down the steps and not up them. It'd be an amazing workout, to walk up and down, the stairs, each day. *(You reckon).*

Arriving back at the hostel, the guests were still having breakfast as I joined them, before starting the morning shift; changing beds and cleaning everything, ready for the new guests tonight. It felt like Groundhog Day, doing the same thing, over and over again every day. Luckily the hostel was challengingly different, with new guest, arriving each day.

THE CRYSTAL PALACE

On one of my first days in town, I set off to explore the town a little more. The walk through the town takes about forty minutes, walking down the left hand side of the road, until the last shop, returning back to the hostel via the right side. I spotted a beautifully dressed mannequin, sitting on a little verandah, at a table, with tarot cards in her hands. The mannequin, dressed like a gypsy, was sitting outside a shop, called the Crystal Palace. The colour purple, first caught my eye, before I realised the shop, was a healing centre; offering massages, readings and meditations. Brochures, in a little holder, by the door, were available. I love all things 'mysterious', planning to check online, to see what's on offer, at this beautiful little shop.

THE READING

I walked back over to the shop, a few more times, before the doors to the crystal palace were opened to finally meet Linda, the owner of the centre. I suppose the easiest thing, would've been to make an appointment, however in the end, everything worked out just fine. Linda was sitting in her little room, with a spare hour, before her next appointment, so I was able to have a reading immediately.

The first question Linda asked was "what was your name" and I replied "Thomas or Pearce" and Linda answered "neither name was right". *Thomas was my maiden name and Pearce my married name.*

I asked "because I'd change it again?"

Linda answered 'yes but it'd take some time, for that someone special, to find me; after being settled and nested first. Surround myself with all of the things I love and he'll find me. Stop looking for him, because he's at least, twelve months away. *(Yeah right – I'm still waiting five years later; because I'm still not divorced or settled.)*

Linda says 'Clear out, all of the negative emotions, after the divorce and settlement, before moving on; to grow into the person I want to be".

Mentioning finances; Ricky would support me financially. I also asked about my health and she said she couldn't see any health issues. Asking about my weight; and how to reduce and maintain it. Linda mentioned the water glass method, using the same principles with food. Bless the food, asking for the nutritious elements, to restore my body, disposing of everything else, for a healthy and trim body. Sounds like a great plan.

Linda mentioned I had to be complete in myself; because my new man wouldn't complete me. We both needed to be complete, in our own sense, so when we meet; we're just two complete people travelling along a path together. He'd become an addition to my life, not a co-creator.

Linda mentioned I'm also very intuitive; discussing my two instances, when I didn't listen to my intuition; with the motorbike rider *(in Chapter 9 – A life has been taken)* and the bar *(Chapter 12 – the Dream Sequence)*. Linda said, now I'm aware of my own intuitive powers, I wouldn't make the same mistakes again. In future, I'd pay more attention; listening to what the little voices, in my head, were saying.

Linda could see me, with a little studio; using my intuitive practice, some multi-layered/textured creative pieces, selling jewellery, using tarot cards and crystals, and serving cups of tea. *Surround myself with all of this creativity at home; with my open garden and having a little craft shop.*

RHYTHM DANCING

I was interested in attending a few events, happening at the centre. The first one was a workshop being held on a Sunday afternoon; arriving at the annex, of the crystal palace, meeting Sally, who conducted the workshop. The workshop was based around the rhythm dances; I was so excited, thinking we were working with ribbons, when we danced. Rhythm not ribbon – Dah!!! I'm always open to new experiences, just going with the flow. The rhythm dancing was based on a holistic approach to life.

I just wish I lived, in a place like this, where I'd study, practice and share my life with other like minded people. There's so much to learn about WHO we were; I want to experience it all. Living in this sacred place, now, was the perfect place for me.

The afternoon session started, as the women gathered, in a little circle, introducing ourselves. Sally had tears in her eyes, telling us she'd waited, a very long time, to find a place, to hold classes; sharing her skills, with other women. Sally was a writer, a book editor, and creator of her own tarot cards.

Sally mentioned a phrase, at the beginning, of each class: "show up, don't show off". All participants started the first session, barefoot, dancing in our own space, to the first song. Dance the way, the music makes you feel, allowing your emotions to surface; memories of sadness, happiness, anger and hurt. Some of the women were banging their fists against the walls in anger, while others were lying in a foetal position on the floor crying.

I really love to dance, in my own unique way, just moving to the beat of the music. I really love to dance around the house with a liqueur and some good music playing. 'This' music was very different, from what I normally listen to, turning inward for reconnection, with no head banging, crying or outbursts of anger; twirling around the room, eyes closed, hoping I didn't bump into anyone.

The second session involved the entire group, bouncing a large balloon around the room. This activity released our adult thinking, returning to our childhood; filled with fun and games. We all laughed, as the balloon came our way; hitting the balloon, to stop it from landing on the floor. This exercise was much harder than first thought. The time spent with the balloon, relaxed us, evolving into our third session; which entailed journaling and drawing in our notebooks, expressing our feelings, allowing whatever emotions needing to be expressed; be expressed, in whatever form.

I've done this exercise many times; since that day to discover, no matter what's written or drawn, it was perfect in every way. I'm such a control freak, so doing these sorts of exercises allows my creativity to be called to action.

I really enjoyed the afternoon with the women, as I meandered my way, back to the hostel at a snail's pace. I wanted to savour the moment, before I had to face people again. I find it difficult after I've been soul searching, to then return to normal life, where everything was the same, but you're now different, on so many levels.

The dance classes were conducted three mornings, each week at 8:00am and when I wasn't on the morning roster, I was there. Music was such a powerful tool, enjoying the connection with this little group. Sherry came to one class with me, as she enjoyed music and loved to dance, with the music touching her soul in a deep and painful way. The class was for you to show up, for yourself, and the whole time, I was worried about Sherry, as she was upset. I introduced Sherry to Linda and Sally; both offering her counselling and meditations, helping with her healing journey.

MEDITATION

Adelia and I attended one of Linda's meditation sessions together. This was Adelia's first time attending a guided meditation session; both of us enjoying the experience. Linda was kind enough, to drive us back, to the hostel, when we were finished.

SIMPSON

The first time I arrived here, off the train, I was amazed to discover bike racks were attached on the front and back of the buses. The passengers loaded and locked, their own bike, into the rack, before they hopped on the bus. When the passenger arrived at their destination, they grabbed their bike and off they went. When the bike racks weren't being used, they compacted against the body of the bus.

There's a public bus service from Cantina to Simpson each day; travelling at least once a week, on a five-dollar-all-day-bus-pass. Each time I arrived in Simpson, I'd walk down different roads, exploring the town, before arriving at the harbour. I found a fantastic coffee place, 'Dolphin Café, serving the best white-chocolate-mocha, I've ever tasted, using white chocolate powder. My days off were spent in Simpson; from about 11:00am to 6:00pm, with enough time to relax and write in my journal.

The café was always the first stop, spending a couple of hours, or if the weather was nice, I'd hang out in the park.

The Simpson town-ship was located on a river, connecting directly with the Pacific Ocean. The wharf and harbour area, were the main tourist areas of the town. A marina, boat moorings and fishing boat fleets were located, a little upriver, from the tourist precinct. At the mouth of the river, on the northern side a massive rock, accessible by road, had two-thousand car park spaces. From the car park, you access the northern beaches, walking up along the coast line, if you wanted to. The whole area was popular with board riders, and beach goers, with a large expanse of sandy beaches. The road continues on, past the rock, towards the mouth of the river, where another car park was located, with access to a rock wall, popular with fishermen.

Across the mouth of the river, a large rock wall protects the harbour, from the direct swells, of the ocean. On the ocean side, there's a lovely beach; inside the harbour, the waters were calm and protected.

The sea lions have a pontoon, anchored in the middle of the harbour, where they all clammier on to rest; making a hell of a racket. I certainly wouldn't moor my boat near them, if I wanted a good night's sleep.

The harbour was lined with wall to wall shops; connected by a dock system similar to Seal Bay in Alaska. The boardwalk follows the river around, discovering everything, your little heart desires. The restaurants serve fresh seafood with cold beer and cocktails☺; cafés selling a wide selection of your favourite ice creams flavours. A salt-water taffy shop, displayed a selection of merry-go-round type horses, in all the beautiful colours of the rainbow. Fashion and souvenirs shops galore, tempt you, to purchase, a memory of your trip. The most amazing shop I found was a building, filled with millions of shells; different sizes and colours, from all around the world. The aquarium located on the harbour; allowing visitors to observe and be entertained by all of the marine animals.

Each time I reached the harbour I'd walk in a different direction so that I'd see everything and then some☺. I walked along the river, discovering the area where all of the fishing boats are docked. A large table was set up, for the fishermen to clean their catch, and dispose of the carcass, into the large industrial bins; smelling *BAD*; beyond belief. The most amazing sight, I witnessed, were the hundreds of grey pelicans, waiting by the bins, for fresh food to eat. I captured a few photos of the pelicans as I looked around.

Along the boardwalk, businesses offered ocean cruises for whale watching; stand up paddle boards and kayaks; available for you to discover, the delights of the area.

One afternoon after I'd finished my early dinner; walking along the dock, watching people, on the water with the stand-up paddleboards. As they paddled in the water, they entered an area, where the sun, was setting directly behind them. I took a few photos of the family and kept walking along the boardwalk, capturing the boats with the amazing sunset colours behind them. After a little while, I noticed the people, from the paddle boards, walking up the ramp. I told them I could email them a copy of the photos, if they wanted me to. So that's what I did. I hope this added, an extra highlight, of their afternoon out on the harbour at Simpson.

I loved strolling along the board walk, occasionally the ruckus of the sea lions, could be heard, as they wrestled for space on the rocks, under the board walk. The harbour was the place to be, for an early dinner, while enjoying a beautiful sunset. The afterglow of dusk, once the sun has gone down, this was my favourite time, with these photos, even more spectacular, because of the reflections on the water.

I love how the clouds turn into indescribable colours of the rainbow, as the sun disappears into the morning, for the other side of the world. Luckily the sunsets, were early, at this time of the year, because it allowed me, enough time to walk back to the bus station, before the six o'clock departure.

With Adelia during my last week; walking along the marina area, we noticed a man painting a large mural. We stopped to look at the mural, chatting with the man who was painting it. A rally meeting was being held, to protest the seismic testing in the area. The mural's size was about four-metres-high and eight-metres-long, with newspaper articles, about the seismic testing, used in the background, behind the ocean scene. The mural was constructed of separate boards; being auctioned that weekend, to raise money, for the group. The local council had given the man permission, to display and paint the boards, in public; and removed prior to the auction, on that Saturday morning.

LOS CANTINAS RESTAURANT

If you didn't know already, California was full of Mexicans and yes there're some great restaurants. Los Cantinas was a great place to hang out, *BECAUSE* they had live bands and made fantastic cocktails. I'm not much of a Mexican food lover, because I've never really had the opportunity to try out the menu; with the wheat, soy, and vegetarian options, *WHAT* do I order.

It was a Sunday afternoon, heading towards the beach for the sunset. The time was about three o'clock, leisurely strolling through town, via the shops. Reaching the intersection, of the main street, I heard music drifting up from the restaurant. I couldn't believe the song 'I come from a land down under' was playing. My theme song, I think it's everyone's theme song, when you're an Australian, travelling overseas, *BECAUSE* most bands play it in pubs and clubs.

Instead of turning right, I crossed the street, to where a band was playing, out on the back deck. There was a good crowd, with lots of people dancing; as I guessed Sherry would be there, but I couldn't see her. I stood at the gates to the deck, looking around, until the song finished; turning around, I started to walk away, when I heard an unmistakable voice, scream out my name. *BELLA!* Of course it's Sherry, dragging me back onto the deck, for an afternoon of toooooo many cocktails, toooooo many bars; arriving back at the hostel at midnight. Tony and Adelia were worried about me, when I never arrived home. I didn't think I had to account for my where-about's to anyone, but realised, maybe I should've let them know, about my change of plans. I gave Tony my mobile number, for future reference should he need to ring me.

BLANCHES

Blanches, was a bar, located in the main street of town, about a five minute stumble, back up the hill to the hostel. Most weeks Sherry, Adelia, Dolly and I would go there, for a couple of drinks, because it was relatively quiet, enjoying the ambience, of sitting at the bar and chatting.

I'm not your average drinker, with my usual drinks being liqueur based cocktails and shots. I ordered a special shot one night, however none of the bar staff had heard of it. The 'good' name for the drink was a 'cowboy'; consisting of scotch, coffee and orange liqueurs layered into a shot glass. The real name for the drink was 'cock sucking cowboy', a definite hit with the girls. Of course, you need quite a few, to make a difference to your state of mine. I didn't like to mix drinks, so that was my drink for the night; with the scotch liqueur I drank straight, unless we went for cocktails as well.

One night Tony, Adelia, and I all went down to Blanches, for karaoke, as Tony loves to perform. Tony sang atrociously, as usual; plugging our ears while he sang. We all had a blast arriving back to the hostel after midnight.

Blanches had a jukebox, and on my final night in town, we put through a heap of money, listening to *OUR* music, while letting our hair down. The lighting was low and dark, as I hid on the dance floor, blending into the shadows, while enjoying myself. Dutchy, the owner of Blanches shared our shots, spending time on the dance floor, partying with our little crowd of party goers. Dutchy loved the fact; the young girls were dancing, becoming an attraction for men, who came into the bar, to look at the pretty girls. The men stayed, spending money on drinks, so everyone's happy. I knew the men were looking at Adelia and Dolly and ignoring us oldies, which was fine with me.

OPEN MIKE NIGHT

One Sunday night, Tony was rostered off, to organise the open mike night at the local brewery. At the hostel, I'd been listening to Tony, practice during the afternoons, and his music was definitely, not my cup of tea. IF you listened to the words only, not how it sounded, you would've liked the song. Adelia and I were on duty, that night, to check in the guests, then at exactly 9:00pm we had the placed secured, and basically ran the ten minutes to the brewery. As Adelia and I entered the brewery, Tony was in his element, performing on stage, with the crowd applauding him, when he finally stood up and bowed.

As the crowd clapped and cheered, (*rather over-the-top, I thought*), Tony had a smile, on his face, like a chess-shire cat. The expression on his face was almost indescribable, as if had he just won an Oscar. Tony stood on the stage, proud and confident, lapping up the applause.

At that precise, moment in time; I discovered a very important message, about LIFE. The lesson I learnt just now; it doesn't matter how good, you are, at singing or dancing or painting or writing. The most important factor; was your belief in yourself, without worrying, about what other people think. Just do it and have the time of your life.

MAY I HAVE A CAFÉ MOCHA, VODKA, VALIUM, LATTE TO GO PLEASE?

I have seen this sign, in quite a few different coffee shops and market places. Yes please, I want and need one of these, each morning, to get me through the day.

The coffee was toooo good at a couple of the local cafes. This daily treat, was one of the contributing factors, why I gained a few extra kilos, during my stay at the hostel.

THE WINERY

Tony asked Adelia and I whether we wanted to visit the wineries for lunch. I'm not sure what happened, but we never left the hostel, until nearly midday; with the wineries at least forty minutes drive away. I mentioned to Tony, I had an afternoon workshop, booked in at 2:00pm. Tony decided we only had time to visit one winery, so I said "this one looks good". I'm not much of a wine taster; liking only sweet whites and liqueurs. Entering the tasting rooms, the aura of the building, was calming and welcoming. The feeling; we're amongst old friends, with a definite Italian influence. All three of us paid our five-dollars to taste the wines, while chatting to an attractive lady who served us.

The winery was started by a man, who worked in the film industry, back in the fifties. The farm; was his weekend getaway, where he and his wife created the vineyard. Recently, their daughter and her husband took over the reins, where a new cellar door, restaurant and outdoor entertaining areas were constructed. The lady server told us, the daughter reinvented a whole new look; changing the label, highlighting a picture of her parents, which they called 'the lovers'.

When the parents were newlyweds, a photo was taken of them, in a beautiful embrace. On their fiftieth-wedding-anniversary, a portrait was commissioned, by a local painter, on behalf of the children, and presented to the parents, as a gift.

I love how a 'picture does say a thousand words' from the poster I have at home. From the expression on their faces, the way their arms are wrapped around each other; their bodies linked. The way they're looking at each other; this was the same passion and belonging, I'm searching for in my partner.

A NEW WARDROBE

I decided, one day, while walking down town, I needed some normal clothes for the Caribbean and Canada, as my volunteer days were almost over. One of the little dress shops, near the hostel, had a sale, with items placed on the discount rack. Usually these racks had nothing that fitted me, but this was my lucky day; purchasing some lovely outfits, to help me enjoy the rest of my travels. I'd lost fifteen kilos of weight, since beginning my trip; excited about my new trimmer body, new hair style; and with the new clothes, I was feeling more like myself again.

I was happy with myself, for the first time, in a long time, and my confidence had grown; feeling mentally, emotionally and physically stronger, than I had, in a very long time. With friends like Adelia, Dolly and Sherry, I enjoyed socialising, as I explored California. Finding 'myself'' at the same time, was definitely a bonus.

THANKSGIVING DINNER

Since everyone was going to be away over the Thanksgiving holiday, we arranged a celebration dinner, earlier in the week. Each staff member invited their friends along, plus any guests who were staying that night. Everyone was asked to bring a plate of food to share with the group. Sherry, Dolly, Adelia, Tony, Norma plus a couple of young men made up the guests for the dinner party.

I cooked up a storm with roast pork and vegetables, with so much food. The two young male guests contributed to the evening, by purchasing a dessert pie and a bottle of wine. A lovely evening giving thanks, for a lovely meal shared together, with my new friends.

ROAD TRIP

For my last week at the hostel, I hired a car, which enabled Adelia and I to tour the Pacific coast line. The hostel was booked out to a private group; Adelia and I received complimentary accommodation at two other hostels, along the coast line.

On the Thursday morning, after finishing our shift, we travelled along the coastline highway '1'. WOW was all I can say - when you see scenes from movies, along the cliffs and windy roads; the coastline was like that. The trip was an amazing adventure, with horrendous traffic, as the long weekend trippers, traffic-jammed the road; plus we tried to stop for photos, as often as we could.

Adelia and I had been praying for perfect weather; we weren't disappointed, witnessing two incredible sunsets. Santa Monte had a boardwalk, right along a ragged cliff face; no more than six-meters from the ocean level. This afternoon was Thanksgiving Day, with a soft breeze blowing; thousands of people out, strolling along the boardwalk, enjoying the peace and calmness of the ocean.

Driving along the road, I felt like I was in one of those movie scenes; where you're in a slow-motion-type sequence. Everyone stops talking; turns to look at your vehicle; to see who's behind the steering wheel. I remember looking at families, with dogs and children; appearing not to have, one care in the world. At this time, at this place, there's peace, love and calmness. The ocean was calm, with a soft swell, heading towards the shore line. The message I received, was that all was forgiven; all's well with the world. The board riders, out on the water, added to this feeling of calmness, as they waited for the perfect wave.

Adelia and I spent an hour enjoying the sand, between our toes, while watching all of the other beach activities. When we first arrived at the beach; I noticed the tide was on the way back in. After a little while I realised a pair of shoes, with a small bag, were going to be washed away, so I moved them up the beach a little, so they didn't get wet. Both Adelia and I didn't notice an arch way, in the large boulder, located about twenty metres out in the water. The man, who owned the shoes and bag, was the photographer, standing in the water, taking photos of the rock. As we turned around to look at the photographer, we noticed the hole; reminding me of a little door. The rock was home to pelicans, seagulls and other birds, preparing themselves, for another quiet night at home.

After about thirty minutes, the photographer returned for his shoes, we chatted for a minute or two. Since the photographer had such a great camera, he offered to take a photo of Adelia and I, which he sent to me via email. Wasn't it amazing, when you do a nice deed for someone?

I learnt; that behind this beach was a large grove of eucalyptus trees; home to millions of monarch butterflies each year. The monarch butterflies travel down from western Canada, to nest and rest here during the winter months. The monarch butterflies from Eastern Canada and North Eastern America travel via a strange route, through the central states to arrive in Mexico, where they invade a whole forest of trees. The story of the monarch butterfly was quite extraordinary, as I learnt about their journey south each year. Sometimes it takes four generations of butterflies to travel from Eastern Canada to Mexico. See more of this story in Chapter 21 – Salmon, Native Birds, Monarch Butterflies.

After the sunset we needed to find the hostel, phoning to get directions; you wouldn't believe it, and it still amazes me; I drove directly there, *WITHOUT ANY 'U' TURNS*. We booked into the hostel, enquiring about restaurants, open for dinner that night. The staff member replied; a free Thanksgiving dinner was available here for all their guests. We were spoilt, with the whole roast turkey and vegetables, with pumpkin pie for dessert. The other hostel guests were from Israel, Canada, Brazil, France, Germany, local Californians, Belgium, Switzerland and of course Australia. About forty people, including staff, celebrated the thanksgiving dinner.

We had non-alcoholic wine and apple cider to toast during the dinner. A couple of the guests, from France, were studying a wine maker's course, at a nearby university. As the hostel had a no alcohol policy, a group of us stood on the footpath, outside the hostel, celebrating this special day; drinking wine out of plastic cups.

After the drinkies on the footpath, the group walked down town to have a look around. Emmanuel and his family owned a winery, in the south of France. Emmanuel, an absolutely stunning man, in his late thirties, I'd describe, as your typical French man. I spent the night chatting to the different people in the group, celebrating the American way of life. We did a sort of 'pub crawl' and found a bar serving cocktails. Adelia and I counted; this was our ninth, consecutive, alcohol intake night. *WE NEED TO DRY OUT*☺.

When Adelia and I searched Emmanuel's winery on the internet, we found an old website with only his parents in the photos.

The following day Adelia and I travelled further along the coastline, which consisted of open beaches, just perfect for board riders. The beaches with its white sand, was perfect for hand holding and sunset walks. Miles and miles of commercial vegetable farms, located right along the coastline, had billion-dollar-views, of the best available land, for the next subdivision. Whoever owned this land was sitting on a gold mine, as the farms continued along the ocean front, for at least twenty miles.

We stopped at a historical lighthouse, which operates as a hostel, with magnificent ocean and sunset views, from the lighthouse keeper's house.

As we headed towards Tremont, for our next overnight stay, I noticed a marina, full of boats; as I needed a break from driving. A road running parallel to the highway, led us towards the mouth of the river, having a brief walk in the sand. As it was almost lunch time, we noticed a restaurant, with a queue of people lined up, out into the car park. Obviously a popular place; as we waited almost an hour, before placing our order, chatting to the people around us. One man asked us how we found this place and I said "we just turned off the highway and pulled up in front". What are the chances of finding, the most popular and award winning seafood restaurant, in the area?

This restaurant certainly knows how to satisfy its customers; with our meals delivered, within fifteen minutes of ordering. My guess, over four hundred people, were dining in the different areas; including the verandah area, where we spotted a table. This area led directly onto the beach via a large sand dune. We couldn't see the ocean, however, a constant stream of people, walked to and from the beach.

I can tell you, the meal was worth the wait, enjoying perfectly cooked fresh fish and chips; as much as I enjoyed watching the other diners enjoying their meals. OMG, some of the meals were big enough, to feed three or four people. The meal sizes were 'so over the top', reminding me of the campaign for 'supersize me'. The meal sizes were totally unnecessary, not to mention unhealthy, to consume that much food, for one person at one time.

We arrived at Tremont at 3:00pm, just in time to find the butterfly park. We had directions of where it was, but with me driving, it was hard to find the tiny, tiny little sign that mentions the butterfly park. I thought it was a building; but instead it was a grove of trees, located in a very small park, with a narrow pathway winding through it. The monarch butterflies stay here over the winter months.

When I visited a butterfly farm; they mentioned the butterflies, would only be active, if there's sunshine. If the weather was a rainy or cloudy day, they're inactive and rested all day.

Walking to the top end of the park; an area where the sun was still shining, a couple of butterflies landed on Adelia's shirt, with a lady commenting, you're very lucky, if a butterfly landed on you. Adelia had two butterflies land on her, so she was very very lucky☺. We kept walking through the park, looking high up in the trees, with a few butterflies flying high up in the air, where the sun was still shining. In the dark shade, of the eucalyptus trees, no butterflies were active, nearer to the ground. I was astounded by how many people, were in the park, looking for the butterflies. I now have another activity to tick off my bucket list.

Eucalyptus trees were found right along the western coastline, reminding me so much of home. A totally unique tree, with unique bark; and the smell of their leaves, was so soothing. The one thing I noticed was the trees were struggling with the environment. The marine layer, basically a cloud mass, comes onto the western coast, during the summer months, staying most of the day. The sun doesn't warm up the atmosphere, beneath the clouds and the weather stays cool. *I met a lady who said, the northern part of California, was warmer in winter, when the marine layer wasn't around as much.* I know a huge variety of eucalyptus, could be planted and not sure why, the correct ones, were not introduced here in California. *I heard recently, eucalyptus plants, have been exported, to every continent, in the world.*

After the butterfly park, I drove to the large cliff face, located on the outskirts of town; astounded by the sunset views. Along with hundreds of other people, we enjoyed the magic of Mother Nature at her finest. We fought for a car parking place, with overcrowded vistas located along the cliff face. It'd be an unbelievable lifestyle to have a house here, with multimillion-dollar-plus-views. At dusk each day, traffic jams occur, as everyone clamours to get the best photos.

As we left the cliffs, after dark, I realised how exhausted I was, as we had been travelling since 8:00am this morning, and now it's after 6:00pm. We found the hostel quite easily, checked into our sixteen-bed mixed-dorm room. It's free, so we didn't mind sharing the room.

After check-in we drove down town; and do you think I could find the freaking supermarket? I was absolutely exhausted, knowing I needed to be horizontal, ASAP. I finally found a car park, which charged ten-dollars for parking. I didn't care, as I wasn't able to keep driving around in circles, to find the supermarket. Adelia and I walked towards the main street, with huge crowds of people everywhere. Of course, it's a Friday night, with the town's official 'turning-on-their-Christmas-tree-lights', were being held. I spotted a café, while Adelia listened to the choir singing. It would've been lovely to stay and be part of the activities; as I think, Adelia would've liked. Adelia had a couple of sleeps in the car, as I drove; she was refreshed, unlike me. *I WAS DEAD.*

On the way back to the car I spotted the supermarket, with Adelia and I both having ice cream for dinner, since we're still full from our late lunch. We bought yoghurt for an early morning snack tomorrow. Back at the hostel, I caught up on my emails, decided to have a shower, and go to bed. I wasn't sure how much sleep, I'd get in the dorm, as from previous experience; people would be coming and going through the dorm, all night long. At 10:00pm I turned off all of the main lights, in the room, put in my earplugs and got a few hours sleep.

The next morning, in the kitchen, I was having a snack, when some Tasmanians walked in. They were the second Australians I'd spoken to, since I left home in April. I was shocked with how different our accent was. I now know why people just want me to keep talking when I first open my mouth, knowing that I'm from Australia. I always found it embarrassing when people guessed where I was from; New Zealand, South Africa, and Britain. No not the British#$%?&. I started saying a quick 'Hi' in a very high squeaky voice, in the hope; people didn't pick up the accent, straight away. I'm definitely not ashamed or embarrassed being an Australian. Quite the opposite, as I can talk under water for half-an-hour or more, without even drawing breath☺.

Adelia and I were rostered on at the hostel, for the morning shift, to start work at 10:30am. Our job was to clean up, after the twenty-five people, checked out of the hostel. The hostel had to be spick and span by five o'clock, being totally booked out that night, as well. Adelia and I came back along the coastline, with a beautiful sunrise, with basically no traffic; because most normal people were still in bed.

As we travelled, the view was unbelievably, breathtakingly, indescribable. The ocean was like a sheet of dusky blue glass almost stationery; except you'd detect, a small shimmer of movement, as the swells headed towards the shore line. The surface of the water was scattered with designs, creating a masterpiece, of a magnitude, beyond words. Adelia and I stopped more than a few times, because we're shocked and amazed by the views; each time the car manoeuvred around a bend. We stopped at a little town (well there's a café and bungalows overlooking the ocean) enjoying a coffee, sitting at an outside verandah, looking out over the ocean. Absolutely spellbound!!!

We arrived back in Cantina, Norma told us to take our time, as the hostel was still full of guests. We enjoyed another coffee and shopped for supplies, before heading back to the hostel, safe and sound after our forty-eight hour adventure.

THE RENTAL CAR

What an incredible feeling, having a car to visit *ALL* of the places, not possible without transportation. You might ask the question, of when we fitted in work with our busy sightseeing schedule. Both Adelia and I had two days off, each week and between 10:30 and 4:30 each day we're on our own time; not wasting a single minute.

BUNGALOW RESORT

Adelia as I were about to leave for a coffee, up along the highway, when Dolly came over to the hostel to visit, so we all went together. I'd driven past the café a few times without stopping, so today we spent time, with a coffee and looking at the view out over the Pacific Ocean.

A large row of bungalows, and motel type accommodation, lined the edge of the cliff; allowing guests staying in these rooms, uninterrupted views, of the incredible sunsets. The track down the cliff face, towards the beach looked very scary; deciding not to tempt fate today. Instead we stood at the lookout, watching the wave's crash, onto the majestic rock formations lining the rugged coastline.

MERTON

With Sherry, we travelled to Merton for the afternoon, as Sherry had a doctor's appointment while the three of us (Adelia, Dolly and I) walked the streets, finding a multitude of shops to explore and bargain hunt. Dolly purchased a fantastic pair of jeans, to suit her perfect size-eight butt. I purchased a new suitcase, to replace my small one, constantly full and underweight. I was accumulating way toooo much stuff to cart around with me. When we were sick of shopping, we found a bar to wait for Sherry. A very cute waiter flirted with the girls, ordering a couple of drinks, as none of us were driving; what a great way to kill time. When Sherry finally arrived, she ordered a drink, while filling us in on her visit to the doctor. Today was Sherry's final visit to the surgeon, to make sure she'd lost enough weight, for the surgery to be successful.

We continued to enjoy our afternoon at the bar and when leaving, I said it's my shout. The young waiter came over as I paid him for the bill plus a tip. Sherry asked how much I'd tipped him, and I said 10%. Sherry said NO, you have to give him more than that. I get so peeved off when I have to pay tips, as in Australia NOONE pays a tip. So Sherry forced me to give the waiter more than 20%. What the@#$%&*? The waiter was friendly and chatty, as I apologised for the under tipping, as I left with the barman happy and me pissed off. Not happy Jan@#$%!The reason behind the tipping was employers pay their staff 'jack shit', with employees relying on tips to make a wage. *IT WAS SO WRONG ON SO MANY LEVELS* and our Aussie work standards; are federal law however there're always people, bucking the system.

TOURING

After a morning shift, Adelia and I headed towards the wineries, to finish the tour, we started with Tony.

We detoured to visit a craft village spending over an hour watching a man glass-blowing. I found it really interesting, and couldn't believe the amount of steps that occurred, before the item was finished. I had my own guessing game going, about *WHAT* I thought the molten glass would finally become; maybe a tall wine glass, a tall flower vase, a small dish, a small wine glass or a bowl. All I know it's going to be purple, oh no it has changed to pink, then brown, then red and ……….

The man placed the long poll into the fire; then out; rolling it onto the bench and picking up colours and shards. In and out of the fire, rolling and pressing on the bench, with the sweat pouring off the man; working hard creating a beautiful piece of glassware. The object came out of the fire every couple of minutes; each time believing, it's finished and I'd get ready to leave. I was being very patient; curious to know, what the final product was. Finally the object was finished; revealed as a vase, about eight inches tall, with beautiful autumn colours.

Now I know how much time, was involved, creating each piece, and why the prices were so high. Was the creation of every piece, as intense in its creation? The artist would definitely need to be dedicated to his craft, as it's hot and dirty work. I enjoyed watching the whole process unfold, as I wandered around the showroom floor, envious of the talent, on display.

When you think about any artist, and what lengths they go to, to create something unique. The time involved with planning, material choices and size of your item, the length of time to complete a piece, could be hours, days, weeks months or even years to create. I bought a couple of hummingbirds as a memento, one for Sherry and the other one for me.

Adelia and I continued with our trip, stopping at a few wineries; to buy a bottle of 'something' for Adelia, to take home, to her dad in France. It was a lovely drive; each boutique winery offered a different view of the valley. The five-dollar wine tasting fee, I didn't pay for, as I was driving (that's my excuse). When we completed the loop of the wineries, we found a sign that said Simpson, arriving just in time for the closing of the Saturday afternoon markets. We continued down to the harbour, for a sunset tour, along the boardwalk, before heading back to the hostel.

CHRISTMAS VILLAGE

Meeting Sherry, for a walk around the Christmas village, where twenty little boutique cabins, offered different businesses, the opportunity of selling their wares. The path ways were lined with fairy lights and each little cabin was individually decorated in a theme. In one little area of the park, the ground was carpeted in blue lights, as lights were wrapped around the tree trunks; every branch decorated with different coloured fairy lights. The whole area was covered with at least a million tiny bulbs. We continued our walk along the path of wonderment, reaching an arch about twenty metres long, six metres wide and four meters high. The tunnel was covered with, panels of lights displayed in multiple colours. I can see why so many people, love Christmas, as the decorations made it all feel so special. I found a beautiful Christmas card to send home to my mum for Christmas. We purchased a Christmas mug, filled with eggnog, sitting on Santa's knee where Adelia, Sherry and I told Santa, whether we'd been naughty or nice.

Around a camp fire, a band was playing Christmas songs as the three of us sat down, listening to the music, while warming our toes with the fire. We stayed for about thirty minutes, finishing our eggnog and singing along with the band. Sherry was funny; actually I think it's something I need to learn. When you come in contact with someone, for the first time, you introduce yourself straight away. This practice was something I've never done, and while we're sitting around the camp fire, Sherry introduced herself to a man, Spencer, who's sitting next me on the little bench seat. Spencer was aged about forty-five, enjoying his company while all four of us chatted, in between songs.

The night air was starting to cool down, as we walked over to a bar at the Tall Timbers Resort, to thaw out. We found a couple of lounges, to relax on, while listening to the band. When we first arrived we chatted to Spencer for a few minutes; and he asked if he could buy Adelia and I, a drink. I said no, as we're not staying very long. However Sherry had other ideas; staying for an over an hour, including me dancing in a room full of people, with bright lights shining.

I hate dancing in front of people; but I was dragged up, protesting the whole way. Of course Sherry was a fantastic dancer and knows how to look sensational dancing the swing. She's a confident performer, being the centre of attention on the dance floor.

I was so jealous; Sherry knew how to dance so well. Learning how to swing dance properly, was one of my bucket list items; like I see people dancing in the movies. Now that's how, I wanted to be treated, on the dance floor; swift moves, showing a girl who was in charge. The only time a man was in charge of me, well maybe, a couple of other instances I could think up☺

ART CLASSES

Since I purchased my water colour paints, pencils and books I've been creating master pieces. One day while at Simpson, I noticed a sign, advertising water-colour classes, placed on a shop window. I filled out the enquiry book, hoping to set up an appointment. The next week I went back to ask if a teacher had been contacted; the man said no one had replied to his email. The next week, I asked again and he said the same thing, but added the classes were very expensive, also mentioning, he had trouble getting anyone, who'd be available, to teach me. The guy quoted me $165 for water colour classes, as I said I was still interested in having a couple of lessons.

Leanne finally emailed me, with one available day, to teach basic water colour techniques, costing $20 for a two hour lesson. How expensive was that? Leanne mentioned she only received the email, from the art gallery manager, on the Monday. *WHAT THE….* I wasn't impressed, as I could've had at least three lessons, using the bus for the other weeks. I attended the class, with the rental car, that week, learning some basic techniques, at Leanne's art studio.

CARE PACKAGE HOME

I'd been gathering and collecting different items, over the last few months, to send a care package home. The cost was sixty-five dollars to send two-and-a-half kilos from Canada; and sixty-dollars to send twenty-pounds from the US. What a difference. I enquired about how long the package would take, to arrive in Australia; the post office lady said two to three weeks. I planned to send the package at the end of November, arriving in perfect time for Christmas. At the post office, I arranged to take home two different size boxes, so I'd decide which size I wanted. I couldn't believe they didn't want payment, in advance; with the box, included in postage price. What the….?#$%

I filled the box with gifts for everyone, for Christmas, including a present for each member of my family; Christmas cards, to be posted in Australia rather from here. I sent home special things, including the glass hummingbird, glass ware, and a beautiful Eiffel tower hand towel, Adelia gave me, as a farewell gift. I couldn't believe when I filled the box, I still had six pounds of available weight.

SPIRITUAL CONNECTIONS

While I was in the east I purchased a guided meditation programme, with the presentation delivered, on a weekly basis, via email. At the beginning, I wanted all of the presentations, but I soon discovered meditating on that particular subject, for the week, was perfect. Looking for direction; making the necessary changes, with the help of this programme. The meditations were based on the charkas, aligning our bodies; using the magical benefits of crystals.

My morning and evening routine, revolved around meditating with my crystals, and affirmations focusing on reconnecting with myself. Relax and centre yourself, close your eyes and focus on what was being said. Energy; Happiness; Money; Love; Luck; Influence; Confidence; and Mental Power were the tools I needed.

The different presentations emphasised, how to be *MORE*, reflecting how we treat and serve others in our community. Random acts of kindness each day; and being a wonderful role model for the community, our families and ourselves. Treating ourselves with respect, flows outwards to the greater community; this in turn, makes us value who we are.

CRYSTALS

My crystals were used for their healing properties, to improve the quality of my life. At each different location I visited, I placed my crystals, out on display, if I had room. I placed the larger crystals around the window sills. I loved having them on display; each day one would say "pick me, please pick me". Placing the crystal, in a little organza bag; in my bra, after reading the crystal book, for the healing offered today.

I had the same result with picking tarot cards on a daily basis. Each day I shuffled the deck, picked a card, using that information as guidance for the day. I had six decks of cards ranging from angels, crystals, flowers and love, using them as a guide for a 'better me'☺

WEST SIDE STORY

One afternoon, in the west village, I was waiting for my chain, to be fixed, at the bead shop. The chain was Ricky's mothers; gold plated with two hearts joined by a clip, was damaged; worried the long, chunky chain, would be lost.

Standing at the door, to the bead shop, I heard this whoop-to-do noise, coming from down the street. I mentioned to the girl in the shop, it might be a streaker. A lady in the real estate office, next door, said if it was a streaker, to let her know. I walked out onto the footpath, but unfortunately, no one was running, down the main street naked. Robyn and I chatted while the lady fixed my necklace, and then we chatted some more, both disappointed our streaker wasn't real.

LIVE YOUR LIFE

Preparing for my trip, I searched for material, to inspire me, during my time away from home. This poem was placed on the bedside table, of each place I stayed at; reminding me each day, of what I'm capable of.

Dance to the music of your dreams; follow your bliss; be sensational; live your passion; seek adventure; learn something new; make mistakes; trust yourself; take a chance; unleash the power of your creativity; speak your truth; lose yourself in laughter; fall in love with life; celebrate the uniqueness of you.

I have shared this poem with many people, using my painting skills, to create a colour wash on paper, writing the words, in an artistic way, to inspire others, to live the life of their dreams. *See more of this story in Chapter 18- Thank you Gail.*

SPEAKERS

When I first arrived on the central coast, I contacted the local Speakers club, to confirm their meetings; missing out on one meeting, because of a long weekend. One morning I met Marie, the president, at Fiona's Café for a coffee. I attended the next meeting, enjoying a new venue, with a new group of people. One man had a daughter, travelling to New Zealand, so I gave him my card, in case she ended up in Australia.

This was my first American club I'd visited, noticing both Canada and America were very patriotic. Both clubs sang the national anthem, at each meeting; instead of the club pledge. A few different practices, at the club meetings, will be shared, with my club back home.

LAST 48 HOURS

The last forty-eight-hours were full of excitement, as I finished my last shift at the hostel. I ran around, like a maniac, seeing and doing all of the last minute things, like sunsets. Sherry wasn't happy I was cooking, my own farewell dinner, at her house. I wanted to do it for her, because she was so busy with school. I cooked lasagne and joined the group of Adelia, Dolly, Sally, Linda and Sherry on the deck, enjoying drinkies, while watching the sunset. Linda and Sally didn't stay for dinner, so the four of us, sat down at Sherry's little table, enjoying a very special time together. I counted my blessings, with this wonderful memory; as the three of them would enjoy more fun times together, over the coming weeks, until Adelia returned to France.

Adelia mentioned she'd never heard of the limbo stick, finding a broom and Lowering the stick down, to some great music. How flexible were the young ones, compared to the oldies? It's a fun game to play in the lounge room, before we made our way over to Blanches, for farewell drinks.

My last morning at the hostel; my luggage was in the car, I attended my last rhythm dancing class, with a sad farewell to Linda and Sally. I waited for Adelia to finish the morning shift, before accompanying me to Merton, for the afternoon. Norma, an emotional person, was at the hostel for a quick goodbye hug; with tears in her eyes, thanking me for all of my work.

The wet drive along the coastline, made the final trip down the coastline, sad; as I couldn't say goodbye to the beautiful blue ocean. We'd planned to go shopping, but the rain was torrential; parking the car, running into the first restaurant for lunch. Adelia and I both had photos we wanted to share; so our laptops came to lunch. It's funny, we both had the same laptop, except mine was green and Adelia's was blue.

After lunch we dropped the car at the rental place, with the young man returning us back into down town. I stayed at a coffee house, with my luggage, while Adelia went shopping for shoes. When Sherry finished work, we transferred my luggage into her car, before guiding us to a nearby bar, for farewell drinks.

Sherry wanted to spoil us, with a visit, to her favourite Italian restaurant. I was very impressed, making ourselves comfortable in the cocktail lounge, sitting up high on the bar stools. The room was pretty quiet, with only two other tables occupied, and one lady sitting at the bar. We sat at the table looking at our menus; with no staff serving us. The barman was busy, chatting up the lady, at the bar, and no other staff were visible.

The bar started to fill up, when we spotted a young waitress, who zoomed past us, to attend to another table. As she went past us she noticed our 'dagger of a stare'; coming back to see if we'd been served. We placed our order for drinks and entrees, explaining to her, we'd been waiting for twenty minutes, and hadn't been served. We weren't really bothered with the wait, as we were enjoying each other's company. Our drinks order arrived quickly, and then finally the right food order arrived, with apologies from our server.

The little cocktail bar was full of customers, as we were totally ignored. We weren't asked whether we wanted any more food or drinks. Our empty plates remained at the table, as we enjoyed our last evening together. Sherry, Adelia and I didn't really have a time limit BUT we were definitely there for a good time and maybe, a long time, or *NOT*. We definitely wanted a couple of rounds of drinks, before Sherry dropped me off, at the hostel.

Finally catching the eye of a waitress, Sherry requested the bill. Sherry looked at me, and told me not to say a word; leaving our seats, walking towards the front door, where a maître de was standing. Sherry asked the man, if he'd find the manager on duty, as she would like to talk to him. Now I have watched a lot of television about how people handle inefficient service. Sherry handled herself quite well, explaining to the manager, she's a regular guest here, with her guests from Australia and France. Our experience was relayed to the duty manager as Sherry showed the manager the docket with a zero tip included on the bill. Sherry wasn't impressed by the service (what service) we'd received. All bar staff and waitresses rely heavily on tips, so you would think, they'd bend over backwards, to please their customers. We were all upset, leaving the cocktail bar, with definitely more tears to follow.

We linked our arms, walking back to Sherry's car, to drive to the hostel. Arriving at the front of the hostel; the heavens opened up, while I transferred my luggage, onto the front verandah. Mother Nature was just copying our inner feelings; all three of us, crying, as I hugged them, goodbye.

Chapter 17

IN TRANSIT TRAIN, BUS, FERRY - NOVEMBER

ON THE MOVE AGAIN

Checking into the hostel, I dragged my luggage, up the stairs, to the second floor; reserving my bed for the night, in a female dorm room, with six beds. After a few minutes, I went downstairs discovering Wayne, a guest from my hostel, was staying tonight, as well. I had a quick look around the downstairs areas, had a shower and got ready for bed, being emotionally and physically exhausted, as it'd been a busy few days.

Being very fortunate the night's accommodation, was complimentary, even though it's only thirty-five dollars; it's still worth enjoying, and being thankful the organisation appreciated its workers.

Another lady joined me in the dorm room; telling me about her life, as a children's entertainer, working on cruise ships and travelling around the country. The cruise ship, works the same way as volunteering; in exchange for entertaining the children, for a certain amount of hours each day; she received full board and food. The lady conducted art classes and face painting, sharing with me photos of her work. I congratulated her, on her talent, wishing her well, as I went to sleep.

At about 4:00am, another lady checked into the dorm; quickly resettling, until the alarm woke me. I transferred my luggage into the bathroom, to redress, before heading to the railway station, only a short distance away. By the time I reached the station, my arms were nearly dropping off, from dragging the luggage up the hill. The incline wasn't that steep, but steep enough, when I had two suitcases and a backpack.

Boy of boy, I need to get rid of some stuff; looking at prices, for another piece of luggage, on the plane, was seventy-dollars, I think. For that dollar value, you can get fifty pounds or twenty three kilos, being cheaper to take it home with me, than posting it home. (*But I was so wrong) See On the Road Again in Chapter 21.*

My train arrived at the railway station, without a dining or viewing car; with the wet and cold weather, I spent most of the time in my carriage seat. I went downstairs for breakfast of yoghurt and fruit to meet up with Alex, a former guest from the hostel. Alex's mission was riding his bike, from Canada to Mexico; however today Alex was taking the easy road, because of the rain. Shsss!! don't tell anyone.☺

SEISMIC TESTING

As the train manoeuvred along the coastline, Alex and I chatted about the seismic testing, offshore, along the Californian coastline; which had been Government approved. ALL marine life, within a certain amount of kilometers, of the blast site, would be destroyed. Alex said there had been protests, with a high court appeal lodged, to stop the company. The latest news, announcing the public had apparently, won the high court appeal.

I'm not sure if the story, Alex told, was true, but it goes like this. A meeting was organised, as people arrived to support the meeting; the marine life out in the ocean gathered as well. The human protestors, located near the pier, started to notice dolphins, seals and whales were gathering just off shore. As the event proceeded, the crowds increased, on land and off shore, as well. Whales were breeching out in the ocean, thanking all of the people, for helping to keep their home safe. It's a wonderful thought; I believe it to be true, hearing the same story, from the man painting the mural, in Simpson. *(See Rental Car in Chapter 16)*

SALVADORAN

I arrived at the Salvadoran train station, hitching a lift on a cart, from the platform to the station building; relaxing for the two hours, waiting for my transfer bus. At the café I struggled with my luggage, in through the door, and struggling back out, the same door, balancing a coffee, with not one person offering to help. What was going on? How rude? No wonder I don't like spending time in cities.

I spent the two hours reading and people watching, moving around each time with all of bags. Finally the bus arrived, enjoying a lovely two hours tour, around the city, until my drop off point. The bus stop was in the middle of nowhere, not knowing how, to get to my motel. I watched taxis go past, waving to them, but they ignored me. After about forty minutes I finally caught the attention of a cabbie; as he completed a 'U' turn to pick me up. He dropped me off at the motel, handing me his card, for when I needed a taxi, during my stay. The cabbie would be on duty to take me wherever I wanted to go.

At the motel, the cabbie unloaded my bags, so I could check in, but the front foyer doors were locked. Alarm Bells No. 1! What was going on here? The attendant let me in; then I walked directly to my room. The whole room had dark curtains and smelt of something unrecognizable. Deciding I didn't care; as I was hungry, only having yoghurt for breakfast and a coffee and chocolate bar for lunch. The attendant mentioned, the restaurant next door, had good food. I decided to try something new; I still regret it, with the meal so hot, I couldn't eat any of it. Lucky I'd ordered a side order of rice and a banana fritter for dessert.

In my room, at least the bed was comfy, and when I woke in the morning, I had shock No. 2. As I entered the bathroom, I noticed black footprints, on the white mat, on the bathroom floor. Visiting the bathroom, during the night, was the evidence, of a few sets of footprints. I looked at the bottom of my feet; a disgusting black colour, from the filthy carpet. Oh yeah, how clean were the carpets? NOT; wearing shoes for the rest of my stay. Not happy Jan.

I slept in, because I could, with a yogurt for breakfast, before I called for my friendly cabbie to drop me down at the movies. It was still raining, as we drove down to the waterfront, where I was thoroughly entertained, spending time in 'escapism mode'. Leaving the movie complex, I noticed a familiar name, walking over to the restaurant, for dinner.

I texted my daughter Nicole, to see what she's doing; discovering she's sitting, in an airfield terminal, waiting to catch a lift, for a sky dive. I told Nicole not to do it, but she didn't listen to me, doing it anyway. I checked my emails, while waiting for dinner to arrive, to find a message, from my youngest son, Christian saying "I should come home, as Nan misses me too much". I've been asked by many people, whether I miss my family, while I've been travelling and I say "NO". I carry all of my family, in my heart, and when I get lonely, I think of them, with the memories, always bringing a smile to my face.

After dinner, I caught another cab back, to my motel room, still with locked foyers and dodgy people hanging around. I quickly locked my door and settled into a chat with my mum for awhile. If the house sitting job, in Canada hadn't eventuated, I would have been travelling back to Australia this week. I was still on that magical carpet ride, full of extraordinary adventures, awaiting my discovery.

Carol, one of the other volunteers, was staying here as well, thanks to my recommendation. What the….%#@. Gail sent out a bulk email, mentioning staying at some fancy motel chain, with the tariff for a room, way out of my league. I emailed the other volunteers, advising them of my plans for staying here, sharing a cab, on Saturday, over to the ferry terminal.

Carol knocked on my door; horrified by what she's witnessing, as I apologised profusely. It was OK in the end, as it's only for one night. Carole told me, how scary it was when she arrived, at the motel, a couple of hours earlier. Carol went over to the restaurant next door for dinner, as she didn't know where I was. Carol had flown into a nearby airfield, more convenient, with cheaper flights, than the bigger airports.

We were awake early, ready to catch the cab on the Saturday morning at 7:00am, with time for breakfast, at the ferry terminal. I thanked the friendly cabbie as Carol and I purchased the tickets, enjoying a bacon and egg breakfast. There were supposed to be five volunteers, on the ferry this morning, all staying the same amount of time, with Gail.

Chapter 18

HOST NO. 10 THE ISLAND - DECEMBER

SANTA NOVA

The Ferry ride was smooth sailing, travelling across the bay, for two hours. The township of Santa Nova was located in a small horseshoe shaped bay, with a small mountain range restricting the township, to a narrow shoreline, along white sandy beaches.

The ferry tied up at the dock, we collected our luggage, with Carol and I picking out a young couple, with shoes dangling off their backpacks, as our fellow volunteers. Shivani and Josh joined Carol and I, meeting Gail; who led us to a small pickup truck, loading our luggage into the back. We all met Jenny, who'd arrived on the island, a couple of days earlier, staying out at the caravan park.

Gail had plans for the ladies to attend a gathering, for the local women, celebrating Christmas. I enjoyed the morning tea, with the other ladies, with a little gift to take home as a memento. I couldn't believe that I was living in a town again, with only a five minutes' walk, down to the main streets with shops, cafés, restaurants and bars.

I am a morning person, walking around the cove, towards the freight dock, with restricted access for residents only. Freight arrives from the mainland, with EVERYTHING needed for the town's survival, transported in.

A cruise ship was moored out in the cove, with small boats ferrying the passengers to the shore. The cruise ships arrive in town for a few hours, almost every day, where the tourists are able to hire a golf cart to explore; shop or enjoy the beach. A large dock area supplied water craft for hire, or organised a whale watching cruise, etc. Unlimited amount of activities, were available to enjoy; and those were the days, I avoided the down town area.

GAIL'S PLANT CARE

Gail was a lovely young woman, aged in her early thirties, working as a landscape gardener, maintaining her client's gardens. Gail had been living here, for a few years, staying in a two bedroom apartment; she shared with her brother and a dog.

THE WORKERS

Gail organised her crew of workers for only ten-days each month. The first-day-of-December was when everyone arrived, to start work. Josh from New Jersey; Shivani originally from India but studying in New York; Carol from San Francisco; Jenny from San Diego; and Bella from Australia.

THE ACCOMMODATION & SWOPPING OUT

We arrived at the apartment, realising there wasn't much room; for seven people to stay with only two private bedrooms, a lounge/dining room and kitchen. Two toilets and one shower, added to the total amount of room, for all of us to survive. Jenny had her own tent, opting for that option. I said I'd sleep in a tent, which was a private space. Carol reserved one lounge, with Josh and Shivani, taking the other two lounges. We were all set, making ourselves at home the best we could.

The apartment located, on the side of the hill, had spectacular views across the cove. Sitting at the dining room table, our view included the hummingbird feeder. The feeder was a constant course of action, with a woodpecker, trying to suck out the nectar. When the woodpecker wasn't there, I'd be delighted to see hummingbirds, coming to feed.

The tent wasn't a very good experience, with cold, wet weather, and the air mattress needed to be inflated, every two days. The job was only for only ten days, so it's *OK,* but then, maybe it wasn't.

On the first night staying in the tent, I got up to go to the bathroom and woke up the whole house, including the dog, as I stumbled past everyone on the lounge room floor. Deciding, in future, I'd pee in the corner of the yard, at least during the night, anyway. Tenants lived on the top floor, but the corner was dark, hopefully they didn't see much, peering out their window at 2:00am.

After three days, Gail's brother moved out; and I was offered his private bedroom, since I was sleeping in the tent. Offering it to Josh and Shivani because they were sleeping on a lounge; sort of happy in my tent, but with the wet weather, I dragged my mattress into the lounge room to go to sleep. Josh decided he'd clean the kitchen or do whatever the hell he was doing, to make so much noise at 10:00pm. I tossed and turn for about an hour, before I dragged my mattress, back into my tent where I happily went to sleep.

What annoyed me the most, about my decision, was Josh and Shivani bedroom had the only shower; with the door, almost permanently closed. Gail's bedroom had the other toilet, through her bedroom, with neither options ideal, for visits to the bathroom.

FOOD AND COOKING

Gail supplied dinner and breakfast during our stay, with lunch at our own expense. With five of us working; some yoghurts and fruit in the fridge, never seemed to be enough, to go around. Josh and Shivani smoked a lot of weed, and were constantly hungry. I wish I was that thin, with the amount of food, they ate. Maybe I should take up the habit, to keep my weight under control☺

Each day, a roster for jobs, was created for duties, such as kitchen assist, cooking or washing up. The roster system was a wonderful idea, helping each other out, with the duties.

Shivani had her birthday during our stay, making it special, with a cake, flowers, wine and a three-course-meal. What a wonderful time for festivities, with my wonderful new friends, enjoying a relaxed night of celebrations.

Dinners were a mix of vegetarian or vegan meals, with different cooks, making interesting meals. For our last meal together, I cooked a vegetarian lasagne with eggplant, roasted capsicum, zucchini, sweet potato, assorted cheeses and my onion jam. Gail cooked a corn bread and the whole meal was amazing. Is your mouth watering!! Plus pumpkin pie and ice cream for dessert.

THE ISLAND SYSTEM

Apparently there're more golf carts than residents, here on the island, mainly because of fuel shipment expenses; as golf carts are battery operated. It's funny each morning, seeing everyone driving around town, in their golf buggy, with coffees balancing on the seat.

One morning I looked up from breakfast, to see a macho guy riding a pink mo-ped. I wonder if the mo-ped belonged to him or his wife's☺

Many tourists, who arrive on the island, hire the golf carts to get around. The ferry ride over cost thirty-five dollars, with forty-dollars was for ONE hour buggy hire.

DINING OUT

With the shops so close, downtown was convenient, to grab something to eat, at anytime. I'd try for a coffee each day, at one of the little cafes, with an espresso machine. Plus breakfast one morning at a café, with enough food left over for another meal.

The bars have happy hour, every afternoon around sunset time; with a unanimous decision to take advantage of this opportunity. The bars along the strip, had bench seats, facing the ocean, to sit back and watch the world go by; as Carol, Jenny and I pub crawled our way along the bars one afternoon. I love cocktails; ordering them at each place; we were all truly primed, arriving for dinner with James.

James, a friend of Gail's, invited the whole crew down for dinner, at one of the local restaurants. James received 50% off all his purchases at the restaurant; from his employment with the company. The evening was lovely, listening to everyone's stories, while overlooking the restaurant, from an elevated floor with high tables, and high bar stools.

FELLOWSHIP ANYONE?

Gail's pastor's invited the work crew, to a pot luck dinner, at his house on the Tuesday night. We all enjoyed the casual stroll along the streets to Jeff's place, where forty people were attending the dinner. For the non-vegetarians, amongst us, we enjoyed pizza and hotdogs.

On Sunday Josh, Jenny and I attended church, for a morning tea, to meet a lady, needing help with some gardening work. The job only needed muscles and willing helpers; making the whole area neat and tidy again. The job didn't take very long, but felt good helping the church community out. *(This was what volunteering, was all about, being part of a community, allowing it to prosper and grow.)*

EXPLORING

Josh, Shivani and Carol were fitness maniacs, spending their time hiking and biking all over the island. Carol hired a bike to explore the island on her own. With the bus service, you place your bike on the front of the bus; pick the place to get off, to explore different parts of the island. Carol and I explored, the same parts of the island, however there's one major difference. Carol used her mountain bike, whereas I hitched a ride in an off road truck. I can think of nothing worthwhile, in exhausting myself, exercising, when I could travel in style.

On the Friday Gail received free tickets on a tour; to the middle of the island. The tours were guaranteed, regardless of how many people had booked. The tour company rang Gail to offer tickets to her workers, making the tour group bigger. Everyone exploring the island, had to buy a membership, except us, because of our volunteer work, we received complimentary membership. Whooa!!!

The inland roads, throughout the island were used by the tour companies, hikers or bikers, as well as emergency services. Another township, Adeline, was located on the other side of the Island, with bus services, commuting each day, between the two towns.

The tour of the island travelled mostly along the fire trails, up and over the top of the ranges, with breathtaking three-sixty-degree views of the Pacific Ocean. I was extremely grateful for the opportunity to spend an enjoyable few hours exploring the area. The one regret was my camera was left back at the house. I didn't need to spend time, behind the camera, to appreciate the experience.

Our volunteering day saw us travel two hours, through the fire trails, to a camp facility, mainly used by school children. Our job was planting trees in a new garden; but they forgot to tell us the area had previously been a bitumen car park. The ground was so compacted; it took twenty minutes, to dig each hole, with a crow bar. There were ten of us, working for over two hours planting fifty trees. The job was physically exhausting, as I struggled with the crow bar. It's a pity they didn't have a bobcat to dig the hole for us in two minutes flat. The plants would certainly have a better chance of survival if the hole had loose soil, instead of a tightly compacted hole.

Cleaning up one of the isolated beaches, was our second day volunteering; however we waited at the wrong pick up point. We all arrived early, waiting for ages, before we headed out to do our own thing. I decided to hire a buggy, for one-hour, for forty-dollars. Driving like a maniac, to see *EVERYTHING* I could, in that time frame. I already had an idea, of the layout of the Island, from my adventures walking, and in the off-road vehicle.

It was funny, driving the buggy on the road, at breakneck speed, zipping up to the top of the eastern side of the cove, then out to the gardens; around the back end of town, where the outdoor sports arena was located. Zooming around the corners, like a race-car driver, to arrive back to the northern end of the cove. Boy of Boy, the energy was flowing, stepping out of the buggy, with one minute to spare; before the extra penalties applied. The buggy company would charge you, for every minute you were late, returning the cart. Man of man, what a drama.

One day, walking near the ferry terminal, the sound of heaven was travelling from the pier, across the water, towards me. I knew immediately, who was making the sound; taking several minutes to locate, the source. I continued walking, towards the main street, breathing in the magical notes, through every part of my body, listening to the music, Josh was playing. I found a bench to sit and listen, as the saxophones' rhythm touched deep in my soul. Nature must be his church, as Josh sat on a rock wall, facing the water; his bare feet in the sand. Josh let his fingers make the magical sounds, appear effortless.

I enjoyed the performance; mentioning to Josh, that when the cruise ships were docked, he should take his saxophone down onto the beach, to make money from the tourists. I noticed Josh down on the waterfront, with his music case open and a few dollars lying inside. I placed five-dollars in the case, as I certainly enjoyed listening to him play.

SPOILING MYSELF AGAIN

It has been a very long trip and a few months (*actually over six months*) since I spoiled myself with a massage. I deserved it, I needed it, and so be it. I booked a foot massage appointment, at the same time as my hair cut and coloured. This was the first time I have ever had a foot massage, except for a reflexology treatment. The afternoon was ever so relaxing, as a neutral colour was applied to my newly trimmed hair. I felt pampered leaving the salon, ready for an afternoon of cocktails and a dinner invitation.

THE WORK

All of the volunteers were there for ten days, with only four hours of work to perform each day. The hours were mostly in the afternoon, as Gail worked her normal day job in the mornings. The afternoon shift, allowed us time away, from the house, to explore.

Most of the jobs we completed were in the gardens, located at the house block next door. The property owners were an older couple, not able to look after the gardens anymore. Gail had taken over the upkeep of the land; established with garden beds; and Gail had chickens and ducks. It's the end of the summer season, as we rejuvenated all the gardens with compost; set up irrigation; planted seeds and seedlings, including potatoes. Fruit trees, flowers beds and shrubs also received attention.

One afternoon Josh and I were given the job of emptying the compost bin, spreading all of the contents, onto the prepared garden beds. With the empty bin, we started the process again adding the tree clippings and weeds. Repair work was needed to the small fences, placed around all of the garden beds, so the ducks didn't eat the vegetables. The chickens and ducks both laid eggs, which Gail sold, to supplement her income. One night a fox entered the chicken pen, with three chickens being lost. Josh and I were given the job of repairing the cage, so the chickens would be safe again.

Our last morning on the island; our commitment to Gail was to clean the entire property. The list included windows; vacuuming, cleaning toilets and bathrooms; cleaning the kitchen and fridge, working as a team, to restore the house, to an orderly fashion.

Our time was finally up, finishing our list of jobs and leaving the property. Josh and Shivani were staying on the island, for a few extra days while Carol, Jenny and I were ready to escape. Carol was flying back to Frisco; Jenny was heading south to San Diego, on the train. We said our goodbyes to Gail, at the ferry terminal, wishing her well.

THANK YOU GAIL

My last night on the island, I presented Gail with a gift, of my poem 'live your life'. As a memento of my time with them I give each host a gift. Gail hung the poem up on her lounge room wall, with the rest of the balloons and streamers, left over from Shivani's birthday.

I received an email from Gail in early 2014, to say my poem had remained on her lounge room wall. Each day she was inspired to live her life to the max. The email thanked me for the poem, as Gail mentioned, she's now heading to South America, to work as an aid worker — something she has always wanted to do. See more of this story in Chapter16 – Live Your Life.

FINAL VOLUNTEER'S DAY

Jenny, Carol and I travelled together on the ferry, back to the mainland, where we ordered a frozen daiquiri at the terminal, to say celebrate our friendship. Jenny headed to the train station and I'd booked a shuttle; Carol decided to stay with me, as she had all day to fill in, before her late afternoon flight. I'd booked my shuttle-ride using Carol's phone; receiving a call from the shuttle company asking where I was. I told the man I was at the terminal, waiting for him. The guy rang again; obviously the booking officer had written down the incorrect ferry terminal, as he was at a different terminal. A lady, waiting at the entrance, had booked a shuttle and had been waiting for almost an hour for her lift. Yes, we're both waiting for the same company to arrive.

Finally the shuttle arrived and I wasn't even on their passenger list, confirming my booking, as we travelled along. Since I was staying at a motel, I didn't care, how long it took, before I arrived at my motel. However, the others needed to be at airport to board their planes, ASAP. I thoroughly enjoyed the drive around the city suburbs, picking up the passengers, dropping them at the airport, before I finally arrived at my motel.

Chapter 19

FREEDOM - DECEMBER

FREEDOM

Well the 10th of December was a night for celebration, after eight months working as a volunteer; I'm finally free of all of my commitments; congratulating myself on a job well done; given it my all, having work ethics second to none, with positive host comments on my volunteer site.

The big question was; will I ever do it again? Never say never. We'll see. I think I'll need to look at different types of work. I really enjoyed the hostel, besides the self-imposed cleaning work. The hostel was a cushy job, with the highest reward, not a compost pile in sight or sixty stairs to climb to go to work.

In 2014 I travelled back to visit; the horse farm in Chapter 6; the cattle property in Chapter 11; and the hostel in Chapter 16 working for a total of four months. In 2015 I worked with a volunteer group for four months through Italy, Greece and France. I would recommend this form of travelling for anyone who wants a different perspective on how different cultures live their lives and how they all sustain their lifestyle.

THE MOTEL

The motel had *GUESS WHAT*? A luxurious queen size bed just for me! Thankfully there wasn't an air mattress or a leaky tent in sight, as I placed my luggage in my room. The room had a microwave, coffee machine and lots of space to spread out. Conveniently close to restaurants, a small shopping centre with a second hand book shop, where I purchased a couple of books. Never let an opportunity go by when you see a book shop, especially when the prices were bargain priced at one and two dollars each. Dinner was at a restaurant across the road, before I lay in bed, watching television. Breakfast was included in the tariff, but I wasn't getting out of bed for anything. With a fantastic sleep I spent a very lazy morning in bed with movies, coffee and snacks.

After lunch I went shopping for my trip, as apparently everything was expensively priced. The hostel owners asked me to buy tamari, as they couldn't purchase it on the island. The owners were vegan, with all meals provided, the same. I'd asked Savannah about bringing my own food, since I had allergies as well. Savannah said "yes"; purchasing bread mixes to bake, plus dried fruit and nuts; always handy when travelling.

My second night, I had a frozen dinner, with a delicious wheat based cake. Boy of boy, it tasted so good. I repacked my luggage, reorganising everything to include the food. My backpack was filled to the brim, as I knew my other bags were going to be overweight; having access to some extra shopping/ storage bags to transfer items into. Of course you have to be careful what you carry onto the plane, especially liquid. Being so easy to remove my cosmetic bag, which was the heaviest item in my bag, but of course, I'd lose it at security.

That night, my Dad entered my dreams, to say Mum was in hospital again. When I rang, the next day, my Mum was at home; glad to hear from me. I know they miss me, but I cannot put my own life and dreams on hold, waiting. Waiting for what? Waiting for them to die first? I could easily die before them, wasting my life *NOT* following my own dreams. My family will be there for me when I get home *OR THEY WON'T*. Can I be certain I'll make it back to Australia alive? What's my destiny? Let's just not go there.

I'M LEAVING ON A JET PLANE AGAIN!!!

I'm leaving on another jet plane, oh boy, here we go again. This time I'm heading south to the Caribbean. It's an early morning flight, checking into the airline, with one extra carry on. I always leave enough time for the shuttle bus transfer, line up at the airline check-in desk and security. When a million people are flying around the world at the same time, you never know how long it'll take. The big city airports were an enormous size, each airline having their own terminal, with hundreds of docking stations, well not quite, but you know what I mean. The terminals are alphabetical, which was handy, if you remember your alphabet☺.

I enjoyed a hot breakfast before my flight to Miami, with no window seat on the plane. Time certainly flies; get it, flies, when you are busy reading, and included a quick nap to rejuvenate myself during the long trip. Starting my day at 5:00am and not arriving until after 9:00pm was a very long day, especially with time zone changes. In Miami the airline attendants asked passengers with large carry-on bags, to check them through, as the plane is at full capacity. I checked in my backpack, before realising I was losing my reading material, food and water. Oh well, what could I do; buying a new book, ordering a nice lunch of fish and plantain at a restaurant. The food was very tropical; the beginning of another culture, how exciting.

THE ANNIVERSARY

My latest book was too close to home for comfort. The book tells the story of a man and woman, with three grown up children, married for almost thirty years. Their marriage was in crisis, without any communication or happiness; with the spark in their lives, a distant memory. The husband blames himself, with the wife becoming more distant, because he forgot their twenty-ninth-wedding-anniversary. The husband started planning a surprise thirtieth-wedding-anniversary party at her father's house. The big wedding, she'd wanted the first time round, but they didn't have the finances. The son was very dubious; how his father could turn their marriage around; so his mother would agree to renew their vows.

The husband spent eleven months planning, asking for the children's help, during the final weeks leading up to the date. The husband and wife spent more and more time together, rekindling their relationship, getting ready for the wedding of their eldest daughter. (*A total sham*). At the father's house, all of the gardens were transformed, repainted, replanted with a total makeover. Their favourite restaurant was catering, and the daughters arranged the dresses, for them to wear.

You are probably wondering why I included details about this book. Well the story was so close, to my own story, except there's no happy ending. How could I go back and forgive him for the deceit and lies? Yes the book husband and wife lost their communication, but it didn't include of all MY stuff; grief, death and stress. There's no chance of my marriage being rekindled, as I've more respect for myself than to return to a man, who doesn't want me anyway. I am one-hundred-percent positive, partners don't have any idea, how soul destroying it was, when they stop wanting you and/or dumps you for a younger model.

The book story shows how; any effort can bring about, amazing results, when the couple renewed their vows, with the blessings of their three children.

Chapter 20

THE CARIBBEAN - DECEMBER

THE ARRIVAL

The plane flew low over the country side, as palm trees and street lighting, came into view; a flush of excitement, raced through my whole body. This was a real holiday adventure; with no work involved no plans, no rosters, and no one telling me what to do. FREEDOM!!!!

The plane was late arriving, taking forever, to be processed through immigration; and collect my luggage. Peter was out the front of the arrivals hall, waiting for me, as I hoped my rental car person was there as well. I'd left a message on their office phone to say that my flight was changed to an evening flight.

Peter contacted the rental car place, who collected us; returning to their office, to fill out the rental agreement and pay for extra car insurance. *I HATE THIS*. I just wish rental car companies would include *ALL* of the hire charges in their price, instead of being a charge for this and that, with costs getting higher. I think the daily amount was nine-dollars extra, for the twelve days, which was not much money, but adds up, when you're on a budget.

The vehicle I'd booked wasn't available, so I had a small minivan to drive back to the B&B. Peter drove me home, as he and Savannah decided, driving at night, was just too dangerous, for someone who didn't know the area.

So the party begins, as I had my first glimpse of the island. It was winter here, with the night air having a warm balmy feel to it, with the car windows down, driving out of town. The journey to the B&B was about fifteen minutes in real time; but the reality of it was; this was the beginning of a real journey of self discovery. The area we drove through was the real deal, as I witnessed the poverty, of those who lived here.

Because I arrived during the night, I had no idea of where I was, as I met Mary-Anne and Savannah. I had a very late dinner; and it's after midnight, before my head hits the pillow. *In Singapore about forty-years earlier; I remember feeling the same ambience. It's the warmth, in the night air that awakens your senses, feeling the energy of the vegetation, and smelling the tropical fruit, ripening on the trees.*

FIRST DAY

My first night's sleep was rejuvenating, even though the bed was quite hard. Usually it takes a couple of days, to get used to a new place. Waking up refreshed and excited about my holiday; planning to explore, as much of the island as I can.

Mary-Anne was free, to take me back down, into the city, to change over, the rental car. The weather was perfect, with Mary-Anne pointing out places I could visit on my own. Places like the bank; the shopping centres for groceries; fuel station *AND* most importantly, the directions back to the house☺

Mary-Anne drove the car back to the rental car place, but the car wasn't available yet, so Carol and I went to a private club for lunch. The Mariner's Club restaurant was located in a marina; where resort styled furniture were placed, around the beautifully, manicured lawns. Mary-Anne had been a member of the club in previous years, but financial commitments, had taken its toll on the family. Mary-Anne had sold everything in Britain, to relocate with the family, with the cost of living, far more expensive than they anticipated.

After a leisurely lunch we drove back to the rental car place, and the car still wasn't ready. We should've just gone home and returned the next day. Mary-Anne and I decided we'd go grocery shopping for supplies, as I needed a few things like *WATER*. I never bothered buying water, as I usually just drank out of the tap. However, it's different here, with the tap water not recommended for drinking. I purchased a large twenty-five-litre cooler bottle, which suited the cooler base back in my room. I'd purchased a few ingredients, I needed to add to my bread mixture and other random stuff and I was set.

We drove back to the rental car place again, and finally the car was ready. By now the time was late afternoon. I'd wasted my whole first day chasing the car around. But all wasn't lost, as I spent the time with Mary-Anne, who unfortunately, had missed an outing with a friend, because she was stuck with me.

When I arrived back at the B&B, I placed all of my cooking ingredients in the kitchen. Savannah advised me the house and kitchen were off limits to guests, as this was their home. The kitchen couldn't be used for any of my cooking, as they were vegans; none of my ingredients could be placed in the fridge or cupboards; the oven couldn't be used to cook my bread. Oh Dear!#$%? Well that's really disappointing, as I'd purchased, all of these ingredients; so I could enjoy my gluten free breads and now find I have basically nothing to eat.

However the dramatics of it all worked out ok, with Mary-Anne agreeing I could use her fridge for my yoghurt, milk, eggs and cheese. Mary-Anne was not vegan, and had her own little fridge and stove where she prepared her own food. Mary-Anne liked all of the normal food, vegans didn't eat. Mary-Anne and I agreed she'd prepare my breakfast each morning. Retuning the other ingredients I'd purchased and got a refund. Everyone was happy – well sort of. Purchasing rice crackers, as a replacement for the bread, and gave thanks anyway.

When I booked the reservation online, it was through a hostels website; assuming (as you do) there's a public kitchen. After written conversations, with Savannah, I also assumed I'd use the kitchen for my cooking. However in reality; this was a bed and breakfast, having to comply with the owners wishes.

BED & BREAKFAST

The B&B was owned and operated by an English/Caribbean family. British born Mary-Anne moved with the family eight year ago; to build a life for themselves, in Peter's home country. Peter worked in the music industry, Savannah worked at the resorts as a fitness instructor, and Mary-Anne looked after the guests. The three teenager children were attending local private schools. The two girls and one boy were quite stunning; with their mother's tall, modelling features, and light milky chocolate complexion. I found it quite fascinating; the teenage boy had long dread-lock-hair, and speaks with a definitive British accent. Yeah Man☺.

The house had been built, over several years, currently furbished on two levels, with the top floor still under construction. The second floor was currently the main part of the house with all of the family's bedrooms, lounge, kitchen, bathrooms, plus three guest rooms. When the third level was completed, the whole of the family would move up, a level, and the second floor area would be used exclusively for guests.

My room was located at the end of the front verandah, with my own private entrance. A beautiful alfresco table and chairs, were available; to sit and enjoy the sunshine and the atmosphere. My room was spacious, with windows on two sides; an ensuite bathroom was located behind the main room, with a shower, toilet, basin and large wardrobe. The room was tastefully decorated with minimalist furniture. You know what? The room was for sleeping only and absolutely no reason why, I'd be spending much time here at all. *YOU'RE ON HOLIDAYS*, don't waste a single second, sitting in your bedroom; go out and explore this fantastic country.

The views, from my bedroom and front balcony, were over the valley, and I could see how the fog and mist, would hang around the valley floor, during the cool winter nights. The country side was lush green, with houses scattered around this little valley. Even though I couldn't see any buildings, I heard dogs barking all of the time; wondering why so many dogs? Savannah and Peter had five dogs; which were for security, to stop people entering your property. During the night you'd hear the first dog bark, then a chorus followed, all around the entire area. I'd been hoping for quiet night's to sleep, but unfortunately that didn't happen, as I ended up wearing ears plugs most night.

Savannah had beautiful fresh fruit and fresh coconut milk, for me on the first morning, as I enjoyed the luxurious taste of the pawpaw, straight off their tree in the yard. Mary-Anne agreed to prepare my breakfast each morning; yoghurt and eggs. A few nights, I had dinner at home, with Savannah cooking vegan meals.

Two other guests' rooms were located, at the back of the property, accessed by a path along the side of the house, past Peter's studio. The B&B had all three guest's rooms full during my visit, which was wonderful for the family; as winter can be quieter times.

Peter's studio was located directly below my room, hearing really nice music, filtering out the studio, on a regular basis.

Being a guest entitled me to some special privileges, such as internet access, but it's all about give and take in these situations. At the beginning of my trip, my computer restarted itself and I spent hours trying, to get the internet, to work properly. All of the family relied on the internet to communicate just like I did. I was grateful the internet, was available for me, to use in the first place.

With any third world country, you don't know, what their particular circumstances, were. One descriptive point, from the online booking system, mentioned twenty-four-hour hot water, would be available to all guests. I thought this was a rather odd thing; not realising water wasn't a guaranteed supply, with water pumped into a tank, for use by the household. I'm always conservative with water, only having quick showers, unless it's a hair day, taking a little longer, because I like the conditioner to stay in my hair, for a few minutes. One day, Mary-Anne mentioned to me casually; during a conversation, the guests were the only ones, to have a shower, in the last two days, because of a water problem. Boy did that make me feel rather upset; they didn't feel comfortable enough to tell me, as I would've understood the circumstances.

The electricity prices were horrendous for domestic use, and everything purchased at the shops, were at least three times the price, compared to the mainland. During my first few days on the island, these were the first awakenings of the moments of truth; as I paid extra for my water cooler.

NO MONEY

Mary-Anne drove me to the ATM, to withdraw cash, for their accommodation payment. The online booking company accepted a percentage, as a deposit with the balance payable on arrival. I'd spent the whole day using my debit card which was working fine. The most amazing thing was, you can pay in either $US or local currency with your cash or card. After transferring money over to my travel money card; discovering the banks didn't accept that card at the ATM's or in the banks. The first day I went into the ATM to withdraw money and I couldn't work out the currency. By the third day Mary-Anne and Savannah were getting upset with me as they wanted their money. I finally went into a bank and they advised me, even if different accounts are linked to the card, the machine only recognises it as a credit card. I had tried a few different banks and *EVERYWHERE* I was denied access.

Now I was getting upset, because my cash, for this trip, was stuck on the card, I could only use with purchases. Finally I went into one of the secure bank boxes, where you lock yourself in, with the ATM. I said a prayer; to work out the machine; the currency, and using a different card. *FINALLY*!!!!! Success at last, unfortunately this card attracts international fees and charges, which is why I don't normally use it when travelling. The travel money card was already converted to US currency. My biggest mistake was not withdrawing the US currency, before I hopped on the plane. Next time I'll be more travel savvy☺

QUARTZ CRYSTALS

To enter or leave the property, I drove along a narrow gravel road, through paddocks with grass higher than the car. It's like a little tunnel, as you manoeuvred up and around bends and gullies. The whole area had a large deposit of quartz crystals, a healing stone. Known benefits include restoring balance in your life and healing many aliments. Of course, that's if you believed in their powers.

In fact everything that's ever been created, whether it's rocks, water, soil, birds, plants, animals and even humans; all have our own healing powers. If you BELIEVE. All creatures great and small have been blessed, with their own 'time line'. Each piece of rock on this planet, has seen the changes, since the beginning of time, and just like us has lived many lives. Some rocks have travelled up, from the depths of the planet, to now sit on the surface. They store the energy of the planet, and all the movements that have taken place. How can you explain the mountains, once on the ocean floor, now stand, thousand of metres about sea level? How can you explain the millions of different stones, discovered around the planet?

This was why I love crystals and nature so much, as you sit and hold, a crystal in your hand, to meditate. Ask the earth, rock, crystal and yourself; what messages can be shared with you today. Be still, mindful and wait patiently for the message. The time spent meditating, relaxing and connecting to mother earth, via crystals, was the most important gift, we can give to ourselves.

Each location I visited, I displayed my crystals, for their energy to be renewed by the sun and moon. The perfect location, I found here, was the breakfast table, on the verandah, where during the day, the crystals sparkled, and during the night, they glistened.

REJUVENATION

My whole body was fatigued from the last eight months of work, even though the mattress was hard, I'm sleeping ok. The barking dogs, each night, didn't annoy me, as much, as I started to feel rejuvenated by all of the crystals; relaxing for the first time in months. Volunteering wasn't just the physical expectations affecting you; it's the emotional and mental effects as well. I placed myself in different situations, 'forced' to comply with other people's demands and expectations. Even though I wasn't volunteering here, I still placed myself in a strange, if not a wonderful location, with expectations of me, even as a guest, were limiting and guarded.

I believe I visited, the different locations, to have these specific experiences, meeting the people who lived there. Just like my favourite song "welcome to wherever you are". I'm meant to be here, in this valley, at this time, to meet Mary-Anne and her family.

Mary-Anne was an incredible woman, full of wisdom with an interest in crystals, tarot cards, healing, psychics and spirituality. Each morning when Mary-Anne delivered my breakfast, we would chat and share experiences.

RELAXING

I spent one day totally enjoying the property, as the energy involved with driving and exploring, was exhausting, as you're never still. A picnic table placed in the garden, under a forest of beautiful shady trees, was the perfect place to set up my art supplies. I knew I had to take this opportunity, to feel the energy of the valley, spending the day painting, reading, sleeping and meditating; feeling much more relaxed and rejuvenated, at the end of the day.

MUSIC

Yeah Man, the music, I discovered, was *EVERYWHERE,* driving through the towns, with my window down, to soak up the atmosphere as every shop, house, car and person had their own music blaring from big boom boxes.

I had a blonde moment one day, *(AGAIN)* realising their music originated from Africa. When you look at the world map, of course Africans would have travelled. Durrrrr!!! The music was certainly an important part of this culture; as it is, to each and every country around the world.

NIGHT ACTIVITIES

One night really late, I was having trouble sleeping as everything seemed to be bugging me. Even with ear plugs placed in my ears, this insistent beep was driving me insane. Finally texting Savannah to see if Peter had left an alarm on, in the studio, located directly below my open window. After a little while, Savannah texted back to say Peter had checked the studio; the beep was coming from some bug, down in the field, and unfortunately they wouldn't be able to control that situation. I almost laughed myself to sleep, as the beeping set the rhythm to serenade me☺ Beep, Beep, Beep just like a heart monitor.

THE SANCTUARY

I have to tell you, one of my favourite birds was the hummingbird *(in case you haven't already worked it out).* When I had booked my stay at the B&B, they mentioned a hummingbird sanctuary nearby. After turning off the main highway, the paved road was getting narrower, as I climbed towards the top of a steep hill. The road was in total disrepair, and basically a goat track by the time I pulled the car, into the parking space; greeted by a man who'd be my guide. Handing him twenty-dollars and my camera, he directed me towards a plastic chair, to take a seat; handing me a mini bar bottle, full of nectar.

The man instructed me to hold out the bottle, in a horizontal position, with one hand; on my other hand, hold out one finger, to act as a platform, for the bird to land. It wasn't long before my first hummingbird, landed on my finger, to drink the nectar, out of the bottle. The variety of the hummingbirds, in the garden took my breath away. Their colours were from bright green, to bright pink, to dark purple, some with long wispy tails. The most incredible thing about the birds, was the size of their whole bodies; smaller than my little pinkie.

The sanctuary had been established by a lady, who decided to feed the birds, with the tiny nectar bottles. The lady persevered for many years, and now the sanctuary's a tourist attraction. Winter was the best time to visit the garden; as during spring and summer the birds were busy with nests and young babies.

The guide captured a couple of great photos of the birds sitting on my finger. This was definitely a very special and unique experience, I'll cherish forever. After feeding the hummingbirds, I walked around the garden, to enjoy the landscaped gardens; spotting a few birds flying around, astounded by how fast they move about.

A lady explained to me that during the night; hummingbirds rest their tiny bodies, in an almost unconscious state to rejuvenate. They need this rest, so they're able to sustain, their busy lives each day. I understand completely, as I believe I need this same level of sleep, to rejuvenate my body each night.

THE HILL

The Hill was a private gated community and resort; movie stars and wealthy people, were amongst the owners. A friend of Mary-Anne's was holding an art exhibition, at the resort, and I was invited along as a treat. I'm not sure what happened, but we're at least an hour late leaving. Mary-Anne and Paul (*another guest*) travelled with me, in my car, after dark, struggling to find the resort, without street lighting. I turned around once, finding the resort the second time around.

The cocktail party was held on a beautifully manicured lawn area, making the ambience of the evening very special, with subdued lighting and spot-lighted trees. Large tables with white clothes were set up; unfortunately most of the food and drinks had finished, with staff packing up. Mary-Anne's aim to get really drunk wasn't going to happen, as we were too late. Luckily a few pieces of hot hors devours, and a nice tropical punch, were still available.

Inside the gallery, three were people exhibiting their art tonight. The first artist, an older man used acrylics; painted abstract blocks and shapes. Obviously the man had talent and imagination; who am I to judge what good art was. The second artist painted landscapes, with the scenes almost as perfect, as a photo. A couple of my favourite paintings were already sold; obviously I had the same good taste. The third artist was an abstract artist, enjoying the experience of sometimes turning my head; this way and that way; to establish the subject matter. The paintings were really different; conducting my own interpretation, out of the colourful brushstrokes. If I dared, I'd cheat, by looking at the title of the painting, to see if I could work out why the painting, was so named.

The evening was a chance for Mary-Anne to catch up with some old friends Pat and Tony. Tony had dementia, sitting with him for awhile; as he retold his life's story.

ROAD SIDE STALLS

I travelled one-thousand-kilometers, during my twelve-day stay. Every time, the one thing arousing my senses, the most; were the aromas, from the road side stalls. The stalls had signs mentioning jerk chicken and fish with local spices. The smells of the fresh cooking meat were so tempting; I regret I didn't try some of the fish; not wanting to risk, having a bad experience, as my stomach wasn't used to all of the spices.

MAYAN CALENDAR 21ST DECEMBER

The world press had been going crazy for ages, about the dooms day predictions; the twenty- first-day of December 2012 would be the end of the world. Just like Y2K!! People in 'the know' knew, the connection was to the Mayan calendar; ending a specific energy, controlling the earth. The twenty-first-of-December was the new beginning for humanity, evolving our spirituality, and personal connection to mother earth.

Mary-Anne and I had discussed the Mayan calendar, excited about the changes to Mother Earth. Even more excited when Mary-Anne mentioned, a party to celebrate the date, was going to be held here with their family and friends. Ask the universe for what you want, and it's delivered. On the Friday night all of the guests arrived with a pot luck dinner, as I'm introduced to the families' local friends.

Damien, a local worker, collected wood for a huge bonfire. Damien's girlfriend, Rochelle, lived in a local village and didn't speak English very well, but she's doing ok. Rochelle enjoyed a liqueur with me, not realising how potent the drink was, drinking it straight, like I did. By the time we were half through the evening, she was well and truly drunk, with my bottle half full. I have to tell you, I drink the 40% liqueur by the wine glass.

The guests brought along a vegan or vegetarian dish, to share for dinner; with incredible tastes. After dinner we moved over near the pool area, sitting around, listening to the drums, with Damien lighting the fire. I LOVE fires, mesmerised by the flames, as the vegetation turned into glowing coals, adding warmth to the night's atmosphere. The almost full moon was present in the southern sky; drifting in and out from behind the clouds, highlighting the evening's activities with its presence.

This evening guests started to relaxed, with full bellies and satisfied children playing in and around the house. Around the camp fire, women started to gather, as the drum beat set the mood. Each woman, standing in the circle, dancing, had a moment in the centre, to announce to the world, their wishes and prayers for the future. I remember Rachelle asking 'for more moments like this'. *Me too.* The drumming had an incredible vibration, echoing through the valley, as the still night air started to cool. One of the young sons joined in the performance, setting the rhythm for people relaxing around the lawns and pool area.

I went back to my room for a refresh, and when I came back to the bonfire, all of the women had joined hands and were standing around in a circle. I broke the connection to join hands with Savannah, adding my energy to the circle. The connection with the local women had an incredible strength, as I joined the prayer for a better planet for us, our families, communities and countries.

EXPLORING – THE ROADS AND THE TRAFFIC

I clocked up one-thousand-kilometers during my twelve days holiday. Oh yeah! Guess What? They drive on the left-hand-side of the road, the same as in Australia. However there's just one little problem; I'd been driving on the right hand side, for the last eight months. There's only one instance, leaving the property; turning left onto the main road, automatically merging onto the right hand side of the road. But it's ok, as I was only going about ten-kilometers-per-hour. The road was full of potholes, so I was going ever so slowly, when I spotted a car coming towards me. I noticed they're locals, as I just casually veered the car, over to the left☺. I waved and smiled at them, both continuing on with our day, without any hassles.

After booking my trip, I searched the internet, for a 'heads up' of what to expect, from my visit to the island. The road conditions were mentioned, with the most important thing, to remember; was driving on the left-hand-side. Another thing; horns sounding, with hand gestures, were GOOD, as the locals use, this form of communication, to say Thank You☺

There's no speed limit (well there are signs, but no one takes any notice), with the locals driving like crazy people. The male members of my family would fit in here perfectly. I found most drivers very courteous; if you're turning right, across the flow of traffic, the oncoming cars gives way to you, so you don't hold up the line of traffic following you. What a wonderful idea☺

The taxis stop on the road, to drop off or pick up passengers, as you wait behind them, if there's oncoming traffic. The taxi drivers had a particular licence, driving back and forth all day long, between the destinations, picking up and dropping off passengers.

Did I mention the state of the roads? The main highway was well maintained except when it entered a town. You had to slow down to basically zero speed; weaving in and out, around the pot holes. One town I travelled through regularly, were in desperate need, of road repair work. This town was located right on the ocean front, level with the ocean; a rock wall protected the town from the ocean swell. I bet, the rough seas and king tides flooded the town on a regular basis.

TRAVELLING EAST

Most mornings were my chill out time, for meditation and resting, and the afternoons were my exploration time. I headed east, towards a bay side town, of Del Mar Sol, before realising I forgot to fill the car, with petrol. The road sign said it was one-hundred-kilometers and didn't know whether I'd make it there and back, so I turned around. I travelled back to a beachside bar, pulling up a chair for an afternoon of relaxation.

There were only a few guests when I arrived, and the waitress directed me to a table away from the crowds, where I didn't want to be disturbed by hawkers. The beautiful little beach had the sand immaculately raked and cleaned by a young man, aged in his twenties; who worked continuously collecting all of the debris, coming onto the shore. I ordered a couple of pina coladas and a late lunch.

I had my journal, which I wrote in for the longest time. The music playing above my head, from a speaker, was very upbeat; didn't mix with a spiritual book I was trying to read, so I just kept writing in my journal.

Three men and one woman, all aged in their twenties, were getting ready to go sail boarding. I watched them over an hour or so; setting up the sails, with continuous instructions to the student. One of the guys was set, carrying his gear out onto the water and off he went; well sort of. I watched him, struggling to get onto the board; eventually disappearing from view. The other man didn't seem too worried about him, as I walked out, to the end of the jetty, to see what's happening. They finally went out in a canoe, to rescue him, then came back to finish the lesson with the student. One of the young men was white, British, I think, with blonde dreadlocks down to his waist. When he was ready to enter the water, he put his hair in a ruffian hat.

The sun was setting, but I was on the north-eastern-side of the island, so the sunset was not very spectacular from this angle; with very little cloud cover, the dusk light, slowly turned to darkness. I was getting ready to go home when a band arrived and started to set up for a session. I was debating whether or not to stay. I'd been there for about five hours already and I wasn't really hungry or thirsty. Silly me, I left a perfect opportunity; to listen and enjoy some traditional music. What The #$@^*? *Never let an opportunity go by, and please start listening to my intuition more.*

TRAVELLING SOUTH

One day I explored the southern cities, driving through the country side; with very little traffic, stopping many times, to admire the landscape and houses, along the way. When you think about the Caribbean, what's the first thing that comes to your mind? For me it's music and COLOUR. It's the bright luminous yellow, orange, purple and pink colour palates, included in everything, from fashion to houses. Now IF I lived here, I'd definitely paint my house, one of the many colours, displayed around the hill sides; as they definitely say Caribbean, to me.

I arrived in the little seaside township of Del Savant, with the whole town full of excitement and celebration. I have to mention that today, was one week before Christmas; the streets were lined with wall to wall people, markets, shops and traffic. The main street, I'd estimate to be about two-kilometers long, taking me over thirty minutes, to drive through the town.

The traffic was bumper to bumper; my car windows were down, enjoying the festive party atmosphere on offer. The streets were full of people shopping; vendors trying to sell their wares. The music was blasting out of the boom boxes, listening to the songs on the streets; just as one song faded, the next one cut in, rapping and tapping my way down the street.

The gravel car park, at the end of the main street; allowed access to the wharf, fishing dock and ocean. The car park was covered with large pot holes, filled with water; deciding not to park here, as I didn't want to damage the vehicle. Stopping for a few brief minutes to look around, before rejoining the queue of cars; heading back down the main street, enjoying the atmosphere once again, as I drove out of town. I would've been 'safe', since I was the only white woman (person) I could see, as I happily stayed in my car. I'm not a window shopper, not wanting to be harassed, to buy items that I didn't need or want.

THE BAY EXPLORATIONS

Songs and movies had been made, about the capital city, and I wanted to see what the hype was all about. Was it the beach side activity parks, the shopping or just the atmosphere of being in the Caribbean that excited me the most?

Parking at beachside activity park for three-dollars, at 10:00am; the only customer there, besides the workers. Visiting the bathroom, with no toilet paper; none of the shops or vending places were open. I walked down along the beach; reaching a six-foot-high fence; with an assortment of palms and other trees, casting shade over the beach. Sitting under the trees for a couple of hours; adjusting my sitting position, to stop the dumbness. I also didn't want to go home with sunburnt legs. The area was certainly quiet, with the bonus of not getting harassed once. Having to pay, for a quite spot, was worth the expense, to enjoy the whole experience. The beach here, in this little cove, was very well protected and I could see how young families, would enjoy time spent here. As I was leaving, a few more people were arriving, to enjoy a glorious sunny day, at the beach.

Driving over to the main part of town; parking my car; hoping I didn't get a ticket or worse; get the car towed away. I crossed the street to look at some shops, selling everything your little hearts desired. Looking for a hat each for my two youngest children, as I'm sure they'd enjoy my thoughtfulness. They'd probably prefer me to bring something else back, but that wasn't going to happen☺ Walking into the first shop, and walking back to the car, in under ten minutes, with my shopping all done. I didn't have room for anything extra, with my luggage already overweight, especially with all the food I had to take back with me.

My next stop was an entertainment complex; opening the door, a blast of music and food aromas ignited my senses, with people everywhere, A large counter, running along the length of the room, with their high bar stools, were perfect to watch the activities, out on the ocean and in the large open auditorium.

Taking a seat at the railing counter, I ordered a pina-colada with a prawn salad for lunch. A group of cruise ship passengers were being entertained by a DJ, while eating their lunch. A few guys *(or maybe girls)* were dressed in costumes, and wearing stilts, roaming the floor, mixing with the crowds and having photos taken. *(Of course for a tip which was how I found this out, but I have a great photo to prove it).*

There were three levels of the resort, with the bottom floor accessing the pontoons, and dock area; where a party boat was being boarded, heading out for an afternoon sailing adventure. Pontoons and huge floatation devices were anchored, in a protected area, just off the beach, in front of the resort. People were diving, sliding and enjoying the activities with their laughter and enjoyment becoming contagious.

The third floor was an open deck, dining area, full of table and chairs, and large umbrellas, with a spectacular view, over the calm ocean waters of the bay; but today it's very hot, sitting in the sun.

My spot on the counter was perfect, until after I had eaten my lunch, and when I came back from a bathroom visit, some people had taken it. Oh well, time to go.

I wasn't ready to go home just yet! Returning to my car *(it was still there)*, turning onto a random road, on the eastern side of town, leading to the ocean front, behind the airport, where the landing lights beacons, were located in the ocean. I sat in my car, with the windows down, on the ocean front, reading my book, and breathing in the ocean air.

I observed; the colour of the ocean was different here, something to do with the temperature of the water. The blue colour, of the ocean, was so surreal, compared to the whiteness of the sand. Definitely a magical place and so blessed to be here.

With a recommendation of Mary-Anne's, I visited a local restaurant, located near the waterfront, for a beautiful breakfast omelette; enjoying the atmosphere, while catching up on my journal. I was the only white person in the restaurant; figuring it's more of a business person's club, as most people dining here today, looked like professionals, having a breakfast meeting.

Most of the resorts; on the island had all inclusive deals, with their guests never having to leave; with all of their food, alcohol, entertainment and activities included in the tariff. The shuttle bus transfers you from the airport to the resort, where you don't need to leave, until your departure. This little piece of information, explains why there weren't many tourists at breakfast here.

Trying to do a budget, of sorts, for my trips; add together the airfares, shuttles and taxis, the accommodation, the car rental, insurance and the fuel. The amounts are staggering, before adding meals and any treats. After I added up the amounts, it worked out at $250 per day, $3,000 for the twelve days. I really hadn't done very much, or visited many places; image my bill if I'd lashed out. Anyway the experience was worth the outlay, when you take into account my entire trip; the volunteering, balances it out quite nicely, as most weeks my purse didn't open once.

White chocolate mocha was my favourite drink; spending time in a modern alfresco café, near the bank, with their new décor and comfortable seats. Just NO WHIP. Why do cafes do that?

TRAVELLING WEST

I headed west, exploring the part of the island, perfect for catching a sunset or two. The town of Rilgen was perfectly located, for sunsets; nothing was standing in its way from here to Australia. Maybe that's a little bit of exaggeration, for a start; we're in the Atlantic Ocean between North and South America.

My first time travelling west, I was signalled, to pull over for a police check. Two police officers, one male and one female, were stopping all traffic. Requesting my identification and ownership papers for the car; advising them it was a rental car. They seemed happy with the paperwork of my agreement, allowing me to go. Thankfully☺.

The entire length of the highway, along the coastline, was basically door to door resorts, having one-hundred-percent access to the beaches. Holy moly, the size of the resorts were the size of a small town, with massive accommodation towers; everything your little hearts desires, was included in the tariff. Well maybe there're a couple of things, not included, if you know what I mean!#@%&? But then again, what do I know.

The trip to Rilgen was about three hours, and the first time I drove into the township, I completed a u-turn at the first round-about and found a nice open beach to visit. A market place was open selling the normal touristy things, to spend your money on, but I wasn't buying. I already had overweight luggage, my gift shopping was done and I didn't need anything for myself. I parked the car and carried a bag with some water, a little money, my glasses and a reading book. As soon as I reached the sand I took off my sandals; walking straight into the ocean; OMG the water felt amazing.

Here was a scene taken straight out of a romance book: A woman reaches the water's edge; the incredible colour of the sky, reflected in her blue eyes, as a warm breeze gently fans her face, ruffling her hair out of place. The continuous waves crashing onto the white sand, sends a new set of foaming liquid, up onto the beach. Out in the water, a man was riding a wave, towards her. He reaches her, pulling her into his embrace, wrapping his arms around her body, kissing her passionately. All thoughts vanished, as passion consumed them; the wave's continuing to crash around them.

This beach would be the perfect place to have a holiday romance. What are the chances of travelling around the world and finding love here?

WAKE UP Bella, back to reality. The incredible colour of the sky was reflected in my blue eyes, a warm breeze gently fans my face as my hair was ruffled out of place. The continuous waves crashing onto the white sand, sends a new set of foaming liquid, up onto the beach. I reached the water's edge, the magic of the liquid, calmed every cell in my body. I looked up and down the beach, with only a few people on the beach today. Noticing some shade trees, up along the beach; I strolled along the water's edge without a care in the world.

Out of nowhere, a lady approaches me, wanting to put aloevera on my skin, for protection from the sun. This lady was a local, with the darkest skin, compared to mine; forced the aloevera onto my back, costing me ten-US-dollars. The lady told me, how she's trying to feed her children. Who knows what her real story was, as she was still on the beach, when I left.

I walked up along the beach, to find a nice spot, under a grove of trees, to relax and read my book. Well I thought it'd be quiet, but I was constantly approached by young men; trying to sell chocolates, fruit, and escort services. A young teenager came up and sat next to me, trying to sell me chocolates. When I said I couldn't eat them, he asked me to give him money anyway, to help him with his schooling. I politely told him "no" and he eventually left. One young man sat next to me, wanting to keep me company, but I told him, I was reading and wanted to be alone. Through a fence, behind me, was another man, said I could sit in his yard, so no one would bother me. I couldn't win.

Mary-Anne told me, (*afterwards*) white women who travel alone, looking for a 'good time' stay in Rilgen. I was definitely looking for a good time; but not with a local gigolo, thank you very much. I sat on the beach reading my book, until the temperature started to rise. No it wasn't me personally, just the weather. I observed a woman in the surf, obviously having a great time with a local man. I'm not here to judge anyone about their choices; just because it wasn't what I'd do. Hey if I was more confident, about my luscious curvy body, then I'd be out in the waves with a gorgeous young man, who would satisfy my every whim☺. This whole situation on the beach could've ended so differently, if I'd given it a chance.

After I left the beach, I drove back into town and continued heading west along the ocean front. Discovering the wall to wall resort complexes, didn't allow any ocean views. The high walls erected around every residence, blocked any chance to enjoy the sunset.

I spotted a place where I'd definitely come back for a sunset photo opportunity. The Palace obviously looked like a happening place, but there weren't any available car parks; returning to the valley.

WESTERN ROAD TRIP REVISITED

My second visit Rilgen was to visit a health spa; wanting to spend time at the ocean, without the harassment; and the owner was a friend of Savannah. Travelling along the ocean road, I passed the Palace, the historical lighthouse, leaving the ocean front, travelling through a parcel of undeveloped land, before reaching another group of hotels and resorts. Sandy's place was located here, as I was directed through the building, towards the ocean front bar, ordering a fruit smoothie with a fresh salad for lunch. Alone at the bar, reading, for quite awhile before a young couple from the states joined me.

So far they had spent three days on the island; telling me when they were walking along the main beach in Rilgen; they were approached by men offering everything including drugs. OMG. Boy of boy that would've been such a scary situation. This information has confirmed I am definitely safer, in a private place like this, than alone on an open public beach.

Continuing to read my book; the weather was warm and as the sun sunk closer to the horizon. A coral reef off shore, has distributed pieces of broken white coral, littering the rocks along the foreshore. Sandy's ocean frontage was only about five-hundred-metres wide, with a fabulous spa strategically placed on the edge of the lawn area. I could image myself sitting there, with a glass of bubbly, toasting a perfect afternoon on this tropical island. The clouds were just showing the right amount of colour, as the young couple captured the moment for me; witnessing another magical afternoon on planet earth. I thanked Sandy for another wonderful afternoon.

On my next visit to this island, I will definitely visit a few more places, with Sandy's definitely on the top of the list, for a few days of massaging, detoxing and relaxing. I need to stay at one of the big resorts for a couple of days, to get drunk and have a bloody good time. Thirdly I'd go for a sunset cruise, along the coast line, on a party boat.

The Australian government's travel warnings for some of these Southern America islands had high level warnings, for certain locations. Over the twelve-days; I visited a lot of places, even though I didn't get out of the car, at some of the towns; I never once felt like I shouldn't have been there, or felt uneasy in any way.

THE PALACE

Pulling the car into the Palace, after Sandy's place, finding a car park easily, as the sun had set and the crowds were disappearing. A party yacht was tied up at the bottom of the stairs, with guests climbing back on board, returning to their place of departure.

Standing near the bottom of the staircase; I was looking up, at a young boy, about to jump off the cliff, into the ocean. His father was standing near me, encouraging the boy to jump. Everyone else around the cliffs and stairs, were anxiously waiting for the boy to jump, as well. When the boy finally reappeared in the water, everyone was clapping his amazing courage. The father hugged the boy, sending him back up to the top of the cliff, to jump again.

I spent a few minutes, on the staircase that appeared to be, newly constructed. The steps were wide enough for about one-hundred people to transverse them, at any one time. The stair case wound its way down, the side of the cliff, with several large platforms, to take a seat or a photo. The staircase was certainly well constructed, with a lot of thought going into the design, with the final platform, almost at sea level.

I got so close to the ocean, I was almost touching the crystal clear blue waters, as this experience was registered, as a memorable occasion. There's lots of laughter and a party atmosphere; mingling amongst the tourists, almost invisible; wandering around all of the areas, enjoying the anonymous escapade of a tourist. Except I was being watched, and pounced upon by a man, who noticed I was alone. Steve was his name, as he immediately went into action, with his hands all over me, kissing and touching me. It was madness. At lightning speed he asked me a million questions, wanted a photo with me, plus my phone number, so he could phone me, which he did. He dialed, my number, from his phone, making sure it's correct. His whole performance was planned out, to the finest detail, so every second, of our brief five minute meeting, could be accounted for. I'd say the whole routine was practiced, polished, and rehearsed for minimum outlay and maximum effect.

I tried to break away from him, saying I wanted to take photos, but he refused to let go of my hand, as he came along too. He wanted a drink, so I ordered a pina colada for both of us, while we sat at a table. He continuously said hello to people, passing by, as our drinks arrived. Steve asked a waiter to take another photo, as we chatted while we drank our cocktails. He lived on the eastern side of town, spending summers in eastern Canada, helping a friend with his business. We talked about Canada and just general chitchat. Once I had finished my drink I hopped up to leave with Steve saying he'd come too. "No" he wasn't coming with me, as I'm staying too far away.

Steve said a friend of his, owned a bar down the road, suggesting we go there, to play some pool. It's his friend's birthday today, and he wanted to say hi. I drove both of us down the road to his friends bar, staying maybe an hour. The bar was exactly what I thought; with a pool table, and surprisingly, a birthday cake. Coins were lined up in order, at the pool table, with ours, being game number three.

Steve wanted a drink so he bought his own; I said I was fine, as I had to drive home. Steve talked to friends, until it was our time, to play pool. I haven't picked up a cue stick for maybe ten years, so the game didn't take very long, for Steve to win.

When we finished the game I told Steve I was going home. He again said he'd go with me. I said "NO". Steve had his bike back at the car park, so I dropped him off with a quick kiss on the cheek goodnight. Probably wondering what he'd done wrong, because I wasn't coming around to his ideas. Steve mentioned he'd show me around the island. I know, for a fact, I won't be ringing him, for anything, as he's just too far away.

It's the connection you sense; nothing to do with, what people look like. There was absolutely no physical attraction, when Steve kissed me. Yes I waited for fireworks; some reaction, but I didn't feel, one ounce of passion, towards this guy. I'm sorry, but something has to be working to have sex with another person.

After dropping off Steve, this was my first night-time driving experience; with the maniac taxi drivers. The taxis would toot, and wave as they zoomed by, at a-hundred-miles-an-hour. This road wasn't familiar, and too scary to drive, even at the speed limit. I enjoyed the slow trip, back to the valley; catching glimpses of the moon, rising up, over the horizon, guiding me home.

My next visit to Rilgen was my second last night, on the island. I waited most of the day for Savannah, to ring with details of a friend, taking me to watch a drumming show. I was ready to go with my swimmers and towel, with the thought, I may cliff jump. A Rilgen resort had their evening drumming show, with available seat including dinner was $85US.

When I arrived at the Palace, the place was packed with tourist, finding a car park. A few people were still jumping, so I got changed. I was surprised to find Steve alone, sitting on a chair near the top of the cliff; approaching him to say hello. Steve was fixated on filling out lotto tickets, for that night's one-hundred-million-dollar Christmas draw. I gave Steve my bag with clothes and keys and went to stand at the top of the cliff to prepare for the jump.

I have no idea WHY I was standing there. I was so excited to be doing this; I wanted to be spontaneous; to take a leap of faith. I had no prior thoughts, of what the outcome would be, as I looked down at the water. *IT WAS A BLOODY LONG WAY DOWN.* Maybe I should've changed to the twenty-foot platform, instead of the thirty-five-foot one. But no; I had to do it. I stood up there in my swimmers, with this amazing strength, and courage and jumped off. The trip flying through the air was liberating, UNTIL I hit the water. The ocean was angry, as I floated quickly up to the surface, taking a breath; I swam back towards the steps. I couldn't believe how much pain I was in, as I reached the platform, climbing up the ladder, with the help of the life guard.

I didn't land very well in the water, and I was in excruciating pain. The rocks on the bottom platform were still warm, from the sun, as I lay down for a few minutes. The lifeguard asked me 'why I didn't have my legs straight'. A lady who had watched me jump, came to check on me, going up to see Steve, as he came down to help me up the stairs. I took about thirty minutes to change into my clothes; Steve drove me to a shop, to buy pain killers. He told me they could be taken every two hours, but when I read the packet, *THE NEXT MORNING*, they were to be taken every eight hours. I had already taken four times the recommended dosage.

Steve drove me back to his house, where I spent the night, on a daybed, on his verandah. Steve purchased some massage oil, which he heated up in the microwave. Twice during the night Steve rubbed my back, to relieve the pain. I texted Savannah, to let her know, I was staying here the night, and would be home in the morning. A couple of times, during the night, I would've gone home, except the doors were deadlocked and Steve had my car keys. In the morning we went for breakfast, and visited the ATM, as Steve wanted payment for the care and massages. How can you put a price on being cared for? Steve asked for four-hundred-dollars US, which was outrageous, but I paid him anyway. When I dropped him back at his house, after breakfast, he gave me another massage. I thanked him for his healing hands, his care and concern, and for helping me. *When I think about what would've happened, if Steve wasn't there? I would've just driven back to B&B and dealt with the pain, with the help of Mary-Anne. I would've saved the four-hundred-dollars and given Mary-Anne something instead.*

LAST 24 HOURS

Leaving Steve; I drove directly to a drug store, speaking to a pharmacist, asking for a pain management plan. I arrived back at the valley, with Savannah and Mary-Anne very concerned; feeling guilty that one of them should have gone, with me; it wasn't their decision, it was mine. I spent the afternoon rehydrating myself, by drinking litres of water, to cushion the shock.

I was in shock. What the freaking hell was I thinking, by putting myself in that situation? I could have easily crippled myself. Never before attempting anything like that, always protecting myself, from risking my life, and now I do this at fifty-three-years-of-age. My body was in shock, I hadn't eaten since lunch time yesterday, except for a sausage, at breakfast with Steve. My body was in 'fight or flight' mode; I wasn't coping at all. During the afternoon, I rested after packing my bags, preparing to leave, for the airport in the morning.

Mary-Anne and I had planned to go out for dinner that night, heading into the city, to a little shack Mary-Anne had wanted to visit; which was closed. Our plan 'b', was the riverboat restaurant instead; moored permanently in the harbour; walking up onto the top deck, we ordered a cocktail. The night air was a little chilly, with a soft breeze travelling across the bay. The stars were sparkling, and the moon shining, as we continued our tour, to the Mariner's Club. A crisp white-cloth decorated the table, was waiting for us, out near the edge of the deck. I'd visited here on my first and last day on the island, with Mary-Anne. When our meals arrived, the fish I ordered was a full snapper, big enough for a family of four and full of bones. I couldn't see where the bones were, because we only had a candle, to dine by. I wasn't very hungry anyway, as it was nearly eleven o'clock at night, wasting my money, on the meal; however I enjoyed the outing with my dear friend.

I pulled in for petrol on the way home; assuming it was a credit-card operated bowser; however after we'd filled up, and the attendant said it was cash only. I'd already passed the last ATM, with just enough 'tip' money, to give Mary-Anne and the family. I'd now have to pay them twenty-dollars less. Mary-Anne said it was ok, after telling her what my plans were for the cash☺

Surprised I didn't sleep very well that night; drugged up to the eyeballs. On my final morning Mary-Anne brought me my breakfast; chatting for ages, exchanging gifts, enjoying a beautiful sun filled morning, on the verandah. Mary-Anne gave me a small piece of quartz, from the property, and my gift was a copy of 'live your life' poem. After breakfast Mary-Anne came back to present me with a black obsidian pendulum.

Mary-Anne mentioned she'd love to take the children to the movies with popcorn and treats. There's enough money in the envelope, to enjoy the outing, as a thank-you, for Mary-Anne's care and friendship.

Peter loaded my bags into the car, saying goodbye to the family; heading to the airport, via the rental car place. I saved enough cash for the porter, at the airport, as he'd have to transfer all of my bags to the airline desk.

I checked my entire luggage, including my backpack, through to Miami, as I could hardly pick up my handbag. Enquiring at the check-in counter about a wheelchair; they said I had too much hand luggage. I had to persevere paying the one-hundred-and-fifty-dollars for the three pieces of checked luggage. I had a coffee, at the airport café, watching almost the entire movie, about local legends, playing on the television. I kept the drugs topped up; sitting in the plane for the short leg was ok.

WELCOME TO AMERICA☺

When I arrived back in Miami I collected all of my bags, to pass through customs. I was hoping for a carefree entry.

The customs guy asked "how are you"
I told him "I have a bad back"
He asked "how did that happen"
I told him "cliff jumping" he laughed and stamped my passport.

I paid the porter to handle my luggage off the turnstile, before transferring them to the drop off point for the connecting plane. I just had one more airport to go through today, and I had to find an ATM, for the payment of the final porter at my destination. I didn't find an ATM, and when I arrived back in California, I asked at the airlines help desk, for a porter to help me with my luggage. A lady called Francis helped me; and since I didn't have any cash, I promised to drop off cash to her in two days, on my way to Canada.

I arrived at the same motel, from a couple of weeks ago. The driver helped me with the bags, in and out of the van, and into reception. I collapsed on my bed, lying down for an hour to stretch out my back, before going over to a cafe for dinner. I could hardly sit on the chair, because it was so hard, with excruciating pain, throughout my body. I forced myself to eat the meal, to absorb some energy. I spent the night with a continuous path to the bathroom, drinking one glass of water, after another, all throughout the night.

Oh I forgot it was Christmas Day in Australia, ringing my mum and dad; brother and my children while I was in Miami. I'd forgotten to take my phone off flight mode, after the next flight; missing an extra couple of calls; only realising two days later, after I arrived in Canada that the phone wasn't working.

Christmas day I spent most of the day in bed watching television and sleeping. I went out into the breakfast bar, to get hot water for my hot chocolate; to find a lady, Priscilla, writing out Christmas cards for all of the guests. I told her about my sore back, and she gave me some emu oil; not even touching the sides of the pain. I asked the desk clerk, at the motel, where the nearest drug store was located. He said down the road about one mile, arranging for a cab to pick me up, wait for me, while I shopped; then drove me back to the motel. I spoke to a pharmacist, recommending different types of pain killers, to hopefully make my recovery, a little easier.

Christmas dinner I went back to the same café, as the night before, enjoying the festivities and the staff were really nice. The cafe was very busy, with people dining-in for their Christmas meal. Oh well, I was there too, so what could I say☺. I went to bed after reorganising my bags *AGAIN* and would still have to check in all three bags, through to Canada.

I spent the entire night again, doing the bathroom shuffle, continuing to buffer my body from the shock. My back wasn't any better, however I was feeling calmer. I woke up for the 6:00am shuttle, arriving at terminal two for my departure; with Francis working at terminal four. I wasn't able to keep my promise, to pay her, for helping with my luggage.

The shuttle driver helped with my luggage onto a trolley; then asking the clerk at the check-in counter for help. He told me, he wasn't supposed to lift any luggage onto the scales; even after telling him about my back, I still had to lift the bags. I paid seventy-dollars for all three bags as checked-in luggage, passed through security, and found a place for breakfast. You never know with airports how long it may take be processed through check in or security. I definitely know the flights don't wait for anyone, if you're running late.

There's not a chance in hell; I would miss this flight to Canada.

This I believe is my road 'Home'. In The Kiss - the link between
this valley, the circle lake and Meadow Glen.

Chapter 21

CANADA – DECEMBER TO APRIL

THE ARRIVAL

During the flight I chatted to a lady, with her son playing in a hockey competition this weekend. I gave her the envelope with Francis's name on it; to drop it off at the airlines when she returned home. I never heard if she got it or not and just hope she forgives me for not keeping my promise. Next time I go there, I'll have to see, if she's still working, at the airport.

I arrived into the customs area, with a gorgeous officer, aged about forty, sitting in his booth.
He asked "why are you here visiting".
I replied "I'm here for the winter since I'd been here in spring and summer".
The Officer asked with a bored look on his face "why?"
I said "because I love it so much".
The Officer asked "do you have family here"
I said "I had a nephew in Stapleton and had friends all over the place".
The Officer asked "Do you have an application in for residency"
I said "no".

The Officer stamped my passport, allowing me to stay until the beginning of April. Whoooooa!!!!! Thank you, thank you, thank you☺. It's such a relief to know I'm back here to look after Steve and Lauren's house.

A porter helped transfer my luggage, to the rental car building; waiting an hour, before transferring my luggage into the car. Not sure whether he's paid by the airport, but I gave him twenty-dollars for his help.

It's hard to believe the Caribbean temperature was thirty-degrees; arriving here to wet and cold conditions, with a five degree temperature. I settled into my little grey car, setting off towards the highway; getting lost and just kept heading east (well I hope I was heading east); basically following my nose, hoping to find the Trans Canada Highway. Finally back on track, each exit off the highway, advertises what services, were available at that exit. I just kept driving until I found the motel sign. Breathing a sigh of relief, I settled back, into my adopted motherland.

Checking into the motel, discovering it's one of the nicest motels, I've ever stayed in; grabbing underwear, toiletries and my pillow.

I walked next door to a restaurant for an early dinner, as I hadn't eaten much today, but I'm feeling a whole lot better. I rang my daughter, as soon as I realised, my phone has been on flight mode for the last three days. We chatted for a few minutes before a shower, watching a little television, with an early night, excited about my trip tomorrow, heading east. Steve and Lauren were arriving about 8:00am; texting them the address and room number; eager to start the next leg of this extraordinary, courageous adventure.

WARNING

About a week before my arrival, I received an email from Lauren, advising to change my plans, with the likelihood the mountain passes, would be closed, because of blizzard weather conditions. I looked at rental cars; costing me an extra $1000 to rent a car out of Langton or Poomlah, plus the extra cost of purchasing a return air flight ticket. I convinced Lauren, I'd take my time driving, as there's no other option, than to drive in tandem with them.

Now this was from a woman who'd *NEVER* driven in snow, let alone a blizzard; zero visibility, with gravel, slush and ice, covering the surface of the road. My car wasn't equipped with snow tyres, or had snow chains available.

The trip started with Steve and Lauren, and Star the cat, travelling along in their big F2000 truck as I followed them. After about one hour, Steve and Lauren pulled into a park, for a bathroom stop, with Lauren deciding to ride along with me, to set the pace over the mountain. The mountain scene around me was extraordinary, with the snow blanketing the whole landscape, into a white winter wonderland. To be honest, the whole drive, through this blizzard felt surreal, like watching a movie, or travelling in some alternative universe. Mesmerized by the fact it *WAS REAL,* truly one of the most magical moments of my life.

My windscreen wipers were going, flat out, trying to keep up with the snow fall. The other vehicles, screaming past me, threw gravel up all over my car; having difficulty with the vision, and as a result I continuously used the water reservoir, to clean the windscreen; running out of wiper fluid. Luckily Steve had a spare bottle in his truck. Silly me, I thought I'd just add my drinking water to the tank (*like I do at home*) and it'd be ok. Oh no, there's special fluid, as normal water freezes, before you need to use it. Fancy that.

My little car was handling the blizzard conditions, with amazing confidence, cruising up over the mountain. I had little snacks in the car, stopping for another loo stop and to stretch. Luckily we had passed through the worst of the weather, with only another hour or so drive, before reaching home.

After the second break, at Adamstown, I returned to the car to find a flat tyre. Oh NO when did that happen? I had driven on the side of the road, up over the mountain, because of all of the traffic zooming past me. I wasn't even sure how many lanes of traffic there were, as the roads were just slush and gravel, without any visible line markings on the road. How scary to be travelling at breakneck speeds, not even aware of WHERE you were on the road.

My back was still quite painful, but I was feeling better, in myself. Of course excited with the incredible journey, up through the mountains, seeing the majestic trees and landscape all covered in snow. With zero visibility, I took micro seconds to look around at the landscape.

MY EXPECTATIONS

When I first thought about coming to Canada, to house sit, my only responsibility was caring for Star the cat; feeding and medication twice a day. Other than that, I had *NO* other responsibilities, except to enjoy myself.

I thought; *WHAT* could I expect from my three months in Canada? What did I want to experience? What did I want to do or see? Over time, I started to think about 'my bucket list' and came up with a few things, I thought, would be achievable.

1. I wanted to explore, as much of the area, as possible. I wanted to drive around the mountains, reconnecting with nature.
2. At least every second day *I HAD TO LEAVE THE HOUSE,* to go exploring somewhere. If I didn't do this one thing, then I might as well have gone back to Australia. Because I wasn't appreciating the opportunity, if all I did was stay at home.
3. I wanted to have a conversation with a man over a nice dinner.
4. I wanted to be kissed passionately by a man.
5. I wanted to sort out all of my feelings and reconnect back to 'myself' ready for a fresh new start, once I landed back in Australia.

There's a saying 'be careful what you wish for'; starting this new leg, of my journey, of self discovery.

TOP VALUES

Maybe my top values may give me an insight, about what was important.

Genuineness – to act in a manner that was true to who I am

Self-Knowledge – to have a deep and honest understanding of myself

Passion – to have deep feelings about ideas, activities and people

Self-Acceptance – to accept myself as I am

Self-Esteem – to feel good about myself

Acceptance – to be accepted as I am

Inner Peace – to experience personal peace

Spirituality – to grow and mature spiritually

Purpose – to have meaning and direction in life

Health – to be physically well and healthy

THE FAMILY, THE HOUSE

We finally arrived in Benton, to the heaviest recorded snow fall, in years. I'll call Benton my home, for the next three months. Steve helped me with my luggage, carrying them over the beautifully polished wood panel floors.

The house was really nice, just two bedrooms; two bathrooms; an office; small open plan kitchen, dining and lounge; laundry room; a back deck area and terraced back yard. The front of the house was also terraced, with a well designed rockery and minimalist plantings, for a low maintenance garden. The back yard, was where all the action happened with lawn, veggie patch and fruit trees.

Of course, *NONE* of this was visible, under the meter of snow covering the whole neighbourhood. Lauren and Steve had been visiting family for the holidays, only home for a couple of days, before heading to Mexico.

The first night Steve and Lauren prepared their own dinner; which I thought was rather rude, not including me in their plans. Eating a pastry; enjoying a long hot shower; and going to bed with pain killers.

The street and house were really quiet, as I slept in a comfortable supportive queen size bed. My back was saying thank you, thank you, thank you. After breakfast, Steve and I organised a new tyre for my car, at the local tyre place. The replacement tyre was sixty-dollars, with Steve replacing it back on the vehicle for me.

Wait a minute, who said anything about shovelling the snow off the driveway, to get the car out of the garage, before I could drive *ANYWHERE*:-). One day after it snowed, it rained, turning the concrete driveway into a slippery slid runway. I reversed the car back across the street; planted the foot, on the accelerator, coming to a stop, with only the front wheels, making it onto the ramp.:-(The car stayed in that same position for three days, before I was able to drive it back into the garage.

BENTON

Steve gave me a guided tour around the township, a small rural town, with basically a main street going straight through the centre of town. The main street was part of the north/south bound highways connecting the USA with Canada.

The town was situated close the US border, with people I met, travelling to get their groceries and fuel. The cost of EVERYTHING was almost half, so why wouldn't you travel the forty minutes each week, to save your hard earned pennies. I had considered this option, but unfortunately being an Australian, on a visa for three months. I wasn't jeopardizing my visa by saving a few dollars.

Even though summer in this valley, was the peak tourist season; the towns were busy during the winter months, with snow birds staying for several months. Usually the temperatures drop to about minus ten; relatively warm compared to the minus forties, in other parts of the country. Canadians stored their RV's, at the storage sheds here, transferring them to the parks, to escape the weather back home.

I spoke to several people, WHY people would leave their homes, to travel during the winter. Residents, who can, travel further afield to southern USA, Mexico or even Hawaii. If you're aged eighty years or older, the insurance for international travel was too expensive for most budgets. So the 'snow birds' come to here, to enjoy a warmer winter, rather than stay at home.

Of course, most of these visitors have been coming here for years, with many rekindled friendships each year. Activities, at local community centres, entertained all of the snow birds with regular dances, open mikes, musical performances and activities.

Motels remain open during the winter months, offering cheap weekly tariffs, for their winter guests. Tariffs were about three-hundred-and-fifty dollars, for a couple, including warm rooms, comfortable beds, kitchens, internet and all the comforts of home.

SALANGIA

The town's lake freezes during winter, which was a beautiful sight, driving along the narrow strip of land, connecting the two sides of the township. I spent many days driving through this tiny township heading east searching for adventures, sunsets and sunshine.

The township and nearby lakes connects with the border of the USA, which was quite amazing how the waters just turn from one country into another. *Just like when I was touring the Thousand Islands in Ontario, where part of the lakes were USA and the other part was Canada.*

NEW YEAR'S EVE

Yeah, like I'll *NEVER, NEVER, EVER, EVER* again spend a new year's eve like that one. Walking alone, into a bar, hoping to find someone, to kiss me at midnight. No matter how lonely I may be, I'm never putting myself in that position ever again, never, never, ever again. Remind me, each December, to keep my promise, to spend the New Year in a better way.

I walked into the bar and the place was a *DIVE*. I should've checked it out, earlier in the week, and went *SOMEWHERE ELSE* for New Year's Eve. I travelled over to Langton, a nearby town to attend their recently opened movie theatre, with complimentary popcorn for every movie ticket tonight. The place was packed, waiting nearly thirty minutes to purchase my ticket. By the time I watched the movie, and drove back to Benton; there was only thirty minutes until midnight. I'd promised myself I would *NOT* sit at home this year, which I'd been doing for probably the last twenty years, usually asleep, well before midnight.

Tonight was different; I was in a new country, with new people to meet, wanting this New Year to be different for me. Starting with the stroke of the hand, on the clock at midnight, I wanted to be different; pre-empted spells or curses, like Cinderella.

A young DJ/karaoke man, was entertaining maybe fifty people in the bar area. I ordered a liqueur, only to be given a cheap alternative, having two in thirty minutes. I sat a long table, next to other people, but they were all mixed up in their own conversations. When the countdown for midnight finished, a young guy of about thirty, was standing in front of me. I looked at him; opened my arms up, shrugging my shoulders, as an invitation. We kissed for about five seconds; chatted for about thirty seconds and then I walked out. The whole experience was humiliating, degrading, embarrassing and never to be repeated ever again. *NEVER, EVER AGAIN. GOT THAT!!!*

SPEAKERS

One of my first phone calls was to the local Speakers club, enquiring about their meeting schedule; with meetings at the seniors centre, each Tuesday night. The characters, of the group, included bush poets, a local councillor, softly spoken ladies, retired gentlemen, a mentally challenged man, a ball room dancer and working mothers. Being an independent observer, I noticed, the members gain more confidence, as they improved their speaking skills. Two and half months as an honorary member; contributing to the meetings as if, it was my club. I acted as chairman for the evening, gave evaluations of speeches, baked brownies and delivered a couple of speeches myself.

I based both of my speeches on my travels, printing out photographs of different locations, which were passed around the table, as I spoke of my extraordinary, courageous adventure. I invited Angie to attend one meeting, as my guest; presenting my second instalment of my travel story. The time shared with this group of people, was enjoyable, entertaining, educational; listening to the member's stories; presented on a variety of subjects.

CALL FOR ASSISTANCE

The second phone call was to David, a massage therapist, asking for an appointment. I've only ever had one deep tissue massage; and didn't have any other choice, as most of the masseurs had flown south, for winter.

I arrived at David's door, receiving cold packs and *TORTURE,* as part of my session. The one hour session was excruciating, with David recommending I purchase cold packs, from the drug store, to expedite my recovery. I'd booked three appointments, each week for three weeks, and then David was also flying south for winter.

By the time David left on his trip, my back was much stronger. As David left, I found help through Belinda and Ann, who were angels sent from heaven, to restore 'me' back to the person I knew I was. Somewhere deep down, in my soul; was Bella, who'd been hidden behind grief, sadness and emotional turmoil.

The chance meeting of Belinda; a naturopath of different modalities, based at a health food shop, was the beginning of my campaign, for better health. Belinda, via an electronic machine, she hooked me up to; read my blood pressure and other important information. I've always had good health, but needed more energy; as Belinda suggested a few different products, available through the shop. Belinda also recommended I make an appointment with Ann, to help me with my emotional and mental concerns.

Ann was a professional woman, trained in an alternative healing practice, helping people on their journeys of recovery, from whatever circumstances had occurred in their lives.

I had had a lot of trauma in my life; I suppose, no more or less than any other person. I try not to let 'things' worry me, with a positive outlook on life. The last few years have been difficult, with my twenty-four-seven business, the breakup of my marriage, together with a multitude of other events in my personal life. Basically I was an emotional, mental and physical wreck, trying to claw my way back, from the depths of the *HELL* that had swallowed me whole.

My first visit to Ann was quite informative, discussing my medical history. My main reason for seeking help was for the recovery, of my back injury. *(Or was it)* During the first appointment, I was shown how to move while protecting the injury, with correct placement of my arms and legs to sit up; roll over in bed; how to sit in a chair, etc. Shown how to 'support' myself, by using cushions to fill in gaps, and cushioning the injury, in bed and while sitting. All of this information, shared by Ann, was so simple, yet so effective.

Of course the physical problems were only a disguise, of a mental or emotional issue. The second visit, I shared with Ann, *ALL* of the major events during my life. This session was the starting point, for my road, to recovery.

Living for fifty-two-years, a massive amount of baggage was associated, with that period of time. I had many events, where my life was at a cross road, or took a turn. Some of these events have been minor changes; others have been life altering; including the death of my youngest daughter. I had a lot of *'SHIT'* to process and work through; in the eight weeks, left of my trip. I booked two sessions each week, with Anne, hoping to complete my recovery, in that time frame.

During my first couple of weeks with Ann, I started to relive, basically the entire events where my daughter died; spending three days in bed with nightmares, aching body, tears, fears; including a roller coaster ride of chaos and heartbreak. In all of my conversations with Ann, I told her the hardest thing I've ever had to do; was telling my children, their sister had died. I also admitted, for the first time, to anyone, I never completely loved my other three children. I had kept a part of me, a small piece, protecting my heart, just in case, any of them died. It was my safety net, to sanity; if I held back, just a tiny bit of my heart, then I wouldn't be completely destroyed, by the grief.

After week three and four of the treatments, I could see some daylight, continuing to work through, the deep dark secrets, my body had been harbouring. Many authors have shared these same beliefs, in books about emotional problems, manifesting in your body. My most recent injury; my back; trying to explain to Ann *WHY* I cliff jumped. How could I explain the reason and significance behind my actions? Boy of boy, I needed some deep meditation and conversations with myself; working through all of these memories.

ANGIE

During my second week at the house, Angie, my next door neighbour, invited herself over for coffee. Angie had been visiting family over the holiday period, and had just returned home. Steve and Lauren suggested we meet, to support each other, with the animals, if either of us needed help. Angie and I discovered we had many hobbies in common, including art. Angie was a member of the local art group, with sessions held each Tuesday morning.

Angie also liked movies; visiting several cinemas together, travelling around the district. Angie loved to dance, regularly travelling for the oldies dances; going along one night, being the youngest person there, by at least twenty years. We had a great night, but I hate dancing in bright lights; self conscious, in the spot light.

Angie and I went to many places together, including a valentine's dinner, costing fifteen-dollars for dinner and dancing. It was a hoot, as the older generation grooved along to the music. We lashed out one night, attending a theatre café; with a delicious three course meal, while being thoroughly entertained by a female folk singer; charming us with incredible stories, quick wit and wonderful banjo playing.

One of the local Benton churches was transformed into a concert hall, on a regular basis, holding a series of concert performances, during the winter months. A local committee obtaining grants to help fund the visiting artists, which in turn, allows the general public to attend the performances, for a reasonable price of fifteen or twenty dollars; both of us attending a performance by a thirty-something musician.

How exciting one Sunday afternoon; Angie and I joined a few friends for an open mike session. The friends enjoyed coffee, cake and music for a grand total price of five-dollars per person. Again the oldies entertained us with banjos, violins, rock-a-billy songs, magical voices and performances; with some acts definitely better than others.

RELIGION

Angie was a member of an alternative religion, inviting me to attend a meeting, with her. The first night was a book club meeting, where each person focuses on a particular message, from the book, incorporating that message into their daily lives. At each meeting, members had the opportunity, to share their experiences, with the group.

The second outing was attending the monthly meeting for the members. I attended two of these meetings, and I cannot believe, how powerful their chant was, with the vibration rising higher and higher. The combined magical voices were like angels singing, with the chants lasting for about twenty minutes, after which time; we sat in silence.

I really enjoyed the silence; the vibration creating an incredible feeling; being part of something, much bigger than just you. Morning tea was served after the meditation, enjoying conversation with the members, over a cuppa tea. I was offered a few books to read, to see whether this religion, held an interest for me. Searching for a new direction in my life; this might be, what I'm looking for.

During one of my drives I came across a road side sign that said: Dreams, Past Lives and Soul Travel – if you believe phone ……..! I noticed this sign one week after the first meeting. How bizarre was that? I believe in all three of those topics.

I started reading the books, discovering this religion doesn't believe in tarot cards, astrology, physics' or crystals. Their belief was; once you found your connection to God, you don't need any other form of communication. This belief may be true, however, all of those 'things' had been a major part of my life, for many years.

I continued reading the books, with incredible stories from people, surviving many hurdles was due to their belief, as I too believe, with faith, anything's possible.

As I continued reading the books, I started to feel parts of this religion weren't what I was looking for. Giving up the tarot cards, astrology and crystals, while studying the books; however I really missed my crystal and tarot connection. In fact, becoming very sick; with severe flu systems, affecting my breathing, not feel very well, at all. I decided, to close the books, to concentrate on *ME*, and that's what I did, returning the books to Angie. Only parts of the religion I believed in; being an 'all or nothing' kind of person, devoting your life to a certain practice, you give it your all.

SOUL MATES

The first time I met Joseph, an immediate friendly connection, was evident, as he sat next to me at Speakers; whispering a quick hello. At the next meeting, Joseph arrived late, sitting opposite me, again, I felt a strong connection; with Joseph handing me, a piece of paper, with his phone number and email address written down. Joseph said he had this overwhelming need to talk to me. I asked him what he was doing now; driving to a café, only to find they were closing.

We ordered a takeout, going back to my house, spending the next eight hours talking. During the night, we shared our lives, over more tea and hot chocolate. I felt an amazing connection with Joseph, and this was the first time, someone has confirmed, the same feelings, I intuited. Joseph had just started a new relationship with a lady, Tanya, rekindling their childhood relationship. Our relationship was friendship based and purely platonic, as Joseph was only thirty-seven, and way too young for me.

It was evident; Joseph and I were soul mates. Soul mates make agreements, to reconnect, each life time, explaining the immediate attraction. *Discover unexplained feelings, towards another person, without any reasoning behind it. The interaction wasn't always positive; immediately causing friction; this ends up being a bad experience. How can you explain 'why' you feel, a certain way, about a person, when you're complete strangers?*

I truly believe the reason I met Joseph, in this lifetime, was to help him, with his relationship with his ex-wife. Joseph had a teenage daughter plus a young son, and after many hours of conversation, about his current situation; I mentioned to Joseph, what I believed, was the right course of action. I suggested Joseph write a simple text, letting Amanda know, he's there for her, in whatever way she needed him. This text apparently worked, as the next time they met; to exchange their son, they spent time sitting in the café talking, with a fresh start for both of them.

Joseph also introduced me to his circle of friends, with the evening meditation held at Donna's place, located just north of town. I was so blessed to meet this group of ladies, who touched my life, especially the beautiful relationship, started with Samantha from the Vineyard. Linda was another lady, working with Reiki, helping animals, and she'd even looked after Star, the cat.

Joseph also introduced me to some of his friends when he had a small party. Linda was there along with Isabella, Michael, Kate and his daughter Kia, enjoying wine and nibbles' along with music. Kia gave a performance; an internet sensation, hitting plastic cups, on the counter creating a rhythmic sound. Michael, also a talented musician, worked with the local indigenous people, specialising in the youth.

Isabella worked for a local hospital, and at the weekends worked at a local winery. We immediately made a lasting connection, keeping in contact, via email, both struggling with our life path. Isabella was definitely a soul mate connection, from a previous time, helping each other, through this lifetime. I believe Angie, Joseph, Isabella and Giorgio were all part of my soul mate family; connected over many lifetimes, on our eternal journey.

The group had an amazing conversation about wealth and how we can all help our communities. If you're a normal 'every day' person, and someone asks you for a donation, and you donate five-dollars, the maximum amount you can afford. If you asked a millionaire to donate, and they gave five-dollars, what would that say to you? Comparing both the contributions, where the generosity of one, far outweighs the other. I mentioned, I don't believe religion, should have a price tag, placed on your beliefs. My mum has an envelope with her name on it; she places in the collection tray, at her church, each Sunday. Whoever opens the envelopes knows the amount she contributes each time. I believe your contribution should be anonymous.

Michael mentioned that sometimes he would attend a church or spiritual meeting. A donation box was available, to place an appropriate donation. I agreed with this idea; where it's your choice to donate, according to the value you place on the experience.

QUILTING

I spotted a quilting shop, located on the main highway, calling in to enquire whether they're offering any classes, during the next few months. I was surprised to learn, the quilters only work in summer, as I thought winter would be perfect, to sit inside and create. However, I must admit this time *I WAS WRONG*. While in the shop, a piece of fabric spoke to me and made me take it home☺. The fabric was a beautiful hand dyed piece of cotton, featuring all of my favourite colours from lime green, to pink and purples, with an amazing design; I just wanted to explore. Arriving back at the house, I placed the piece of fabric on the end of the kitchen counter, hanging down like a curtain. While watching television, I'd visualize what I wanted to create. Since the fabric wanted to go home with me, maybe it had an idea of what I could create.

I spent the next three months turning the fabric around, on each side, to see which view was the best, and what inspiration it created? Absolutely not one message was relayed to me, until after I arrived back in Australia. *I'd been collecting bits and pieces of 'stuff' for the last fifteen years. I now had this collection, waiting for divine intervention, to start the project. I spoke to a lady, who said, when I have all of the necessary pieces, I'll then be ready to start. Until that time, keep your eyes open, and keep adding to the collection, which was what I've been doing. I cut the fabric into four equal pieces; using masks and laces from Italy; beads and jewellery from USA; off cuts of hand-died ribbons and fabrics from my vast collection from over the last forty-five-years of sewing.*

COFFEE SHOPS

On my bucket list I promised myself to leave the house, at least every second day, to go exploring, with the coffee shops, usually my destination. The most distance I travelled in one day was four-hundred-kilometers. My usual morning schedule were for chores and spending time at home, with the afternoons my exploration time.

During January, I spent many afternoons sitting in nearby cafés, huddled in the warmth, watching the world go by, while the blizzards and bad weather made it impossible to travel too far. At the beginning I tried out the local cafés in Benton, because of the distance. I found the Rectory Café, located in an old church, had the perfect lounge chair, for sitting and writing in my journal. The Rectory also had a book exchange, swopping out books; reading books from authors, I wouldn't have read if I paid full price for the books.

The George's was my favourite café; as I believed this was where, I'd meet a man. At the back of the café, an armchair had an uninterrupted view, of the front door. I usually visited the café, after the busy lunch time period, to spend a couple of hours, with a coffee and quiet solitude. If I arrived before lunch, my favourite chair was occupied, by another lady. Our arrangement worked out well; she had the chair in the morning and I claimed it in the afternoons.

George's café was owned by Hella and George, with Jimmy the waiter, helping out most days. Hella prepared all of the meals and George served the beverages. I enjoyed their hospitality, telling them, they'd be mentioned in the book, I was writing.

My aim was to visit George's, at least three times each week, waiting for this new man to walk through the doors. Finally, he walked into the café, immediately recognising him, as the man I was there to meet. *(See more about our meeting in The Kiss later in this chapter)*

Domm's Café was located in Manoria, on the banks of Kashra Lake, a twenty minutes drive from home. I visited the café more than a few times, to enjoy their coffee, for a change of pace. A steady flow of art exhibitions were displayed in the café, including the art works of Rose, a friend of Angie's. Friends of Rose's put together an exhibition, of her current art works, using a caustic wax medium, with spectacular effects. Unfortunately, heating the wax has caused Rose to have serious health issues; with her passing away not long after her exhibition.

Each time, on my travel days, at least one coffee shop opened until late in the afternoon, with my drink of choice, being a white-chocolate-mocha. Some of coffee shops I visited were located inside a store, selling furniture, clothes, skin care and jewellery. These little cafés were my favourite, serving home-baked goodies, enjoying a sweet treat. Most of the cafés displayed works from local artists inspiring people, *(Me, of course)* to rush home and pick up a paint brush.

Alison, one of the local ladies, displayed her art at the Mantra Café. I loved to be absolutely, fabulously, amazed; enjoying the ambience, while looking at the water colour prints on one wall; then turning around to see the acrylics, on the other. I had a tough time, trying to decide, which medium I liked the best.

SKI DAY

One Sunday Angie and I drove up to Mountain Peaks Ski Resort, with the distinct purpose, of finding *SUNSHINE*. Angie drove her car, because it had four-wheel-drive, needed to climb up the mountain, into the resort area. How spectacular to see the blue sky, with the resort crowded, with a ski competition in full swing. Thousands of people were taking advantage of the spectacular day, on the ski fields; we sat out on a deck, enjoying a coffee, with the sun on our faces, before looking around the resort. A ski hill for juniors drew our attention, watching the children, travelling down the slope, on inflatable devices. How my grandsons would enjoy something like this.

The resort offered motel style accommodation, as well as apartment complexes for guests to escape for a little while. How I'd love to try skiing, the only thing was, I've only worn ski boots once before, about thirty years ago. That experience was a total disaster, which I may never repeat, but I can never say, never.

We enjoyed a light lunch before heading back down, into the gloom and doom of *HOME*. We called into a charity shop in Langton, purchasing new clothes. I visited this shop a couple more times, finding really nice warm jackets, which travelled back Australia with me. Sorting out my luggage, for my return trip to Australia, I discarded my excess clothes to this store.

ICE HOCKEY

Angie and her friend Marilyn were keen hockey supporters, attending the local arena to watch their hockey team play, on two occasions. I've never been to a live game before; it was so exciting to see all of the action. The junior team played the first night, with a senior's team playing the second time; action happening in the stands with kissing competitions and raffles.

The second game night, I was sitting next to a couple, who used a cow horn, almost every five seconds. Luckily my ear plugs blocked the noise, from my right ear; otherwise I wouldn't have any hearing, at the end of the night. The man with the cow horn, was the spitting image of a friend of my parent's. Each time I looked his way, he was looking at me, it was quite bizarre, the resemblance, between this man and my friend.

I have since read a book series, where this type of encounter, was mentioned in great detail. I should have spoken to him, to share 'something' with me. I find it so strange, these intuitive messages and signs; are ignored or treated as insignificant. However, I now realise I NEED TO LISTEN AND ACT on them.

SPECIAL CONCERT

Each time I drove past the Langton Entertainment Centre, I noticed the sign advertising the Treaty concert. A couple of days before the concert I purchased a ticket for only thirty-five-dollars. I arrived early with absolutely no coffee, food or drinks I wanted to consume. The love of watching people I didn't even take my camera or phone into the concert. *If you're spending all of your time, looking through camera or phone lenses, then you're missing out on the actual event.* I'd checked out my seat down on the main floor, about fifteen rows back from the stage. I waited, until the preshow entertainment started; with my sore back, I didn't know how comfortable my seat would be.

Staying up on the main floor, a couple of girls stood near me, with one of them trying to work out her new phone. I offered to take a photo of her, but she said she was trying out all of the different functions. The girls were from Noverlone; as I mentioned, I'd stayed out by the lake. The girls relayed a story, about the hippies, growing pot, out in the forest areas of Grosvenor. *(From Chapter 8 - this information didn't surprise me)*

When the preshow entertainment started, a very talented solo guitarist, performed on stage. He could've definitely benefited with a backup band, as most of his songs sounded the same.

When the band Treaty appeared on stage, OMG, the blast from the speakers almost sent me flying, back against the railings, of the ice rink. The volume and power of the music was incredible, not to mention the women's voices, who were both aged in their sixty's.

Their songs came flooding back to me, *EXCEPT* they forgot to play my favourite one. The evening flew by; the volume of the music, pounding on the outside of body; in tune with my own pounding heart. The crowd on the floor around me were all standing up, I did too. With hardly any room to move, we all faced the same way, basically spooning each other and moving in unison.

At the end of the evening I ordered a white mocha from the local café, before heading home, as I was looking after Leila (the dog) tonight. I let Leila out, for a bathroom break, tonight and then again in the morning. Angie was dancing with friends and staying the night to attend church in the morning.

ART GROUP

You hear stories of artists inspiring others; well Roxy was that person, my favourite art instructor; inspiringly crazy with her dress sense and art style. Conducting a special class with the art group; our challenge was to create a masterpiece, using a sheet of masonite, primed, ready for our use; purchasing the necessary acrylic paints.

The size of the board was 400mm wide and 1400mm high, with a self portrait theme, based on 'cubism'. The piece of board was too big to fit in my suitcase, choosing to paint a picture for Samantha, who owned the winery. I'd taken a photo of a group of nuns; part of the scarecrow competition, in Santina, California. *(See Chapter 15 – scarecrows)*. This image was perfect, for the crazy shaped head, for the main portrait of the nun, playing a guitar, with a church steeple, in the background. Including an impressionist shadow of Max the dog, a Buddha and the magic eyes from the mountain; Samantha believes are watching over her land; and the sun's rays highlighting the sky.

I worked out; pretty quickly, I'm not a very patient painter. I cannot believe how much time; it takes, to create a finished product, with so much trimming and finishing off. Just like painting a wall with ninety-percent of the work, done in fifty percent of the time, with the ten-percent finishing touches, taking just as long.

Asking advice about what colour paints I should buy; some people say; buy the prime colours and mix them together, to create your own shades. Others say; buy the individual colour so there's no mixing. This time I purchased only the prime colours; finding it difficult mixing the same colour batch, each time. I ended up buying the right shade of paint I needed, eventually adding to my collection.

My nun painting was finished, with Roxy recommending adding a bit of 'bling'; placing a couple of shiny glass beads for her nipples, underlining her breasts, for cleavage. I was really proud of my effort, presenting the finished painting, to Samantha, to hang up on the wall of the winery.

Visiting Samantha in 2014, the painting was hanging up, on the wall, just inside the cellar room door. As you're leaving the room, the painting was directly in front of you. Samantha said there were lots of comments, about the painting, with most people loving the glass beads. My intention was never to be disrespectful.

My favourite medium was water colour, enjoying the softness of the effects, on the paper. The water colour paints creates magic when you add, what? *WATER*. Many talented women and men attended the classes; with Katherine, an older lady, paints from a photo, to create incredible life-like portraits. Mary had her portfolio on her phone, using different mediums, to create amazing paintings, as she shared with me her collection. Norma was also a wonderful artist, winning competitions with her paintings. Beryl had an incredible talent using different mediums. To join the group you pay an annual fee of five-dollars; definitely a great bargain, plus two dollars each week. The members of the group volunteered their services, to conduct different workshops, for an additional cost.

One of my favourite days was a collage class, finding it funny when the teacher tells you to bring things for a collage. Driving two hours, each way, to visit a craft shop in Poomlah to purchase things, I thought I needed. Only to find out, I just needed old magazines to rip pages apart; glue to stick it all together. I purchased different paper, flowers, wooden letters, flowers plus the boards. Creating two different projects; one as a vision board for a lover and the other was a winery inspired one, again for Samantha.

Back at the house, I'd taken over the kitchen table, with all of my art. Usually eating my meals, in front of the television; I balanced a coffee, somewhere in the middle of the mess, when I was creating.

I really enjoyed the love vision board, finding pictures from magazines, creating a wonderful scene, to attract a lover. Setting the board up as a desk mat, an office worker would use, placing a square sheet of thick cream paper, in the middle of the board; with a coffee-cup stain, highlighting the use of the mat. Along the bottom edge, I glued a row of miniature pink roses; on the top right hand side, a gazebo; a spray of glass flowers, laid across the top of the board. On the bottom right-hand-side, I attached a book of poems, I'd written, as his favourite book. On the left hand side of the board, I glued a valentine's dinner invitation, cut out from a local paper; the word 'love'; made out of wooden letters, was placed beside the invitation; with a dried rose lay on the top of the dinner invitation. A pink heart shaped, glass pendant was placed on the board, ready to be gift wrapped. On the bottom left hand side of the board I had a hand written card to my lover. Saying:

To my Darling,

I just want to tell you, how lucky we are, to have found each other.
You are an amazing person and I am so blessed to have you in my life.
I love and cherish you, for the way you make me feel.
I have waited so long for you, and cherish the times we share and
look forward to spending the rest of our lives together.

Love from your
Bella

Alison, a talented local artist, was offering classes at the Salangia Art Gallery, where I signed up to attend her water-colour 'pouring' class. Mixing different coloured paints, in a jar, and then pouring them onto the paper, to see what's created. I poured the coloured water onto the paper, creating a spectacular effect, with absolutely no idea of what I was doing. To this day, the painting was still waiting for divine intervention.

Learning quite quickly I wasn't experienced enough, to participate in the class, however I enjoyed *LEARNING* what was possible, hoping some of the talent, from the teacher and the other participants rubs off on me. Just a little☺. I've worked out; before you start a painting, you really need a 'plan' or an idea of where you want objects placed, so your picture turns out, similar to your vision. I think the whole process, of creating masterpieces, comes with practice and experience.

Jerry a regular 'snowbird' visitor, also a very talented water-colour artist, was offering a two day workshop on water-colour techniques. I purchased proper water-colour paper, along with a list of other items required for the class. OMG how talented was this man; just waving his brush around, this way and that way, and wallah, a finished painting, in five-seconds flat.

Jerry's idea of using a flat, round or oval ceramic dish, as your palate was unique (*I think*). Placing large blobs of paints along the outside edge; using the centre, of the dish, as your mixing palate. I loved this method of painting; when you wanted a fresh start, just wipe the centre area clean.

Learning, the paper and paint, you use, has to be a good quality to achieve a good result. I lashed out, when I arrived back in Australia, purchasing my own oval dish, full of paints, sitting on my dining room table, ready for a brush stroke and water to create my next masterpiece.

THE VINEYARD

After I met Samantha at the mediation session, we exchanged email addresses. The first time I visited the Vineyard, we shared a dinner of a fresh salmon steak, from upstate BC, where Samantha's sister lives. Arriving early, to tour the property, located on a large sloping block. The house, cottage and chapel where already established at the back of the property, amongst a forested area. Samantha and her partner planted all of the grapes, at the front of the property, protected by a deer fence erected around the vineyard. A cellar door and production areas were built in the middle, with a large underground cellar, using natural temperature control, to store the vintage. The area above the cellar, had been beautifully landscaped, with flowers beds and lawns.

At dinner, Shaun a long time friend, made the evening enjoyable; listening to their life's story. Shaun was a street kid from Garland, before making his money; with property developments and real estate deals. This was how he met Samantha, a real estate agent; together Shaun and Samantha created a profitable partnership, buying and selling property.

Shaun had an interest in crystals, alchemy, and astrology; full of stories about his life, with his artist wife. Shaun and Glenda live out of town, on a property, raising horses, which Glenda paints.

Samantha purchased this property, to fulfill her dream, as a wine maker. Visitors to the winery, comment on the vibrations and energy here, with the winery located on sacred land. A large 'eye' located in the mountain range to the east of the property; Samantha believes, is mother earth watching over and protecting her land.

Shaun was certainly knowable about many subjects; learning more about the three principal's of alchemy: plant, animal and rocks; opening my eyes, to new ideas and possibilities. According to alchemy; grape vines are the highest energy plant on earth. When the earth was happy, the vines are nourished, the grapes are full of energy, resulting in amazing tasting wines. The Vineyard was living proof, of this belief, with award winning wines, as testament.

I offered to help Samantha bottle up her wines, when she mentioned her plans for the following week. Large vats, of last season's vintage, were ready to be processed; with good friends like Linda and Donna, plus a couple of men, helping. The first day I emptied three-hundred-and-fifty bottles, onto the table; for the bottlers to fill; then the capping, with the final process; the labelling. Working well together over the three days; filling the cellar, with amazing wines. I know each night, after the work at the winery, I slept very well.

I loved all of the quirky names, Samantha used, for her different wines, based around the Chapel theme. Samantha offered a case of wine, as a reward for all our hard work. Unfortunately, only three bottles were allowed in my luggage, back to Australia, having no other option, than to drink the rest☺. I received a couple of cellar-door wine glasses as a memento.

ROAD TRIP EAST

The main highways were cleared, by the snow plough, on a regular basis, leaving my exploring until about 10:00am, as the morning traffic on the roads, and the overnight weather would've cleared.

Each time, arriving at the traffic lights, at the intersection of my street and the highway; which direction will I go, left or right? Turning right then I'd arrive in Salangia; asking the same question. Going straight ahead wasn't an option as the USA/Canadian border, was in that direction.

Which direction left or right? Choosing left, I'd be heading east. In the first month, I drove up to a lookout, on the eastern side of town, with panoramic views of the valley. This lookout was my favourite spot, waiting for the sun to set, capturing the colours of the clouds, enhanced in the reflections, on the half frozen lake, beneath me. Occasionally sharing the spot with tourists, who stopped quickly, to snap a photo or two. During January the turnout had a cleared path through the middle, with the sides of the road covered with meters of snow. Carefully, carefully I'd climb out of the car, snapping the photos, before returning to the warmth of the car.

At the lookout, looking to the right, the vineyards and orchards are located, along both sides of the lake. The incredible majestic snow covered mountains, lining the western side of the valley, gave me a chance to enjoy the sunsets. In the mornings, you could sit here, watching the shadows slowly disappear, off the western ranges, as the sun rises.

When looking to the left, the landscape consisted of open farm land, rather than orchards and vineyards. As the border crossing was nearby, the United States landmass was the bulk of landscape, in my view.

The first time I continued past this spot, was in search of *SUNSHINE*. The whole month of January had passed by, and I hadn't seen the sun *ONCE*. I knew the sun was still shining, above the fog mass, covering the skies, each day. I needed the sun, as there's nothing more magical than the sun shining on the mountains, the lakes, the trees and *ME*.

As I left my regular photo spot, the weather turned, climbing up through the mountain range into blizzard conditions, with zero visibility, with snow falling. Luckily this time, traffic along the highway, was zero. Was I the only crazy person, driving today, in this terrible snow storm?

After coming to the summit of the range, I noticed a sign for a ranch that had a carved animal as part of the sign. At first glance it looked like a sheep, with fresh snow as his fleece, *which I thought was amusing*. The sight made me want to stop for a photo, which was when I realised the animal, was an elk.

I wasn't scared of driving through the blizzard conditions, just very cautious, continuing to drive through open plains, with houses scattered about the country side. The road continued down a mountain range, with switch back curves; arriving at a small town called Helmslock. A couple of shops, service stations and a few houses were all I could see, through the fog and low cloud cover. In the middle of the day, the street lights were on; illuminated signs, from the shops windows were visible, as I drove through the town.

My mission of finding sunshine today was a miserable failure, deciding, this was as far as I was going to travel today. Completing a U-turn I spotted a café, with an illuminated coffee cup sign, and a warm fire to lure me in and keep me cozy. With my journal, filling in details, of my extraordinary travels, enjoying the ambience of this logging town. A lady and gentleman in the café chatted for a while, before I headed back home.

My next adventure east was so much better, travelling over the same roads, with the sky a majestic blue colour; in complete contrast with the white earth; spell-bound by the intensity of the sun, shining on the white open fields, like an ocean of glistening diamonds. Farm houses, with sheds, machinery and animals, adding their presence, to the photos of this open grazing land.

I continued driving through Helmslock; reaching Blakely, a little town with an historical tunnel as a road side stop. My camera couldn't zoom in close enough, stepping off the road; landing in a ditch. I'd never really stepped in snow before, discovering its light and fluffy, which was why; I was standing in the drain, waist deep, in snow☺.

Laughing out loud, wondering what would've happened, if the ditch, were any deeper. I could've been stuck there for how long? Maybe at the end of winter, someone would discover a vertical body, frozen to death, in the ditch. Oh the dramatics of it all☺. Within thirty seconds, of back-tracking my steps, I returned to terra firma. I didn't get any closer to the tunnel that day, waiting until another time, to have a closer look.

My destination for today was Augusta, finding a little café open, in the main part of town; enjoying a warm soup, while absorbing the Canadian way of life, in a new location. After lunch, I walked along the main street, finding a little crystal shop that was closed. I might return here, for a visit, when the shop was open.

The next time travelling east, Blakely was almost free of snow; entering the township, slowing down, I spotted a church, located up high on the side of the hill, overlooking and protecting the township. Mesmerised by the church; I'd painted one similar to this, in art class. Travelling along the street, I stopped the car, at the side of the church; excitedly, grabbing my camera, walking around to the front of the church. Reaching the large set of entrance steps, the doors flew open, with a man standing in the doorway.

I was shocked and surprised, by this gesture of welcome, as the priest stood there. The priest walked down the stairs, to greet me, inviting me into the church to take photos. I didn't know what religion was practiced here; asking the priest. The church was Christian, welcoming all denominations.

I told the priest my religion was the same; currently living in Benton at the moment. The priest said "I must know the priest". I said "no I didn't know him, because I'm not a practicing church goer, at the moment". The priest was a little taken back by my response, as I left the conversation at that. I certainly don't have to justify, my actions, to a complete stranger.

The priest and parishioners were at the church, to clean or repaint something. I climbed the stairs to the choir balcony, at the back of the church, to capture the décor of the church; highlighting rainbow colours. Admiring the stain glass windows; and how the sun's rays, reflected light, through the windows. The priest offered me postcards, of the church, when I told him I'd just painted a church, very similar to this one. Samantha was surprised when I gave her the postcards, as her chapel, may have been crafted after this church.

Leaving the church, the thought process, started to kick in. *What just happened? Arriving as the doors are flung open, to welcome me back into the church. I'd been struggling on many levels, really opening myself up, to different experiences, trying to work out, what I needed.*

Having devotion, to a religion, was a life style choice; I haven't been regular church attendee for thirty-odd years; disillusioned, with my religion, for many years, and many reasons. Firstly, the death of my daughter; forgiving God, was a very hard thing to do. Then the corruption, in the higher church ranks, protecting priests, from sexual abuse and paedophilia allegations. The church's hierarchy, asking the general public, to please forgive the fact; tens-of-thousands of children, had been sexually abused. The innocence lives, of those children, were destroyed, by the church leaders, who were supposed to protect them. Did my visit to the church reinforce my opinions, one way or another? This experience was definitely negative; not willing to accept the church's deception, on humanity, at this time.

I continued my day trip to Augusta, purchasing a few items; from the crystal shop, and wild salmon for dinner. Having a meal or just a coffee, when I travel, shares my wealth with the local communities. Enjoying a coffee, worth five-dollars, each week equals thirty-five-dollars, spending over five-hundred-dollars for my trip. This item was a luxury, when you add it all together; especially adding the fuel costs as well.

When I left Augusta, a sign to Crystal Lake, caught my attention, turning off the highway. It wasn't long, before the unsealed road, had metre-high banks of snow, on the either side of the road. I discovered many roads, leading down to houses; with lake side views, of this still frozen lake. Since I only had all-weather tyres on my car, I wouldn't be turning down any of the roads, to explore any further. I noticed a boat ramp sign, with the road looking very interesting; however I kept driving to the end of the road, where the snow plough turns around.

One afternoon, the sky was looking very promising, for some spectacular sunset photos, bypassing Benton, driving up towards the Crystal Peak Ski Resort, located on the eastern ranges. Crystal Peak was visible, from my lounge room window, if the clouds were high enough. The visit to the ski resort, I'd been planning with a lady, Cheryl; cancelled by bad weather, each time. Hiring the equipment, we'd catch the chair lift, up to the top peak, walk around taking photos, and hiking back down to the resort; however our plans never eventuated.

So today, driving, climbing higher and higher up on the mountain, stopping to take photos of the view. The further I travelled, the state of the road, went from sealed to gravel, then finally ice covered. There was very little traffic, reaching the car park, with my little grey car handling the conditions perfectly. Relieved the resort was still open, but no food or drinks were available, as they were closing. I chatted to one of the ladies working there, before I drove back home. I always consider my safety and other road users when travelling; and if there's any concerns, I definitely would stop and turn around.

ROAD TRIP WEST - ONE AMAZING DAY

That morning, anticipating my drive west, over through the next valley, for a three-to-four-hour drive. I travelled through this area, on my first day, driving through the blizzard. Today, I wanted to have a look, at this area; with the snow melting, the spring weather was definitely in the air.

My precise route was planned, travelling down to Salangia, with the intersection near the border. This was my first time travelling west, driving up along the mountain range, stopping at the first road side vista. The view was mostly to the south, as the northern view was blocked, by a large rock formation. Looking towards the east was the whole Salangia valley floor; full of the vineyards and orchards, divided by several small lakes and streams. The enormous mountain ranges on each side of this valley, has created a salad bowl of activity.

I travelled west, for another few kilometres, spotting a lake; immediately pulling the car over. I walked back along the road, absolutely awe struck by the sight, of white circles covering the lake. I captured a few photos, looking at the large sign that mentioned the details, of the native ownership, of the land.

My next 'ah ha' moment came, about ten minutes later, reaching the summit, of a mountain pass, leading into the next valley. There weren't any cars following me; again, immediately pulling the car, off the road, to look at the view. As wispy clouds covered the highest peaks the mountains; I noticed a road, winding down, around the valley floor, sensing this was my road *HOME*.

I stood at the summit for a few minutes taking in the view, spellbound, before continuing to drive through this valley; showing the early signs of spring; very little snow was left on the ground; fresh buds on the trees; a rapid flow, in the rivers, was carrying the snow melt. I stopped again, to capture the views, breathing in pure Canadian air. What was the slogan - super …..! WOW

Rounding a bend in the road, the township of Galatia came into view, with a road up on the side of the hill, was calling out my name. As I entered Galatia, the road was still calling out my name. The voices were loud and clear *TURN HERE NOW*. Without question, I turned off the highway, following the voices of my intuition, driving through the town's road system, before finally reaching, the unsealed road, that appeared to be going WHERE? The road displayed water filled potholes; looked rather slippery, with mud patches.

Remember, my car, was fitted with all-season's tyres; continuing to climb up the mountain track. And climb I did; driving into snow country, the road covered in half melted ice. I had decided, if the road deteriorated, for the car to safely handle the conditions, I'd turn around. Arriving at the summit of the range, I kept going to see where I'd end up. Now driving down hill, taking everything very carefully, I spotted a familiar sight; I knew exactly where I was!! The road was leading directly back home to Benton, with Samantha's mountain eyes, being the familiar sight.

I laughed to myself, the whole time, continuing back down into town, checking on Star, before I kept to my plan, to travel west today. My chances were fading fast, since I am exactly where I was, two hours ago.

Instead of heading south again I headed north through Manoria before turning west. Travelling over roads, the car climbed back into the mountains; discovering the high mountain areas still in winter mode. I came across a lake, where the highway wound its path, around the frozen edges, for many kilometres. The windy road was snug against the rock face, feeling like a rally car driver, swerving in and around the bends.

Noticing a few cars, parked on the side of the lake, with couple of young women standing near the cars; with a group of men, sitting out on the lake, ice fishing. Parking the car; the girls and I decided we wanted to join the men, so one of the men helped us onto the ice.

What an incredible experience, for the fishermen, to take a chair, thermos and food; drill a hole in the ice, to fish. The view of the lake, from this perspective, was breathtaking with a light breeze softly whispering past us; feeling the coldness, of the ice, through my shoes. Looking around the lake, in all directions; the sunshine was warm on my face, while creating blinding reflections, on the surface of the lake.

Talking to the different men for several minutes; before I kept driving, stopping in Adamstown, looking at a couple of shops. Fleuron, the next town, I'd travelled through here in December; unfortunately I don't remember anything, about the town. Pulling into the first café, I ordered lunch while I caught up with my diary. Fleuron was my final destination for today, as the time was 2:00pm; with at least a couple of hours driving, to return home via Galatia, to complete the loop of today's travel.

This area was certainly beautiful, stopping several times, staring at the mountain ranges. I noticed a torrent of water, flowing in the river systems; continuing to travel east, until I reached the circle lake again. Spending the entire day, trying to work out why, rings were in the lake. This lake's appearance was bizarre, as every single lake, I've ever seen, never had visible rings.

This morning at the circle lake, I noticed a sign, for a house for sale, on the opposite side of the road, photographing the details of the selling agent. Curious about where the house was located I drove through the open gate, on a sealed, windy track, towards a large shed on my left, up around the next bend, arriving on a level piece of ground. A house was situated on my right, and straight ahead, the entire valley, looking north, lay before me. OMG I couldn't believe the view; quietly and quickly turning around, driving back down the road and back onto the highway.

My reaction to the view was 'shock'; fascinated, intrigued and curious about my findings from my adventures today. Stopping at Salangia, I checked if Liza was working today; with an hour to fill in, I walked down the street, to a café, ready for a relaxing coffee, after such an adventurous day.

Reaching a window, of a real estate office, I noticed Amanda, listed as an agent. I thought this was definitely, more than a coincidence; approaching the counter, I asked the receptionist about the house; with the only details, the property, opposite the lake, along the western highway. Waiting only a moment before Amanda introduced herself, giving me a brochure of the house. I arranged for a viewing of the house on Wednesday.

HOUSE FOR SALE

I was so excited; I didn't give Amanda the correct email address; ringing her on Tuesday, to confirm our meeting, for Wednesday. Amanda sent me the full details of the house, with the owners, visiting, to look through the property, to check the state of the house, as tenants had been living in the house, for the last few months.

On the Wednesday morning, I met Amanda to look through the house. No expense was spared, with top end quality fittings, fixtures, floors, everything was very well presented. The house had three bedrooms, plus a rumpus room area, easily converted into another bedroom. The most amazing feature, about the property, was the view of the valley. Thirteen acres of land were located with the house, and five acres were located, across the highway, with the boundary touching the circle lake. OMG the deal just keeps getting better. We travelled over to the parking lot, looking around, but found it difficult to see exactly where the boundaries were located.

There'd been talk, between the native communities, about purchasing the land, for a visitors centre. However the funding wasn't available, for the purchase, of the land. The owners had lived in the house for a couple of years, but relocated, to care for elderly parents.

I wasn't impressed by the state of the house as we walked through; not vacuumed or tidied, in any way; especially with five days notice, to clean up.

WOW I'm flabbergasted with what's being offered to me. The house was amazing, with my mind going at a million-miles-per-hour on what I could do here. There was only just one, very small, detail stopping me; the $990,000 price tag accompanying the package deal of 'all my dreams come true'.

ROAD TRIPS NORTH

Luckily the main roads and highways, to the north, were maintained each day; clearing the snow and ice. I visited Manoria, Langton, Poomlah quite regularly for coffee, the movies, concerts and art supplies; and with Angie I visited the thrift shops, church, book club, ice hockey, a dinner music show and lunch with church friends.

I'm grateful of my adventurous spirit, turning the car, up along a road, and see where it ended. There were always alternative loops to travel, with the country side, spectacular, whether it was snow filled or green pastures; exploring, to see what's offered.

There were many different roads to take, in life, as well as on the highways. One day I turned onto Dove Lake Road, via the observatory, where huge communications panels take up a large parcel of land; at the 'T' intersection I turned left.

This road travelled through some beautiful country side, with open plains, enjoying the beautiful spring weather; stopping for photos, at twin frozen lakes. This road, linked back, onto a major highway, recognizing the lake, where the men were ice fishing, the last time I drove through here, heading west. Today the weather was perfect with clear skies; the sun shining on the still frozen lake; with very little traffic, on the roads, today.

Parking the car in a turn out, I grabbed my camera and started walking back along the lake. I wanted to get a photo, of the lake, from a long angle, walking to the next bend, the next bend, the next bend, until the angle of the lake finally changed. I'm not sure, how long I walked, maybe a couple of kilometres, before I stopped.

The moment I stopped walking, there wasn't one sound to be heard; a stillness was evident in the air, without any wind whipping around the edge of the lake; no noise from approaching traffic, from either direction. Silence. Feeling as if the world had stopped, for this precise moment. Gathering a strong voice, I yelled out "Dominic" five times. I felt a spiritual connection to Dominic, as a distant hawk screeched a reply, with the words vibrating around the lake. *The moment was perfect, to let go of the emotions, attached to Dominic, as my heart has ached for his family, especially his mother. My heart has ached, for my son, Christian who I don't think, will ever fully recover from, his best friend's suicide.*

I often wonder whether Dominic heard me that day, out on the lake, just like when my name "Bella" found me, while I was staying at the cattle and alpaca farms. *(Chapter 10 and 11)* Can people hear from the other side? Do you believe, our departed loved ones are watching over us, protecting us and guiding us to a better life? I'm becoming more aware, our loved ones are watching over us; truly believing we're never really alone.

One of my first purchases, after arriving in Canada was a GPS. With really bad directional issues, especially since I've lived in the southern hemisphere. You might not agree with me, but my sun travels in the north; and it's hard, to cope with, the sun travelling in the southern skies. People joke about the 'land down under' getting confused, working out where north, south, east and west are located. So the simple solution was the GPS, pressing the *HOME* button, always arriving where I started from.

I travelled to Poomlah a few times to visit the craft shops; with Angie, when we were guests at a church meeting, in Nonverlone, where I met Adam; driving through here while looking for my dream house; and meeting Henry, Nikki and the family for lunch.

Many times I stopped at Maple Lake, watching the swans nesting, on the water, over winter. In late February, the lake was fully frozen, spotting a couple of windsurfers/catamarans, travelling from one end of the lake to the other.

Travelling with Angie one day, she showed me an alternative way, to travel from Langton via Eastern Lake Drive, travelling level with the water. Looping up via the highway, one way and come back, travelling towards the Manoria township; the houses and landscape reflected in the still waters of the lake. Pulling over each time; climbing out of the car, enjoying the view, as these, are the moments that take your breath away. Just breathe☺.

REIKI

I truly believe our lives are predestined; with the universe, pointing us in the right direction. Being intuitive; continuously seeking to discover the right life path, to be travelling along.

Picking up a magazine, at a bus station, in July, I placed it in my bag, never giving it another thought until finding it in my luggage, with all of my memorabilia. With all of Ann's help; healing and Reiki were in my thoughts. Completing a course in Australia, many years ago; visiting the horse farm, with the main intention, of being mentored by Trudy.

I opened the magazine, dated summer twenty-twelve, to see *WHY* it had been brought to my attention; on the first page, was an advertisement for Reiki; sending an email, enquiring about a course. Tina replied a new course was commencing on the first of March. The course was being held, on a Friday night; and during the day on Saturday and Sunday. The cost was three-hundred-and-seventy-five-dollars, which I agreed to pay. I booked my place, after consulting Angie; she'd look after Star, for the weekend. The distance was two-hours each way, not wanting to add those extra hours driving, onto an already long day.

I arrived in Poomlah on the Friday afternoon, staying at a motel, fifteen-minutes' drive away, from Tina's home. *This was the same road, Angie and I travelled along, when we visited Adam after church. See Extra Communication in this Chapter.*

I dined at a local restaurant, filling in time, waiting to go to Tina's, spending a couple of hours talking between ourselves, about who I was, where I was on my spiritual path; practices and what I already knew.

Saturday morning I woke up early, spending time studying how Reiki was created, many years ago. Driving back at Tina's; delighted to meet Julie, a student of Tina's, learning and practicing, the principals of Reiki. Julie and Tina had many different modalities, they specialised in, along with Reiki, for a holistic approach.

Saturday morning was spent looking at the different symbols of Reiki for me to be inducted on the first level after lunch.

CRYSTALS

We spent Saturday afternoon working with crystals, with many crystals scattered around the room on tables, shelving and window sills. Tina obviously used crystals in her healing work with patients and students. This weekend, I brought from home, a selection of my crystals, in an organza bag I use when sleeping, or carry with me, in my bra during the day.

Tina, Julie and I worked on a crystal grid; a hexagon shaped star, using the power of the grid, to reinforce your affirmations. We spent individual time drawing our desires, writing down our own visions, and dreams. I selected seven of Tina's crystals, learning the affirmations, to support my deepest wishes.

Tina mentioned master crystals worked, at any chakra, especially quartz crystals amplified all other crystals. Including this crystal, as part of your treatments, creates a more powerful response.

The three of us spent many hours, just talking, sharing our own experiences about life. My eyes, heart, soul and mind were opened to a life; filled with compassion, healing, love and acceptance of who I am.

KNOWER & NURTURER

Many times, I'd say something, and Julie and Tina would look at each other, in a secret acknowledgement, of my own discovery. We all agreed I'm a 'knower'; just knowing 'stuff', magically downloaded, from the secret files of my soul.

In her healing work Julie used the five elements chart; using the natural elements of wood, fire, earth, metal and water. Julie shared a chart to help with knowing how everything was connected. I am an earth person, nurturing the earth; a protector and earth link for my family.

I asked Tina about my weight, as I've never balanced, at a normal weight. Tina said I'm a nurturer, with my weight, perfect, to nourish others.

BODY CLEANSE

I mentioned my illness over the last month, with flu type symptoms, with voices released, each night, while I slept. One night, so concerned about my health; I thought about visiting the hospital, worried I had phenomena; balking at the idea, of it costing me six-hundred-dollars, for a doctor's consultation. The voices were heard, after releasing all of the air out of lungs, and before I breathed in again. It truly felt like, the unsaid words from my past, were being released, set free from the hurt, sadness and betrayal.

Tina mentioned that as soon as I committed to this course, my body starting preparing itself, for a new level of spirituality and healing. After Tina's explanation, I totally agreed with her, the voices were definitely my body releasing words that should've been spoken, from all of my lives; previous and current.

SECOND LEVEL

My second day of the course was filled with wonderment, as Tina and Julie introduced me to the level two symbols with an incredible morning, with these beautiful souls, being inducted into the next level. This whole experience was more than I could've ever hoped for, filled with deep gratitude, for this journey, of self discovery.

TOTEM ANIMALS

Recently one morning while out walking, with snow still on the ground, Tina found an owl. Normally Tina wouldn't go down this steep hill, because it wasn't 'safe', a voice encouraged her to take the path. Tina had spent a few minutes, descending the hill, when she found an owl, lying on the ground. Tina knew the bird had recently died, collecting its body; holding it close to her heart, she walked home, placing the owl in her freezer. Tina consulted a friend, whether she could remove some of its feathers, as a keepsake. The friend replied yes and mentioned which feathers to remove. Up until this very morning, Tina hadn't even realised, the owl only had one wing. Her partner gathered the owl this morning, for burial in their garden. I could relate to how Tina was feeling, as it'd be the same as, when I helped Grace, with the dead cat. *(In Chapter 10)*.

How do you recognise your totem animal? Tina said a totem animal was what you feel attracted to. I've always loved birds, especially kookaburras, however over the years I started seeing dragonflies everywhere. Travelling on the Americas, I've been intrigued by hummingbirds, with their amazing agility. Still confused about what my totem animal was; with an affinity to elephants, giraffes and wolves intrigue me.

TREATMENTS

After lunch the course was wrapping up; time to participate in a healing session. Julie was first, as Tina prepared the room with soft lights, candles, crystals and a deep meditative state; guided to use my hand positions to feel for blockages. It's quite a daunting task to have a person trust you; with practice, all of the techniques become more natural, as I felt Julie's energy, through all of my senses.

Lying on the massage table, Julie was the healer, spending a lot of time working on my back (*neither of them knew of the cliff jump, until after the treatment*); drifting off to sleep quickly, the healing being absorbed, into my subconscious mind. Magical bells ringing aroused me, from my sleep.

Sitting up on the bed, I experienced sharp stabbing pains, on the right hand side of my stomach. Tina was sitting in a chair, struggling to breathe, started to cough; pulling an invisible piece of string out of her mouth. Tina looked my way, telling me, I needed to speak up, as there're words, I needed to say. Tina asked "what were the words you haven't spoken?" Ricky, was my first thought, as Tina mentioned, the messages were soul deep. Over the years, I've given Ricky, the grace of silence, about our marriage breakup, out of respect. However the main reason was for the protection, of our children, as I've seen marriages; where families are destroyed, by the actions of the parents.

The reason for our marriage breakup should not be shared, with the children, because that knowledge would change, their opinion and relationship, with their father. I believe it's my way of protecting them. Yes Ricky has been a kind husband, supporting me on my journey to find myself again; however he wasn't an honourable man.

I was encouraged by Tina and Julie to find a tree, a cat, a mountain or lake to release all of the anger, frustration, sadness, hurt and emotional blockages. There were five rules to help clear all of your past lives events; the affirmation process starts when you think, write, visualize, speak and reaffirm the process during your meditation. I need the courage to speak these words with passion and powerful intent, heard by the universe, as the link, to move forward with my life.

NATURAL HEALER

I truly believe each and every one of us, are healers, in our own right. Our thoughts are our weapons, in the fight, for world peace. When each person prayers for peace, it creates a vibration, released into the universe; the vibration growing stronger and stronger, as more and more people join in, similar when people sing Om. With love in our hearts, giving the intention of love and healing, to those in need.

INTUITION AND SOUL MATES

Soul mates were a discussion, I mentioned to Tina and Julie; needing clarification of the unexplained feelings and meetings, experienced over the last twelve months.

Tina explained that:

1. The boat arrival in Alaska – in Chapter 4

    Martin from Alaska chose not to communicate with me over that weekend.

2. Meeting the two men both aged, in their thirties, with previous life connections with.

    It wasn't a co-incidence Brett and Joseph, both started new relationships, just prior to meeting me. Brett Chapter 11 and Joseph Chapter 21.

3. The dream sequence from the east where I chose not to walk into the bar to Meet my lover in Chapter 12.

    If he was my new soul mate partner, nothing would keep us apart.

4. The motorbike accident when the young man pleaded with me to help him.

    I chose not to pull over and help him in Chapter 9.

5. The older man who visited me in my dreams in Australia in January; then again at the horse farm in August and I found his house, in March.

    This man has followed me across the globe. Was the letter, to his family, at the green house, what he wanted me to do? To tell his family what?? That he's OK and safe. (See more of this story in Dream Sequence later in this chapter).

All of these instances, Tina and Julie clarified, I wasn't *CRAZY;* these feelings were actually real and not to be taken lightly.

BELLS

Aroused from the attunement I heard, what I'd describe, as the purist sound I've ever heard. This beautiful serenade sounded like tiny bells, crystal glass clinking, guitars strumming, and a harp playing; to a melody of angel singing. Tina purchased these palm sized, egg shaped musical instruments from a friend who makes them, out of an assortment of shells, bones, sand, soil and crystals.

KRISTY

Julie mentioned my daughter Kristy was with me; no longer a baby, but a mother figure; watching over me. Struggling so much since she died; kept wondering, if she wanted to be with me, she should've stayed, with me, in real life. My heart was destroyed, into a million tiny pieces when she died, and only now twenty-seven-years later, was my heart starting to mend.

My heart has been super glued, back together again, making it strong and secure; so tough, nothing would penetrate it. The exterior of my heart needs to soften, for love to penetrate; otherwise I'll end up a lonely old lady, with a cold hard heart and no one to love.

IRISH HISTORY

I mentioned my love of music, as Julie started singing a song; Tina joining in, singing an Irish folk song. Her eyes were sparkling like diamonds; she was the queen of the land, her hair hung down over her shoulders, tied up in a black velvet band. I couldn't believe they both knew this folk song, from Ireland. When I watched it, on the internet, it tells the story about a man, who ends up in Van Demons Land (Tasmania). This particular experience was quite bizarre; as my heritage is from Irish decent.

THANKS YOU AND FAREWELLS

The Sunday afternoon session finished, hugging both Julie and Tina, for this amazing weekend, catapulted to my highest spiritual plane. My belief in 'knowing' was more than enough reason to celebrate. Tina presented me with a certificate and a beautiful crystal; rock hounded from the mountain range near her property. I cannot think of a more wonderful experience, than to meet these two incredible women.

Tina looked, right into my eyes; "I see you". Finally, when someone sees, the real you, it's a blessing. This phrase was mentioned, in one of my favourite movies; regularly using this phrase when I see plants, flowers, trees birds and other things that catch my eye.

A quote from Tina:

A healing practice was like a garden…
Each client was a unique and individual flower, unfolding in its own rhythm.

I'm a unique flower unfolding into my own unique rhythm.

DISTANT HEALING

My dad called, letting me know, mum was back in hospital. I meditated; cleansed and prepared my bedroom, with my Reiki book opened ready to perform a very special ceremony. This was the first time using the distant healing symbols.

Gathering my thoughts; called in all of the angels, guides, archangels, all of my mum's friends, relatives and anyone she'd ever cared for, during their living years. Surprised when listing all of my relatives, one of my uncles I'd forgotten about, popped into my thoughts. Yes, I'm sorry Uncle Bill. I asked them to remain, with my mum, in her hospital room, until she's fully recovered. I phoned mum a couple of times, checking, she was coping ok; receiving the best news, when my dad said, she's really happy in hospital this time. I knew, without a doubt, my prayers had worked, with all of her loved ones, protecting and caring for her, just like she'd cared for them.

SONGS

When driving anywhere, I wanted to connect through all of my senses, usually without the radio on. One day, two songs came on the radio, within a couple of hours of each other, with the words striking a chord with me. I stopped each time to write down some of the lyrics.

1. Live like you are dying – skydive, fast cars, love the most, be everything you can be
2. Don't settle for less – fireworks, don't give up no matter how long it takes.

KNOWER'S ARC

As my departure date loomed, I started thinking about my life; on my return home. What could I do to share my life, my skills and my healing with the greater community?

I often had intuitive dreams; one idea was setting up a shrine at my home in Australia. Knowing the perfect spot, where I'd always felt a connection. At one time, I wanted this particular spot to be included in my garden, but it wasn't possible or practical. The shine was a large mound, about five acres in size; shaped like a pyramid, with massive granite boulders scattered around the whole area. Rocks were naturally placed in circles, in many different locations around the site. The whole site was timbered with a large variety of native ground covers, shrubs and trees.

Every time I went over to this particular spot, to collect rocks for my garden; I would stand on the large granite boulders, feeling the energy and my connection to mother earth. I could hold meetings here, where different vistas were available, depending on what I wanted to do.

The name, in a vision was, Knower's Arc; as I know things, never really knowing where the knowledge comes from. With the arc, the connection between, my farm in Australia and the lake in Canada, were almost, on opposite sides of the earth, to each other. *(See more of this story in The Kiss later in this Chapter)*

I visited the site; at my farm and it's the perfect spot, to set up my shrine.

FOOD

This area was an incredible part of the country; had it been summer time, I'd have a fruit basket full of delights, from the produce grown in this area. However the area was covered in snow; the fresh food was imported from the States, Mexico and maybe even further afield.

Most of the winter I cooked bulk soups and stews; purchasing and processing all of the necessary organic ingredients, into a slow cooker; portioned and then frozen. For meals I added pasta, bread, fish or meat to the mix for variety. Breakfast was mostly yoghurt and fruit; lunch was usually toasted sandwiches.

My coffees were milk based; classifying this as a meal; as the mugs were generally huge. At the cafés I occasionally enjoyed a soup; but basically the restaurants didn't provide organic food. I'm happy to allow myself the milk, but certainly didn't want to subject myself to food, unless I knew the ingredients. Being intolerant to wheat, soy and peanuts I needed to be cautious, in case of an emergency visit to the bathroom. The reaction can be only twenty to thirty minutes, from when I ate something 'wrong'. I'm sure everyone knows; it wasn't a good position to be in.

SALMON, BIRD HOUSES AND MONARCH BUTTERFLIES

I received a brochure about a wildlife series; conducted by a local conservation group, excitedly I studied the programme to learn more about the area by attending these presentations, being held at the Salangia Town Hall on a Saturday afternoon. I asked Angie if she wanted to go, to the first presentation, about the monarch butterfly. Arriving early, we enjoyed a coffee at the Mantra Café, while looking at Alison's paintings, hanging on the walls.

I thoroughly enjoyed the butterfly presentation, highlighting how the western Canadian butterflies, make their winter home, in California. *I HAVE BEEN THERE.* The eastern Canadian butterflies; travelling through the Central American states, follow a sweeping, predetermined path, before arriving, in a mountain region of Mexico. The incredible plight of the butterflies, takes many generations, to successfully arrive in Mexico. The local economy was reliant on the visitors of the winged kind, in the sky; and the two legged earth walkers☺

The second presentation focused on the local birds, and how local residents, are encouraged to have bird houses at the properties. I've noticed the boxes, in different locations; never knowing how vital they were, for the survival of native birds. The local areas were being logged of natural forests and destruction of woodland areas; with birds losing their natural habitat, to nest. I was definitely more appreciative, of the value, of the boxes, after this presentation.

The third presentation highlighted local salmon; attending these presentations, to be informed; becoming aware of communities challenges, and this was certainly a fact finding afternoon. Apparently, many years ago, a dam was built just over the border, in Washington State. This dam blocked access for salmon, to spawn in the local rivers. The last few years, an organisation had been working, to enable the salmon's return to this region.

The first step was making a gate, in the dam wall, allowing the fish, to access the waters, above the dam wall. The fish continuing their journey, along hundred of kilometers of linked lakes, rivers and channels; the whole region was now accessible, again.

This vast network of water-ways, were managed by a local authority, supporting the fish on their journey. One year, the residents of Maple Lake, were advised the lake's water was being raised, to allow the salmon, to access the channel, connecting the next lake.

During my travels I have seen the salmon run, watching the fish fling themselves, through the air, to transverse the waterfalls. It's an incredible sight, with this movie, highlighting the plight, of the local salmon. I believe one day, in the not too distant future, people will be able to fish in the local lakes, catching their own wild salmon, for dinner.

When I travelled back here in 2014 I read an article in the local paper, that someone wanted to register, a commercial salmon fishing operation, in the local lake. What the $#%^&@#

The lady presenter endorsed the local salmon farm, after recently visiting the facility. OMG there's no way fish, forced fed, was in, any way, natural. A normal salmon takes many YEARS to reach the optimum size. Artificial ingredients are fed to these fish, which in turn we're *EATING*. The salmon farms, in Australia, use a dye to colour the flesh pink, to look like the Atlantic salmon.

I cannot believe governments, around the world, allow these facilities to operate. There's more than enough food, in the world, to support the human race. If the one half that overindulges, stops eating the excess, then the other half will have enough. Stop allowing genetically modified crops; fed to all animals, grown for human consumption, ALONG with all food crops, humans eat directly. Don't get me started, as the rest of this book will be about my principals and morals, about how the governments, are killing our planet, along with all of the inhabitants, including animals, the waterways, marine life, forests, bird life and humans. Amen.

IN BOX

I've had numerous conversations about the 'in box' in your life. What! What's an in box? An in box, was basically your life; as each day we 'deal' with things; events, problems, children, family, work. The scenario goes like this:

You wake up in the morning, you've slept well, feeling invigorated, rolling out of bed to greet the day. Sunshine is streaming in, through the windows; you feel FANTASTIC. After a shower, you make yourself coffee and breakfast. NOW this was before interacting with the outside world; you have a smile on your face; a skip in your step.

THEN you turn on the television, the computer, pick up the phone or read the newspaper. Now your life's changed forever; the outside events control, your very next thoughts. You learn what's happened, from all corners of the globe; guaranteeing disasters, killings and tragedy were highlighted.

You turn on your computer, checking your emails 'in box', from friends, families or work colleagues; even from people you don't know. You scan the list of emails, for anything important; attending to them IMMEDIATELY. The junk ones are deleted; 'dealt' without a second glance.

A process of elimination takes care of the news from your email account. Now the phone calls or texts from friends are processed. After this, you are up to date, with your morning.

NOW ask yourself, "HOW are you feeling", maybe thirty minutes or an hour has gone by. Are you still feeling on top of the world, cheery, happy, still with a skip in your step? I bet you feel deflated, and that's why, I'd rather stick my head, in the sand, and NOT communicate with the world at large.

So you don't check your emails, phone and texts a hundred times a day. You don't turn on the television. What effect or affect does this action have, on your mental, emotional and physical body? Think back to how you felt, first thing this morning; image how different, the world would be, if everyone minded their own business; concentrating on looking after themselves, their families and their communities.

This scenario isn't achievable, in normal, everyday life; but how about one-day-a-week. Turn off the television, the computer, the telephone; be with yourself (and the family of course). Go walking, hiking, gardening, sit with a book; start a new hobby you always wanted to do, such as painting or knitting. Go forward, in slow baby steps, discovering, how EASY it was to create, one peaceful day. Tell me then, how wonderful you felt, at the end of that day? The next step; increasing the length of time, connecting more with yourself, and less with the rest of the world☺.

MOON MADNESS

I have watched the moon, each and every month, nearly all of my life; except I've never seen the man-in-the-moon. How jealous, I've been, when people, in the movies, say "there's the man in the moon". The northern hemisphere has shadows, on the moon's surface, slightly different, than my view, from the southern skies. During my stay here in Benton, I had three full moons; the first two were clouded over; with the final moon approaching, I promised myself, to make it, special. I looked at the weather forecast; the prediction was mostly clear, with light cloud cover. I wanted to watch the night's skies, without interference from the city lights, and a clear view of the moon, rising over Crystal Peak in the eastern mountains.

Parking my car, on the side of the road, above Benton, I wasn't disappointed; the night sky was clear, except for some light wispy clouds. For the first time, in my life, I witnessed something magical. It wasn't the man in the moon that I saw; but each of my family members' faces, appearing on the surface, of the moon; the wispy clouds creating the illusion. The illusion, of my children's faces, appearing with delightful expressions, kept me enthralled, for over an hour. I've never experienced anything, more special, than watching a life changing event, unfold in the moonlit sky. *I have a very creative imagination, if you didn't know already* ☺

WOMEN'S DAY

Catherine, a lady I met, through Speakers; organised a local event, held in every country, around the world; raising awareness, of sexual abuse against women. I attended the event where women shared their stories and presented information on how *WE* can all help. The woman's shelters located in Benton and Salangia, were supported solely by donations, from the community. This afternoon's event raised vital funds, through raffles and donations, to keep the doors open. I attended this function, with many of the women I've met, since I arrived in town.

This organisation continues to raise awareness, of this vital programme, to stop the violence against women, all around the world. Now was the time to stand up, voice your opinions and support others in need.

WINE TRAIL

Working for Samantha, at the winery, I was given a charm bracelet, with a little angel attached, as a gift. Visitors to the region were encouraged, to buy a bracelet, adding beads from each winery, as they toured the area. I proceeded to obtain a few more charms, as I travelled around the area, on my last weekend; with most of the wineries having their official, opening weekend over Easter. I spent a lovely couple of hours visiting the cellar doors, discovering a new loop road back from Manoria to home; with a full bracelet, with memories of my time, in the valley.

HENRY AND NIKKI

I received an email from Henry, mentioning he's visiting Poomlah, the following week, for a meeting; asking if I would join him; to meet the family. I said yes, as we found a nice little restaurant spending the afternoon chatting, as I met all of the children, who were all home schooled. In July when I met Henry, his wife Hilda, was almost full term, with her latest pregnancy. However the delivery, of a little girl resulted, in a still birth. How sad for Hilda and the family to cope with this tragic event. I know how it feels, to lose a child; and now six months later, the wounds were still raw.

What a lovely day out, meeting the family; as my first impressions were totally different. You wonder, sometimes, IF people are telling you the truth. When I first saw Nikki and Henry together,

I thought she was his girlfriend; looking about twenty-three or four, but in reality, Nikki was only fifteen. It was an incredible coincidence how we met, in the first place, meeting at the train station in Greensboro, discovering we were twins, born on the same day and year. *See the full details in Chapter Seven – Train travel continues.*

MOVIES

I enjoyed watching movies, always have, always will. The local video shop had rental movies, which I checked out every week or so. Enjoying the pay TV at the house with unlimited movies, without leaving home; I'd curl up on the lounge with Star, as we cried, laughed or were amazed by what was showing on the TV. The home renovation shows were my favourite; loving how the designers could visualise the spectacular vision; out of the mess.

DREAM SEQUENCE

It all started with a dream, in Australia, in January, when an older gentleman visited me. In the dream; I was standing in front of a house with green and white sidings. The front entrance steps was accessed by a narrow pathway; surrounded by lush green lawns. Flowering shrubs along the front of house enhanced the beauty of a well maintained garden. Standing at the front of the house; an older gentleman, with a welcoming smile on his face; came around the side of the house to greet me.

In the July, travelling on the bus, through the Canadian country side, north of Nonverlone; my inner voice told me to grab my camera; with the premonition, the house, from my dream, was located here somewhere. I searched the area that day, but was unsuccessful in my search.

In August, while I was staying at the cattle farm, the man visited me again in my dreams. Staying in the cabin; I woke up to go to the bathroom; but couldn't get out of bed, because a man was sitting at my kitchen table. I went back to sleep and woke up later realising that I'd been dreaming and this time; for real; the man was sitting at the kitchen table. I recognised him; as the man from the green house.

Finally in March the following year, I left home in Benton, early in the morning; driving four hours to explore the area north of Nonverlone. From the highway, I suddenly recognised THE HOUSE, located about four-hundred-meters from the highway in a grove of trees. The house was just south of where the voice had told me, 'get out your camera' and I had passed the house that day, while travelling in the bus.

I pulled the car off to the side of the road, totally amazed and astounded that I'd found it. Driving into the house yard and stepping out of the car; a couple of friendly dogs, greeted me. I knocked on the door, but no one was home; I sat in a chair, on the verandah, writing a note, which I tucked into the side of the porch door.

The note mentioned, my dream, about an older gentleman, who'd lived at this house. I included my email address and phone number, in case someone wanted to talk to me. Walking back to the car, and opening the boot, to replace my pen and paper; one of the dogs, was ready, to jump into the car. I believe the dogs knew me, as the old man obviously had taken the dogs, for rides, in his car.

Disappointed no one was at home, but not deterred, from believing, the man had lived in this house. Believing my message; left for the current tenant, to let them know the man was still here, looking after the garden and watching over them. Why did this man come into my dreams, on the three occasions? What was the purpose? Just to leave a note? Believing the note was important; I'm truly blessed to do this for the man, in my dreams. *The man hasn't appeared in my dreams ever again.*

I desperately needed validation of my intuitive insight, to understand my life's journey. Why was I receiving all of these messages? Do these intuitive feelings actually mean something?

A TRULY REMARKABLE ARTIST

When I met Samantha's friend, Shaun, he mentioned meeting his wife. Glenda paints landscapes and animals, in bright colours, using ground crystals, on massive over-sized canvases.

Arriving at her house, located on a rural property, where they raise horses; I walked into Glenda's art studio, she was painting a deer with a doe, in glorious tones of blue. The studio had blank canvases, of different sizes, stacked up against a wall, ready to create the commissioned paintings, for art galleries all over the Americas.

Glenda uses photos, on her laptop, as a guide to paint the scenes; showing me the ground crystals before adding it to the paint. I looked on-line to see her art collection, featuring horses and portraits of indigenous locals; so awe inspiring. Glenda buys two-litre-sized tubs of acrylic paints in the right colour; there's no mixing, just blending. I was very appreciative; Glenda made time, out of her busy schedule, to talk to me; taking home a small piece of ruby, as a souvenir of my visit.

STAR

Writing in my journal, I couldn't believe I started mentioning about Star the cat. At the beginning Star wouldn't even let me near her. I'd place her bowl down on the floor with her food; saying "thank you Bella, thank you Bella" attempting to pat her. Star constantly hissed at me for weeks, before she started to come around. It's hard to know, what to do with her, as I wasn't really a cat person. However in most of the volunteer places, I attracted *CATS*.

Star had been unwell, giving medication to her, twice a day, with her food. I looked after her the best I could; hoping one day Star would finally like me. Over the three months with Star; she let me pat her, brush her fair; rub her tummy and I think she did like me, eventually. A couple of times I ate bacon and eggs, and ice cream; Star seemed to like these, as she licked my plate.

The first time Star came into my room, I placed her blanket, down on the bottom of my bed, for her to sleep on. I slept on the right-hand-side, of the bed, being closest to the door. Well Star had other ideas; I slept on the left; she slept on the right, before eventually sleeping above my head. I can tell you, this was a little outside my comfort zone, but what can you do, when the cat rules the house. *I've been told that when a cat sleeps, above your head, she's protecting you. I wonder what she was protecting me from.*

The funniest thing happened during my visit to Benton in 2014. While staying with Angie, I looked over the fence; spotting Star sitting on the verandah. I called out her name; looking up she had a horrified expression on her face. She sat there startled; not sure what to make of my visit; probably hoping I wasn't looking after her again.

EXTRA COMMUNICATION

Angie and I drove to Nonverlone, to attend a meeting, of her church group. As the meeting started, it wasn't long before I was distracted by a little boy's voice coming into my mind, from a man, sitting on the other side, of the room. I'd noticed him, sitting there alone, wondering, whether the lady, conducting the meeting, was his partner.

This little boys voice, said to me "Hey, here I am", jumping up and down, waving his arms to attract my attention. I looked over to see what's going on; returning my attention, to the lady presenter.

"Hey you, I'm talking to you" said the little boy's voice again. This time I looked over; saying in my mind "yes I can see you, but I'm listening to the lady, so please excuse me"; then returning my attention to the lady presenter.

At the end of the meeting, Angie greeted her long time friends, grabbing my arm; leading me across the room, to meet her friend Adam. Of course, Adam was the man, whose inner voice, was talking to me. I said hello to Adam, and the conversation was interrupted, by a lady, inviting Angie to join her for lunch.

Adam mentioned he had a turkey dinner, at his home, if we wanted to join him, for lunch. Angie said she'd love to see Adam's house; following him home in tandem. Adam lived out of town; I cannot believe, I'd driven, past his house, each time I drove, from the sustainable host's farm, near Grosvenor to Nonverlone.

Adam's house was located, on the hillside overlooking the valley, with terraced gardens and lawns, making the block more accessible and productive. The two-storey, family home, was built by Adam many years ago; now sharing his life, with his dog Jasmine. Adam was divorced, retired, spending his time growing vegetables, reaping the fruits from a large orchard. Jasmine was the love of his life, together with his church friends.

Adam showed us around the property, before enjoying lunch; sitting in the kitchen, looking out over the valley. The first thing I noticed, in Adam's lounge room, was a large poster print of Uluru, and other Australian memorabilia. Adam spent a year, touring around the country, when he was twenty-something; visiting relatives who had settled in Australia.

After lunch we looked around the garden, before heading back home. Since we travelled up along the highway, Angie suggested we go back a different way. The road was sealed tarmac, but little more than a goat track, in some places. I totally enjoyed the drive as it started to snow, high up on the mountain range, before rejoining the main highway, south of Poomlah. *(I passed by Tina's house along this road).*

Adam asked for my contact details; maybe planning a trip to Australia, to see his distant family. I spoke to Adam, for his birthday, a couple of days after we first met. The next time I met Adam, was at Angie's for Easter dinner. Adam joined me, Angie, her two sons, with their families for Easter Sunday dinner. Lasagne was my contribution, for dinner, and after our meal, we walked around the town, to stretch our legs. The family loved to look around, their old stomping grounds, with Adam, Jasmine and me tagging along for the ride.

For most of the walk around town, I had Jasmine's lead; walking together. On their way home to Nonverlone, in the car, Jasmine became sick; Adam rushing her for an emergency consultation, finding a tumour had burst. I left a message for Adam, on his phone, sending love to Jasmine.

Adam and I had a unique connection; at Angie's I handed him a letter, detailing my story about that first day. I knew Adam would understand the story, because of his beliefs. When we spoke on the phone, he said he felt a connection, as well. However his thoughts were only, for his precious Jasmine. I mentioned to Adam, I might call in to see him, on my way to the Vancouver Airport.

That morning after leaving Benton, driving along the Namangan Lakes, heading north; I had this overwhelming feeling, of dread. Over the last few days Adam had spent all of his time with Jasmine, the vet not knowing whether, she'd survive, the operation that morning. I pulled the car off the road, with an unbearable pain in my chest. I believe it was my physical connection, to Adam, and his reaction to what the doctor was telling him. I sat in the car, for a few minutes, before being calm enough to continue driving. I expected the news to be sad, except it wasn't. Jasmine had survived the operation, however Adam's reaction, at the news was so intense; it was borderline grief.

I left a message for Adam on his phone, debating whether to hang around or keep travelling. Adam rang to say he'd be home at about three o'clock, please call in for a coffee. So that's what I did! I arrived at his home and had a little 'nana nap' while I waited, for him to return, with his friend, who had a trailer full of wood.

After the wood was unloaded, we had a coffee and a chat, with Adam offering me dinner. We ended up having a wonderful meal of salmon and salad. *This dinner was one of my bucket list items 'to have a dinner conversation with a man'.* Adam and I spent a long time talking, including a discussion on my upcoming divorce. Adam offered me some advice; I asked him, to grab me a piece of paper, so I could write it down. Adam's advice was: before you ask anyone a question or share anything with them; ask yourself these three questions first: 1. Is it necessary, 2. It is the truth, 3. Is it kind.

I've used this advice, over the last few years, in many different circumstances; proven to be words of gold, valued beyond measure.

After dinner, Adam and I settled in the basement, to watch the latest installment of a national music contest, we'd both been following. At the beginning of the show, I was sitting next to Adam, on the lounge. By the time, the show finished, I was sitting at one end of the lounge and he was at the other. I went to the bathroom, towards the end of the show; questioning myself, 'what I'm doing 'here'. Obviously Adam's thoughts were only with Jasmine, who was due home the next day.

Upset with myself; walking blind here; basically throwing myself into this situation. Without, what? Caution? I don't know how to explain my actions; throwing caution to wind, to just see, where things lead. I did feel safe with Adam; I certainly wouldn't be here, if I didn't think so. Take a chance, girlfriend.

When I returned to the lounge room, Adam asked 'what I wanted to do'. I said "you can either offer me a bed, for the night or I'll keep driving". Adam offered me a bed, grabbing a few things out of the car, having a shower, and finding a nice guest bedroom, to call my own for the night. I had a good sleep, until about four, waking up, to go to the bathroom. Adam woke up as I walked past his bedroom, whereas I went back to sleep until seven. As I came past Adam's bedroom the second time, the little boy's voice suggested; I climb into bed with Adam to comfort him. I DID NOT climb into this man's bed to comfort him.

What's the reason for the overnight stay? To take Adam's mind, off Jasmine's operation; I believe the main reason, for our reconnection, was his advice; a wonderful and valuable gift I've used in my everyday life. After breakfast we hugged; me heading towards the Vancouver airport via Ploomaks and Adam was heading directly to the clinic to pick up Jasmine.

I told Angie about my experiences, with Adam at the meeting; and she told me, she was encouraged to attend that specific meeting, inviting me along as a guest. Jasmine did make a full recovery from the surgery, but sadly passed away early in 2014. Adam had a wonderful woman in his life and I'm kept updated, with his life, through Angie.

THE KISS

The day was Good Friday; the time was three o'clock, and the place was my favourite café, George's. I was the only customers in the café, enjoying a relaxing coffee, writing in my journal. George was in the kitchen, cleaning up alone; when I heard a conversation begin, before a man appeared in front of me. The man stood there with a huge grin on his face, as he was introduced to me. His name was Giorgio, who continued to stare at me, with a silly look on his face. In his own words, Giorgio believed *'I'm one of most beautiful woman he had ever seen'*. Wow what a compliment; what else could a woman want?:-).

I immediately knew, Giorgio was the man, I'd waited almost three months to meet. This meeting was part of my life's journey; an important rendezvous for me, in this life time. George offered Giorgio some food, as he sat down and started talking. The reason for the visit today was to deliver, a bottle of grappa, as an Easter present. Giorgio's meal arrived, as I shared with him my story, chatting between mouthfuls of food.

Giorgio was a musician; lived in Manoria with his father; was single (*which was important*). His heritage was Portuguese, having lived in Europe, before moving to Canada in his teens with his family. George stopped cleaning, as the two men picked up guitars. Giorgio has a rough raspy voice, singing a couple of legendary songs.

Giorgio and I continued to chat, before he asked what I was writing about. I told him about my journal that would eventually form, the contents, of a book. Giorgio said I should write down this quote:

The story of life was quicker, than the wink, of an eye. But the story of love was hello, goodbye until we meet again.

I finished writing down the quote, Giorgio suggested I should write down his name and phone number as well. Giorgio had charisma plus; knowing how to impress the ladies. Well he impressed me.

We left the café together, agreeing to catch up later. I arrived home to find a message, on the phone from Joseph, inviting me to a 90's party, on Saturday night. The only person I knew, who might be interested, was Giorgio; calling his mobile phone, leaving a message.

That night; nicely tucked up in bed, Giorgio phones me, asking to join in some karaoke. I said "yes", getting dressed, to visit Joe, who lived in the trailer park about fifteen minutes south of Benton. It wasn't until after knocking on the door, that I thought, maybe this wasn't such a good idea. Here I am; at ten o'clock at night, standing at a door, where I've only known one man, for a few hours, knocking on the door of another man's house; who I didn't know at all. What was I doing here? Again I'm letting my intuition guide me, to see where it leads. The door opened, with Giorgio introducing me to Joe, spending the next five-hours singing karaoke, dancing and talking.

Joe had an enormous collection of karaoke songs, purchased over the last thirty years, including movie-style karaoke songs. I loved the fifties, sixties and seventies, reliving the moments of our childhood. Giorgio and I even danced to a couple of the songs; with swift moves on the dance floor as well. :-) It was such a great night; I must tell you, I love music. I love singing, but have never sang in front of anyone. Well I've sung in the car, when driving the kids around. The regular comment, I usually received, was "don't give up your day job". Finally leaving Joe's house at 3:00am, with Giorgio agreeing to catch up with me, later today, which was Saturday.

I slept in, before heading for a coffee, in Manoria, while waiting for Giorgio to answer my text. After an hour, I didn't waste my time, waiting any longer; touring around the wineries, collecting my bracelet beads.

I didn't hear from Giorgio until Sunday; agreeing to meet him, for a coffee, at George's at 1:00pm. I already had Easter dinner plans, leaving the café at 3:30pm. The dinner was important, with my last chance to spend time with Angie and her family; Adam and Jasmine were going to be there as well.

I got a text from Giorgio, arriving about one minute after I left; too bad, so sad. I'd waited hours for him, and he knew about my dinner plans. I texted Giorgio back, with no idea what time I'd be finished with dinner, saying 8:00pm.

Two sons, their wives, along with their children, joined Adam, Angie and I for a lovely afternoon of fine food and wonderful conversation. After dinner we walked around the block and helped with the cleanup before Adam headed back home.

I went home, changed my clothes and met Giorgio, at local pub; the second time visiting there. The first time was New Year's Eve, five days after I arrived, and now; two days before I left.

Giorgio was playing pool, when I arrived, giving him a quick kiss hello. I didn't want anything to drink; Giorgio finished his game of pool and drink, before we left together. Giorgio had been invited for Easter lunch at a friend's house. It's now 9:00pm; Giorgio suggesting we call by to say hello. I followed Giorgio in my car, to his house, in Manoria; where Giorgio introduced me to his father, Martine. Giorgio drove us to Langton, to visit his long time friend, Sarah. Of course the Easter celebrations were well and truly over, when we arrived, Sarah offering me a coffee. Our connection was another significant meeting for me. (*When I revisited in 2014*)

Giorgio and I didn't stay very long at Sarah's house; at nearly midnight when we returned to his house. We sat in the car, chatting for ages, before I received 'my passionate kiss' from my bucket list. Boy oh boy, Giorgio certainly knew how to kiss, with the moment lasting for ten minutes. A bizarre thing happened, while we were kissing. The outside lights, of the house, continued to blink, on and off, as if the angels wanted me to know, they were watching and applauding, my luck; in finding a perfect, passionate kiss.

After the kiss, I mentioned to Giorgio about the lights; he agreed it was quite bizarre. Saying goodnight; the time now 1:00am and Star was still outside. I needed to make sure she's safe, as her parents were due home today, Monday.

When I arrived back at the house, I regretted, for a few minutes, not accepting Giorgio's invitation to join me, back at my house. WHY? Sex has to be more than, the physical attraction and enjoyment. Call me crazy, but there has to be, more to a relationship, than that. Just like Steve in the Caribbean, I'm just not into one night stands.

Agreeing to meet Giorgio for lunch on Monday, there's a pattern forming here; with Giorgio, living in his own, warped sense of time and space, hours and hours late. When I arrived at the Café, the men's club was there, at their usual table, with Joe. I joined them waiting, waiting, and waiting. Wasting my precious, precious time; waiting for Giorgio until two o'clock. I didn't want to spend, my last day, sitting in a café, talking to strange men; when a beautiful day, was waiting to be explored, wanting to spend my last day looking around the valleys and lakes.

I was driving my car, today, showing Giorgio, my favourite places, I'd discovered, while living here for three months.

We finished visiting the valley, grabbing a takeout dinner, before heading towards Meadow Glen, to visit a property, Giorgio owned. Driving for thirty minutes, Giorgio directed me, to turn off the main road, onto an unsealed muddy road, with large pot holes full of water. This road had seen a lot of traffic, in the last few days, since it was the Easter holidays. I was certainly putting my little car, through some challenges, climbing higher and higher, up along this rough, muddy track, before finally arriving at a lake.

We stopped the car, climbed out to an unbelievable vista of dark-brown, coloured water. Huge air pumps, located out in the middle of the lake, were restoring the balance; enabling the fish to survive. Looking out over the edge of the water, an uninterrupted view of Crystal Peak, off in the distance; spotlighted in the late afternoon sun, with the snow having a golden glow.

Giorgio and I grabbed our snacks, standing beside the lake, taking in the breathtaking solitude of the mountain area. The snow had melted, from this location, with camp sites visible, across the lake. We walked along the lake's edge, taking photos of the deciduous tree trunks; silhouetted against, the cobalt blue sky.

The night air was changing the temperature, down a notch or two; quickly losing day light, driving down, this rough track, back onto calmer sealed roads. Locating the entrance of the property, Giorgio opened the gate; driving through, waiting for him to rejoin me back in the car. Remember, I had a baby, two-wheel-drive car. Looking at the steep, unsealed road, with huge ruts and loose gravel; refusing to take my car up the road; and reversing back down, through the gate and back out onto the road.

When attempting to drive up the hill, into the property; I felt a warning, advising me not to enter. The feeling was like I wasn't allowed to enter; the previous sacred men's site. *(Call me crazy, that's my story, and I'm sticking to it:-)*

After conversations with Giorgio, over the last few days, he knew that I was an intuitive person. Asking if I had any thoughts, about the four-hundred-acre property, he had for sale. Giorgio showed me where the boundaries, of the property were, which included both sides of the road. I'd driven on this road a few times, driving the loop between Benton and Manoria.

Each time, I have driven, along this road, I'd sense, the exact boundary of Giorgio's property. I sensed a change; an invisible energy source, marking where one place ends, and another starts. How do I explain the change? As a native Canadian, my connection between the circle lake, this property and the valley, over the mountains, with the road, leading to my homeland, felt real. Had I been here before? All of my senses say YES.

Giorgio and I returned to Benton, with takeout chips and a hot chocolate for dinner; definitely a cheap date, spending three-bucks on dinner. I drove Giorgio back to his car, at the café, where we said goodbye. Enjoying the time spent together, sharing beliefs and life time stories. I felt a connection to Giorgio; more of a friendship, than a romantic one. *My intuition was spot on; the reason for our meeting, would take eighteen-months to come to fruition.*

ON THE ROAD AGAIN

Steve and Lauren were due back on Monday, as I started preparing for my departure, sorting out everything I'd accumulated, placing each bag into the car. The charity shop scored unwanted items of clothing. Angie scored, a massive amount, of art supplies and the extra food. *Angie thanked Steve and Lauren for sending me to be her friend during those few months.*

After finally leaving my commitments to Steve and Lauren I was on the road again, enjoying a few days of action packed adventures ahead of me; before my departure out of the country. Saying my final goodbyes to Hella, George and the men's club at the café I hit the road Jack!!! My end plan was to re-visit places from my trip with my Dad, mainly the area near Ploomaks.

But before then I parked my car at the Poomlah Airport; jumping on a plane bound for Garland. You may ask why I'm flying there. The reason; my favourite singers, The Scampers were performing there. Bored one day, I searched the web; finding out what James Cummings was doing; hoping he might be performing somewhere close by, since he lived in the area, but he was down in southern America. What was my other favourite band doing; The Scampers were touring, with the concert tickets costing only eighty-five dollars. Then add on return flights, accommodation, shuttle bus; both ways to the airport, plus the airport car parking. So a rather expensive twenty-four-hours; justified, as *A ONCE IN A LIFE TIME EXPERIENCE.*

I landed in Garland, caught the shuttle, arriving at the hostel, with a private room booked. I travelled light with only a change of undies and bra; wearing the same clothes over and back. The stadium food available was the normal 'shit', having a hot chocolate and chips for dinner.

OMG the concert was unbelievable, with my favourite singer Robby; so hot. The big screens allowed a close up look at his features, to drool over. My favourite part of the concert was when he performed 'the rose petal song', laying down on the semi-circle stage, entertaining the woman in those seats, with an up close and personal experience. What I would've done to be in one of those seats. I left the concert with a smile on my face, walking back to the hostel.

I was very spoilt, as a Christmas gift that same year, receiving a ticket, to The Scampers. Garland was the first concert on their world tour and Brisbane was the last one. There's no comparison between the two shows, with their performance totally different, both were incredible, as far as I'm concerned.

Waking up the next morning to find it's snowing, in April; walking over to another hotel, for breakfast, while waiting for the shuttle. Before I knew it, I'm back at my car, without any hiccups.

I left the long term car parking and headed towards Nonverlone and this was when I caught up with Adam. *See the full story in Extra Communication in this chapter.* After staying at his house, for the night, I drove towards Ploomaks, wanting to visit a special lake, located somewhere near there. When I arrived at Ploomaks, I entered the lake into the GPS, which directed me over the top of a mountain; through unsealed, muddied, iced roads with massive pot holes, and snow. I passed a beautiful red lake, knowing there would've been a better road to take, but I really enjoyed my off road expedition; finally rejoining the main sealed highway, arriving at Pascoe Lake.

The high altitude of this area meant Pascoe Lake and the surrounding landscape were still in a winter wonderland. The very low cloud cover obscured most of the landscape, with the whole area, almost in darkness. This lake was one of my favourite places I visited with my dad in 2005. The memories of beavers, ducks and wild birds; enhanced the magical deep blue colour of the lake. The sixteen hours I stayed here, the last time, I enjoyed a beautiful sunset and sunrise.

Today the whole area was deserted; parking the car, and stepping out; I looked at the lodge where we'd stayed. Walking down to the little bridge, crossing the lake; sadness and regret filled my soul. Oh how my heart was breaking; that I had to return to Australia. My heart was forever linked to these amazing mountains. How could I possibly return to Australia, when I know I belonged here? Today's journey was finally affecting my soul, coming to terms with the fact, the countdown to departure, had begun.

My final hours were spent travelling with overcast skies, with the weather reflecting how I was feeling inside, sad with clouds, mist and tears. Travelling down through the mountain passes, I felt insignificant, in comparison to the size, of the landscape, towering above me. The Trans Canadian highway travelling through the Rocky Mountains was a majestic experience, stopping along the way, in amazement of the scenery.

I stopped for an early dinner just outside the outer city limits of Vancouver. The last few days have been a whirlwind of activity. Wait a minute; what about the last twelve months?

Entering the outer-city area I got confused, missing the turnoff for the airport, taking the long way around. I still had hours to fill in, before the plane left at midnight. On schedule arriving at the rental car place, empting the car, and loaded up a trolley with four pieces of luggage, which I should've cut back to three; costing me an extra four hundred dollars. *OH SHIT.*

Chapter 22

EPILOGUE - APRIL

LAST MOMENTS

My trip of a lifetime was almost over; now homeward bound, on the midnight flight, where the journey started almost twelve months ago.

What's happened in my life, over this period of time, has been my extraordinary, courageous adventure. I'm a different person on so many levels; changed by the people I've met; the places I've visited; with the experiences that have taken my breath away. The tears, the pain, the hard work and exhaustion, combined with a tiny bit of guilt, of being able to travel and experience these amazing places. The overwhelming joy, I felt, for my hosts, with my help, they've created a life, full of their own dreams. The gratitude was evident, in the embraces of genuine affection, shown towards me, for a job, well done.

Have I made a difference, in the lives of the people, I've met? YES!!!!! I believe everyone changes forever, by circumstances each and every day. You cannot go back in time and un-meet someone. Each exchange during your life changes the universe. Sometimes it wasn't evident, while other interactions are intertwined forever, linked for eternity.

BUCKET LIST

How successful was my 'bucket list' of my expectations for my trip to Canada?

1. I wanted to explore as much of the area as I could. I wanted to drive around the mountains and spend time in nature and reconnect with the Rocky Mountains.

   Yes I travelled over eleven-thousand-kilometres during my three month stay. Experiencing the winter wonderland of the Rocky Mountains;
   Stood at vista views, lakes, and crests of mountain ranges;
   Walked along frozen rivers and lakes;
   Tackled off-road locations with gusto in my little car;

Watched sunrises and sunsets from as many different locations as possible;
Sat at parks, listening to the birds; and
Walked as much as I possibly could, breathing in as much pure fresh air as possible.

2. At least every second day I HAD TO LEAVE THE HOUSE and go exploring somewhere. If I didn't do this one thing then I might as well have gone back to Australia, because I wasn't experiencing Canada if all I did was stay at home.

    Yes I definitely scored a tick for this one. See my answer above, plus my bank account substantiates my coffee shops addiction; driving all around the country side, meeting so many wonderful people in the process.

3. I wanted to have a conversation with a man over a nice dinner.

    Yes I had a wonderful conversation with Adam over dinner; one day before my departure. See Extra Communication in Chapter 21

4. I wanted to be kissed passionately by a man.

    Yes I had my one passionate kiss with Giorgio, four days before my departure. See The Kiss in Chapter 21

5. I wanted to spend time sorting out all of my feelings and reconnect back to 'myself' and ready to start my new life, once I landed back in Australia.

    Yes I spent an incredible amount of time (and money) visiting Belinda, Ann, David, Tina, Julie and Angie where I shared my life's story. I spent many hours in cafes writing down my deep and meaningful thoughts. Spending hours in meditation with Reiki and crystals; using my tarot cards for guidance each day. I'm so much stronger now on all levels of my emotional, mental, physical and spiritual well being.

MY TOP ACHIEVEMENT LIST

My favourite room –	Sleeping on the Docks in Alaska – Chapter 4
	A close second was Wanda's 5*cabin – Chapter 11
Favourite Host –	Wanda from the cattle farm – Chapter 11
Favourite Place to have visited	The Caribbean - a holiday destination – Chapter 20
Favourite View –	Waking up and looking at the snow capped mountain in Alaska – Chapter 4
Favourite Sunsets –	The sundog, the lobster boat and moonrise on the east coast – Chapter 14
Favourite Sunrise –	Flying from Density to Windstrome, seeing the sun rise up over the islands in the bay - Chapter 3

Favourite Sight –	Seeing all the snow capped mountains on the flight to Alaska on a clear crisp spring morning – Chapter 3
Most inspiring moment –	Climbing the wildflower fields at 2,910 metres; looking down on the glacier – I had waited all my life to do this - Chapter 9.
Take my breath away moment	Lincoln Lake– a picture postcard moment so perfect – Chapter 9
Most incredible moment –	Cliff jumping – what was I thinking!!! Crazy!!!!! – Chapter 20
Hardest job -	Veggie Gardens in Chapters 4,6,8,11,14
Most satisfying job -	Wanda's garden with the preserving and baking – Chapter 11.
Most exciting new skill -	Looming the scarf – I am wearing it now – Chapter 10
Most entertaining person	Heather the nanny from Alaska – Chapter 4
Most Famous person seen -	Tied between my favourite actor Ryan James and my favourite singer Robby from *The Scampers* – Chapter 7 & 21
Saddest goodbye	Sherry, Adelia and Norma from California and Mary-Anne from the Caribbean – Chapter 16 & 20

If I could turn back the time travel clock during the last twelve months, my regrets were:

1. Cliff jumping – I don't know where my mind went to, to contemplate something so foolish; Chapter 20
2. I would have stopped at the motorcycle accident; - Chapter 9
3. I would have stepped into the bar in Ville Lauer; - Chapter 12
4. I would never have gone to the bar on New Year's Eve. Chapter 21

A NEW DAWN, A NEW DAY

My heart was heavy with sadness, for the ending of such an incredible year. My emotional body was excited about returning to my family; looking forward to seeing my mum, who I believe, has missed me the most. Seeing Charlie my eldest grandson who turns four today. Thomas was small enough to be cradled in my arms; now eighteen months and walking everywhere.

Of course there's my children Justin, Nicole and Christian who I'm sure would've missed me maybe#$^%#? Just a little! My father and brothers may have missed me as well.

My thoughts go to Ricky my ex-husband, who's supported me financially, on my quest to find myself again. Without his incredible generosity, I wouldn't have been able to re-discover my true self.

As my excitement for Australia reaches fever pitch; I'm excited about returning to my house and garden; reconnecting back with my little piece of heaven; Knower's Arc. For certain, my garden has missed my passion and loving touch; poured into its existence, over the last thirty years.

As the plane landed my patriotism, for being Australian, rose with pride. Am I *HOME* or a just visitor here? Grabbing my luggage and being processed through immigration; my first order of business was a mocha coffee, savouring the taste and enjoying what's so totally unique about Australia. I don't know what it was; in my heart and soul, or was it in the air I breathed.

My outstanding, extraordinary, courageous adventure was now officially over. Will family and friends recognise the changes in my emotional, mental and spiritual well being? Recognise how different I am, from the person, who hopped on that plane, this time last year? Will my son remember to pick me up at the airport? ☺

Searching the world for validation of the person I wanted and needed to become. It's only when I returned home that all the pieces of the puzzle were arranged to display the Bella masterpiece. The creation of a beautiful soul, the true magnificence of an incredible women; who's ready to explore the next chapter of her extraordinary and courageous life.

This is my current home in Australia – Knower's Arc My link between Australia and Canada

Printed in the United States
By Bookmasters